newuniversal

EVERYTHING WENT WHITE

newuniversal
EVERYTHING WENT WHITE

WRITER: Warren Ellis
ARTIST: Salvador Larroca

COLORIST: Jason Keith
LETTERER: Virtual Calligraphy's Rus Wooton
COVERS DESIGNED BY: Patrick McGrath
ASSISTANT EDITOR: Daniel Ketchum
EDITOR: Axel Alonso

COLLECTION EDITOR: Jennifer Grünwald
ASSISTANT EDITORS: Cory Levine & John Denning
EDITOR, SPECIAL PROJECTS: Mark D. Beazley
SENIOR EDITOR, SPECIAL PROJECTS: Jeff Youngquist
SENIOR VICE PRESIDENT OF SALES: David Gabriel
PRODUCTION: Jerron Quality Color
BOOK DESIGNER: Patrick McGrath
VICE PRESIDENT OF CREATIVE: Tom Marvelli

EDITOR IN CHIEF: Joe Quesada
PUBLISHER: Dan Buckley

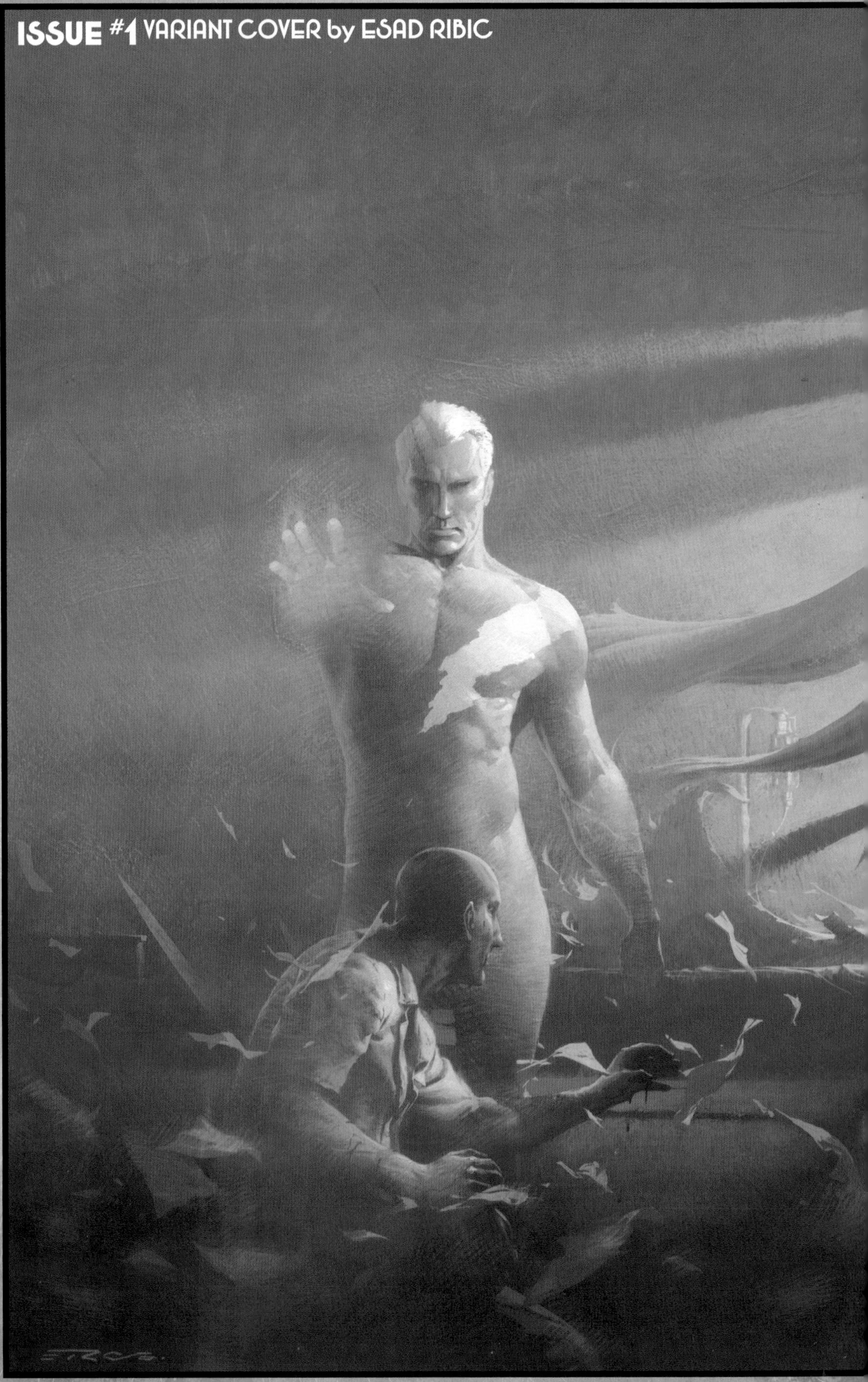

ISSUE #1 VARIANT COVER by ESAD RIBIC

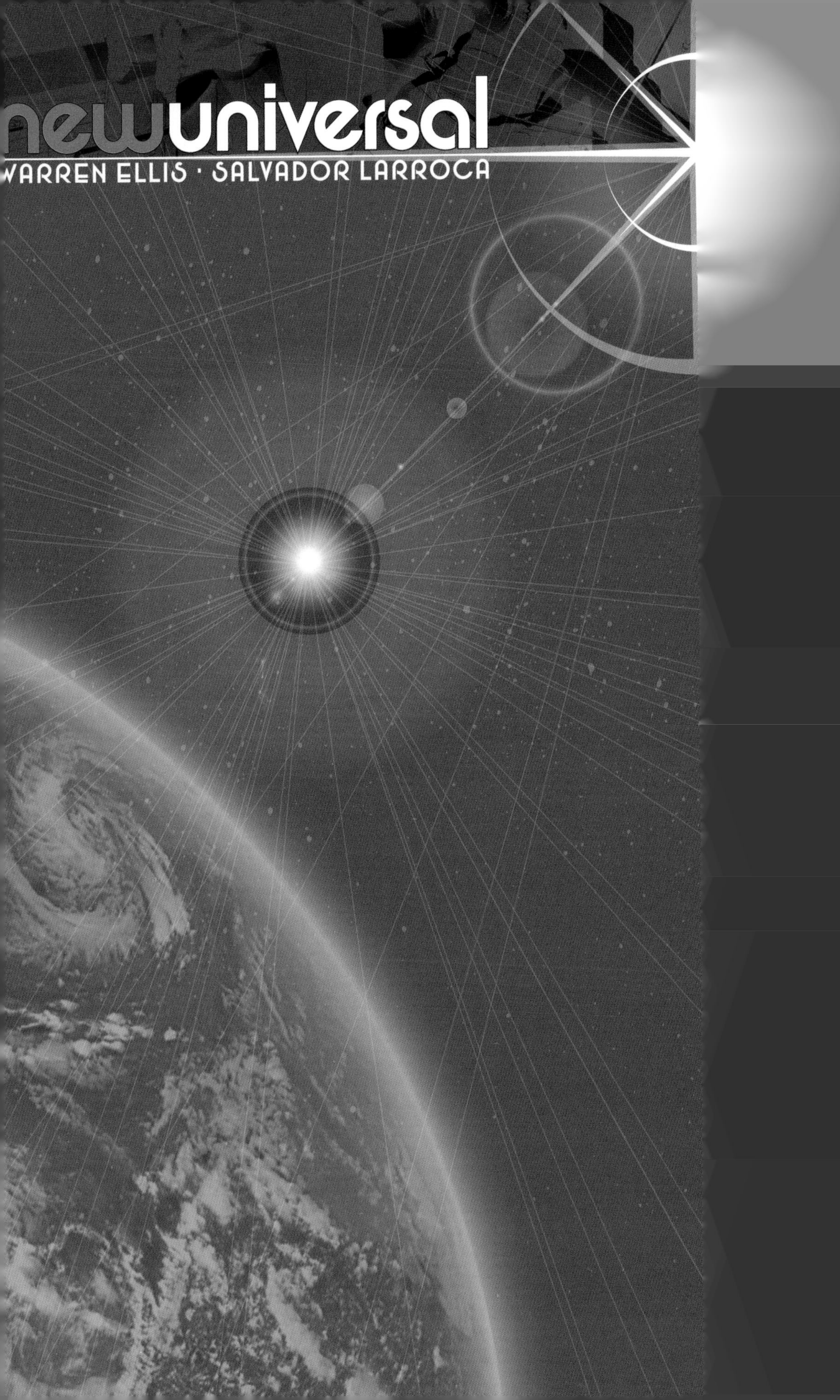
newuniversal
WARREN ELLIS · SALVADOR LARROCA

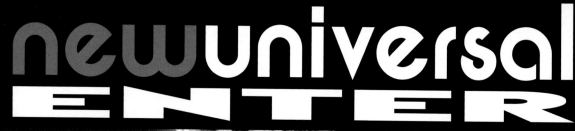

newuniversal
ENTER

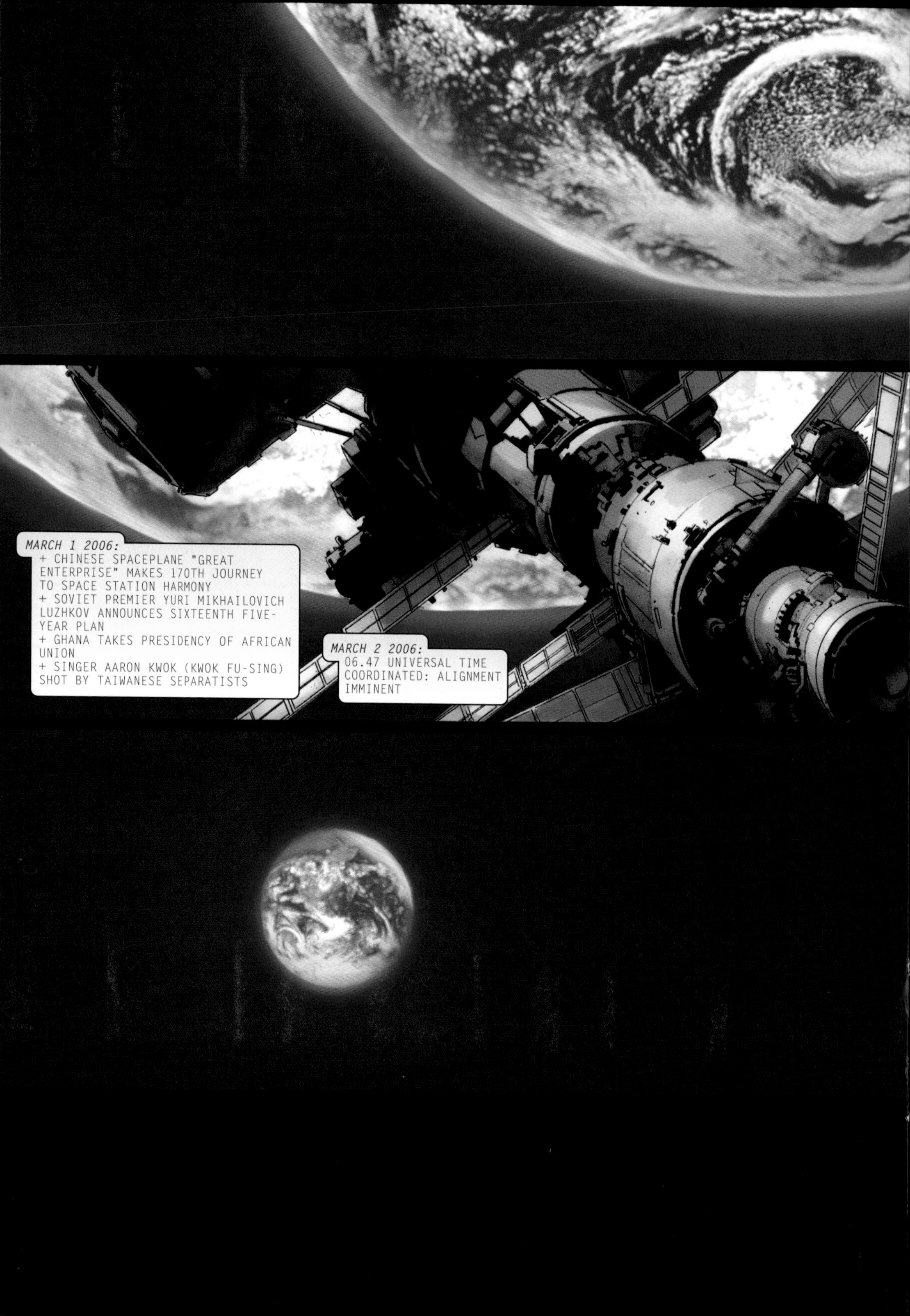
MARCH 1 2006:
+ CHINESE SPACEPLANE "GREAT ENTERPRISE" MAKES 170TH JOURNEY TO SPACE STATION HARMONY
+ SOVIET PREMIER YURI MIKHAILOVICH LUZHKOV ANNOUNCES SIXTEENTH FIVE-YEAR PLAN
+ GHANA TAKES PRESIDENCY OF AFRICAN UNION
+ SINGER AARON KWOK (KWOK FU-SING) SHOT BY TAIWANESE SEPARATISTS
MARCH 2 2006:
06.47 UNIVERSAL TIME COORDINATED: ALIGNMENT IMMINENT

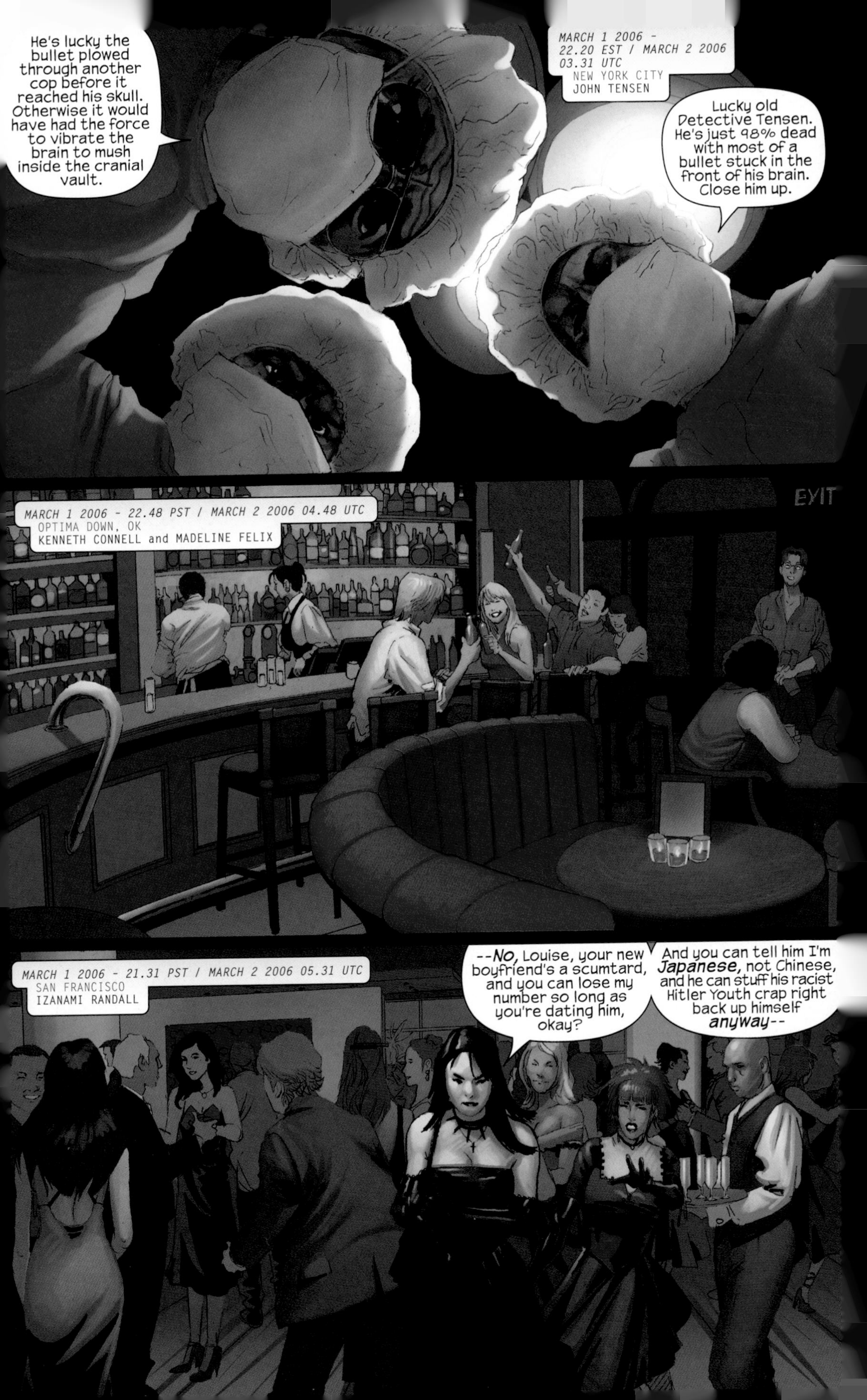
MARCH 1 2006 - 22.20 EST / MARCH 2 2006 03.31 UTC
NEW YORK CITY
JOHN TENSEN
He's lucky the bullet plowed through another cop before it reached his skull. Otherwise it would have had the force to vibrate the brain to mush inside the cranial vault.
Lucky old Detective Tensen. He's just 98% dead with most of a bullet stuck in the front of his brain. Close him up.
MARCH 1 2006 - 22.48 PST / MARCH 2 2006 04.48 UTC
OPTIMA DOWN, OK
KENNETH CONNELL and MADELINE FELIX
EXIT
MARCH 1 2006 - 21.31 PST / MARCH 2 2006 05.31 UTC
SAN FRANCISCO
IZANAMI RANDALL
--*No,* Louise, your new boyfriend's a scumtard, and you can lose my number so long as you're dating him, okay?
And you can tell him I'm *Japanese,* not Chinese, and he can stuff his racist Hitler Youth crap right back up himself *anyway*--

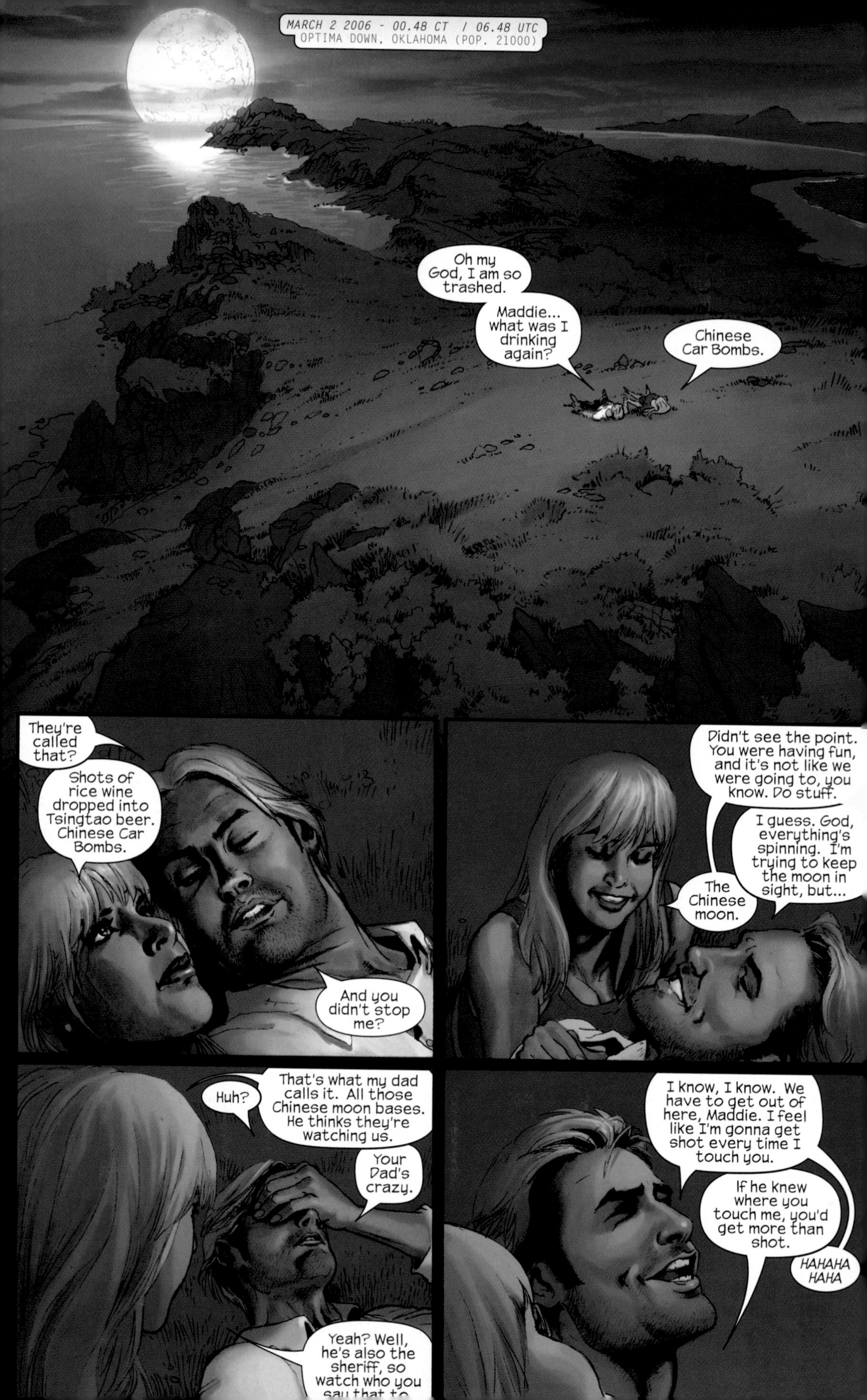
MARCH 2 2006 - 00.48 CT / 06.48 UTC
OPTIMA DOWN, OKLAHOMA (POP. 21000)
Oh my God, I am so trashed.
Maddie... what was I drinking again?
Chinese Car Bombs.
They're called that?
Shots of rice wine dropped into Tsingtao beer. Chinese Car Bombs.
And you didn't stop me?
Didn't see the point. You were having fun, and it's not like we were going to, you know. Do stuff.
I guess. God, everything's spinning. I'm trying to keep the moon in sight, but...
The Chinese moon.
Huh?
That's what my dad calls it. All those Chinese moon bases. He thinks they're watching us.
Your Dad's crazy.
Yeah? Well, he's also the sheriff, so watch who you say that to.
I know, I know. We have to get out of here, Maddie. I feel like I'm gonna get shot every time I touch you.
If he knew where you touch me, you'd get more than shot.
HAHAHA HAHA

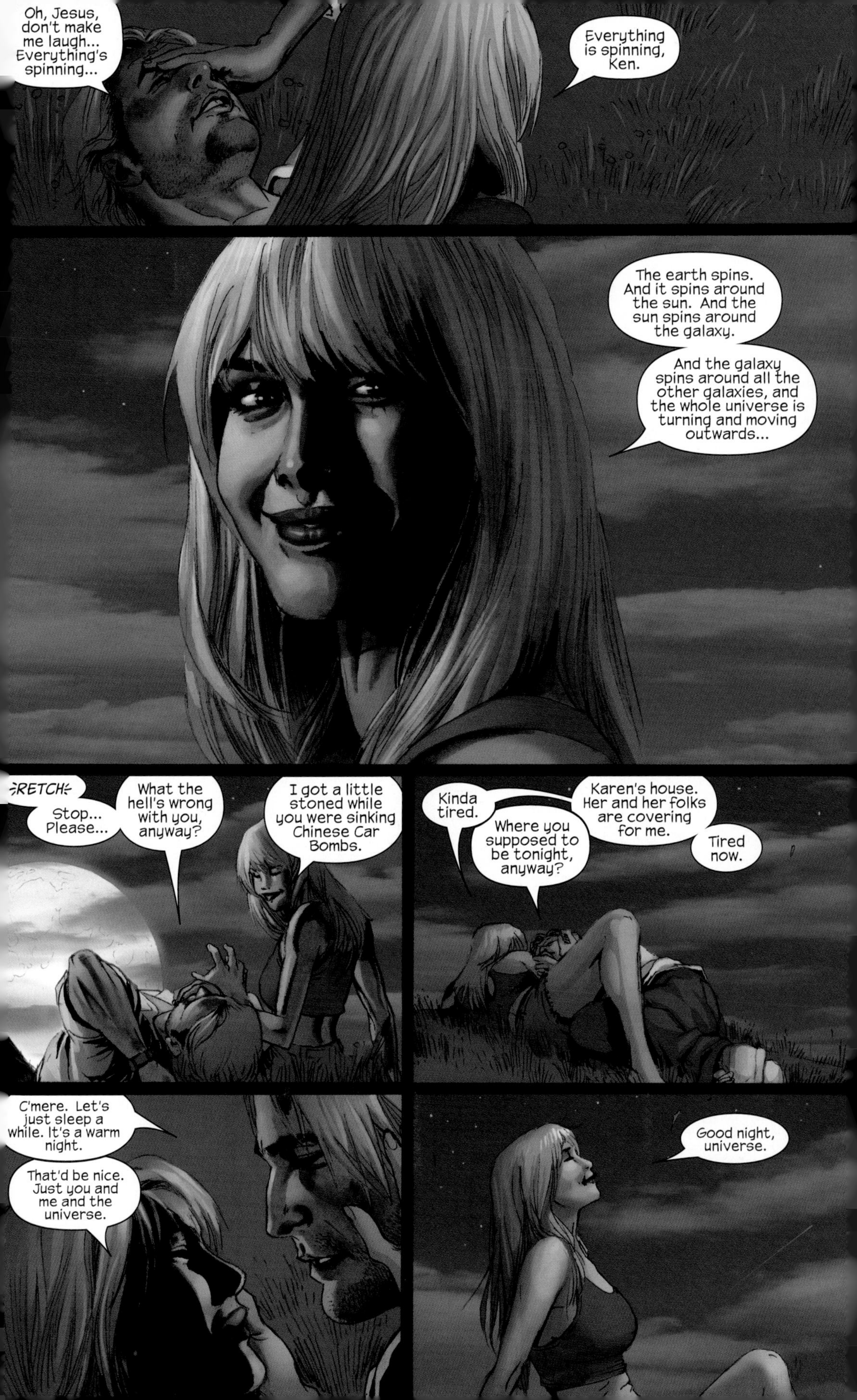
Oh, Jesus, don't make me laugh... Everything's spinning...
Everything is spinning, Ken.
The earth spins. And it spins around the sun. And the sun spins around the galaxy.
And the galaxy spins around all the other galaxies, and the whole universe is turning and moving outwards...
RETCH
Stop... Please...
What the hell's wrong with you, anyway?
I got a little stoned while you were sinking Chinese Car Bombs.
Kinda tired.
Karen's house. Her and her folks are covering for me.
Where you supposed to be tonight, anyway?
Tired now.
C'mere. Let's just sleep a while. It's a warm night.
That'd be nice. Just you and me and the universe.
Good night, universe.

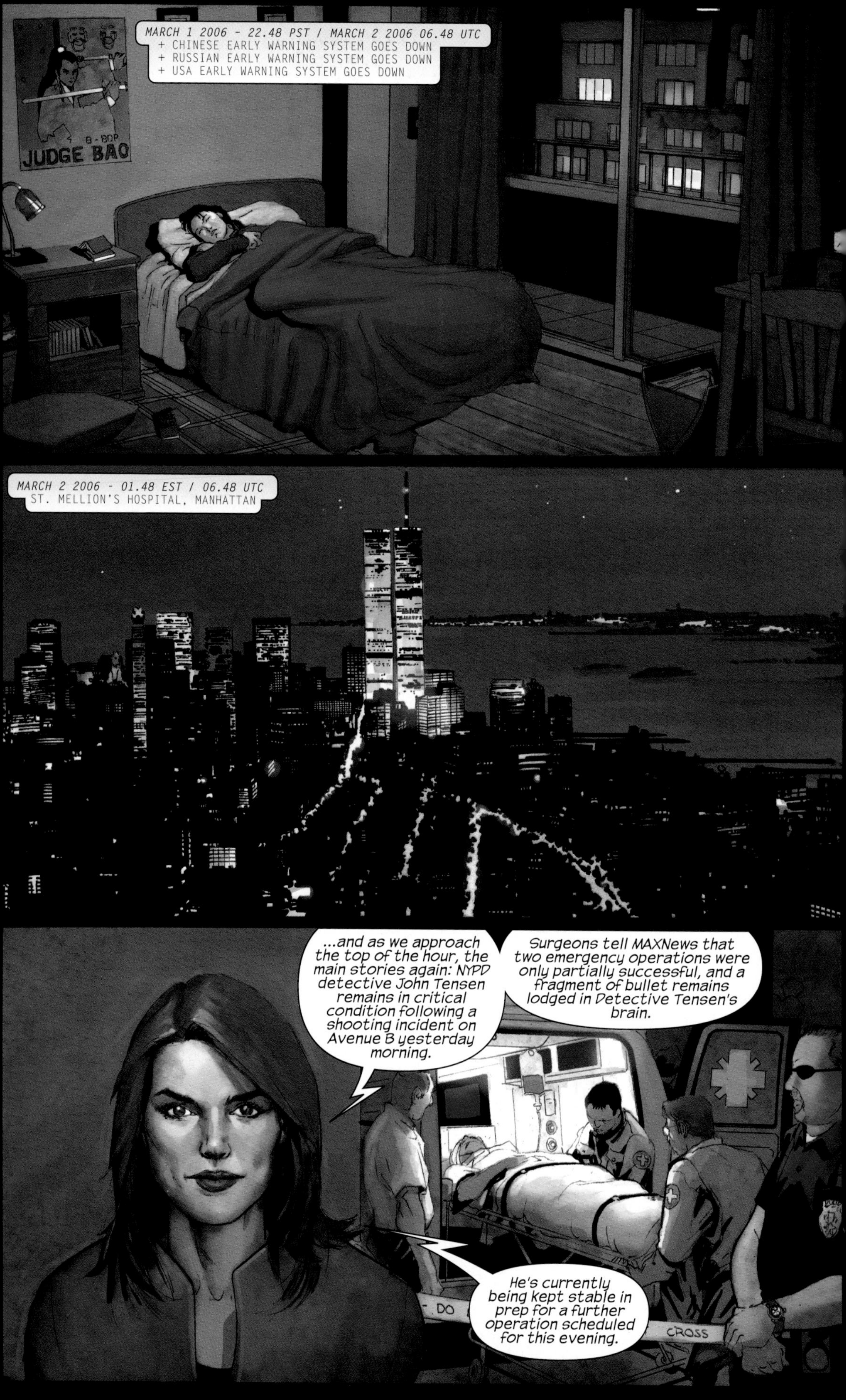
MARCH 1 2006 - 22.48 PST / MARCH 2 2006 06.48 UTC
+ CHINESE EARLY WARNING SYSTEM GOES DOWN
+ RUSSIAN EARLY WARNING SYSTEM GOES DOWN
+ USA EARLY WARNING SYSTEM GOES DOWN
B-BOP
JUDGE BAO
MARCH 2 2006 - 01.48 EST / 06.48 UTC
ST. MELLION'S HOSPITAL, MANHATTAN
...and as we approach the top of the hour, the main stories again: NYPD detective John Tensen remains in critical condition following a shooting incident on Avenue B yesterday morning.
Surgeons tell MAXNews that two emergency operations were only partially successful, and a fragment of bullet remains lodged in Detective Tensen's brain.
He's currently being kept stable in prep for a further operation scheduled for this evening.
DO
CROSS

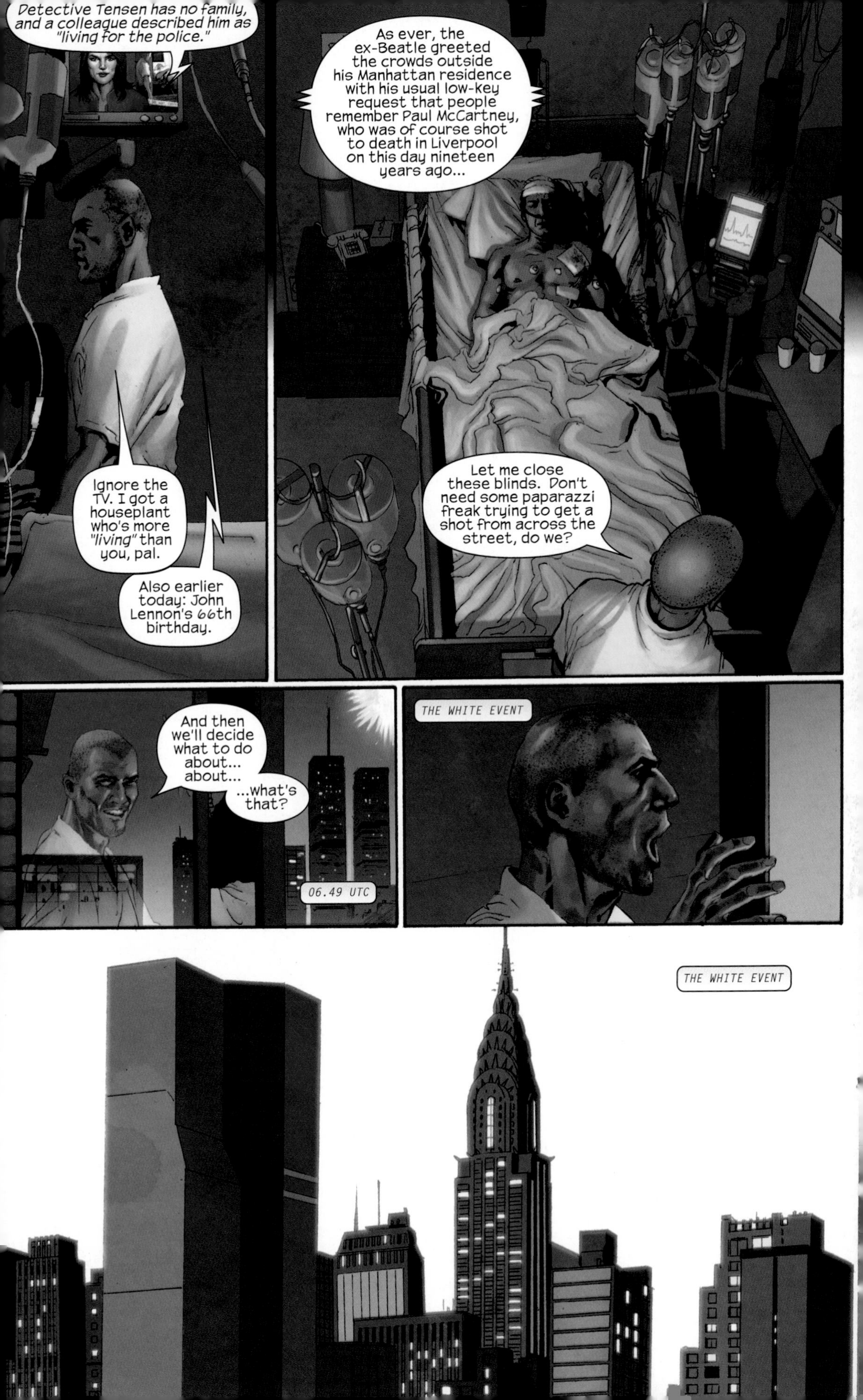

Detective Tensen has no family, and a colleague described him as "living for the police."
As ever, the ex-Beatle greeted the crowds outside his Manhattan residence with his usual low-key request that people remember Paul McCartney, who was of course shot to death in Liverpool on this day nineteen years ago...
Ignore the TV. I got a houseplant who's more "living" than you, pal.
Also earlier today: John Lennon's 66th birthday.
Let me close these blinds. Don't need some paparazzi freak trying to get a shot from across the street, do we?
And then we'll decide what to do about... about...
...what's that?
06.49 UTC
THE WHITE EVENT
THE WHITE EVENT

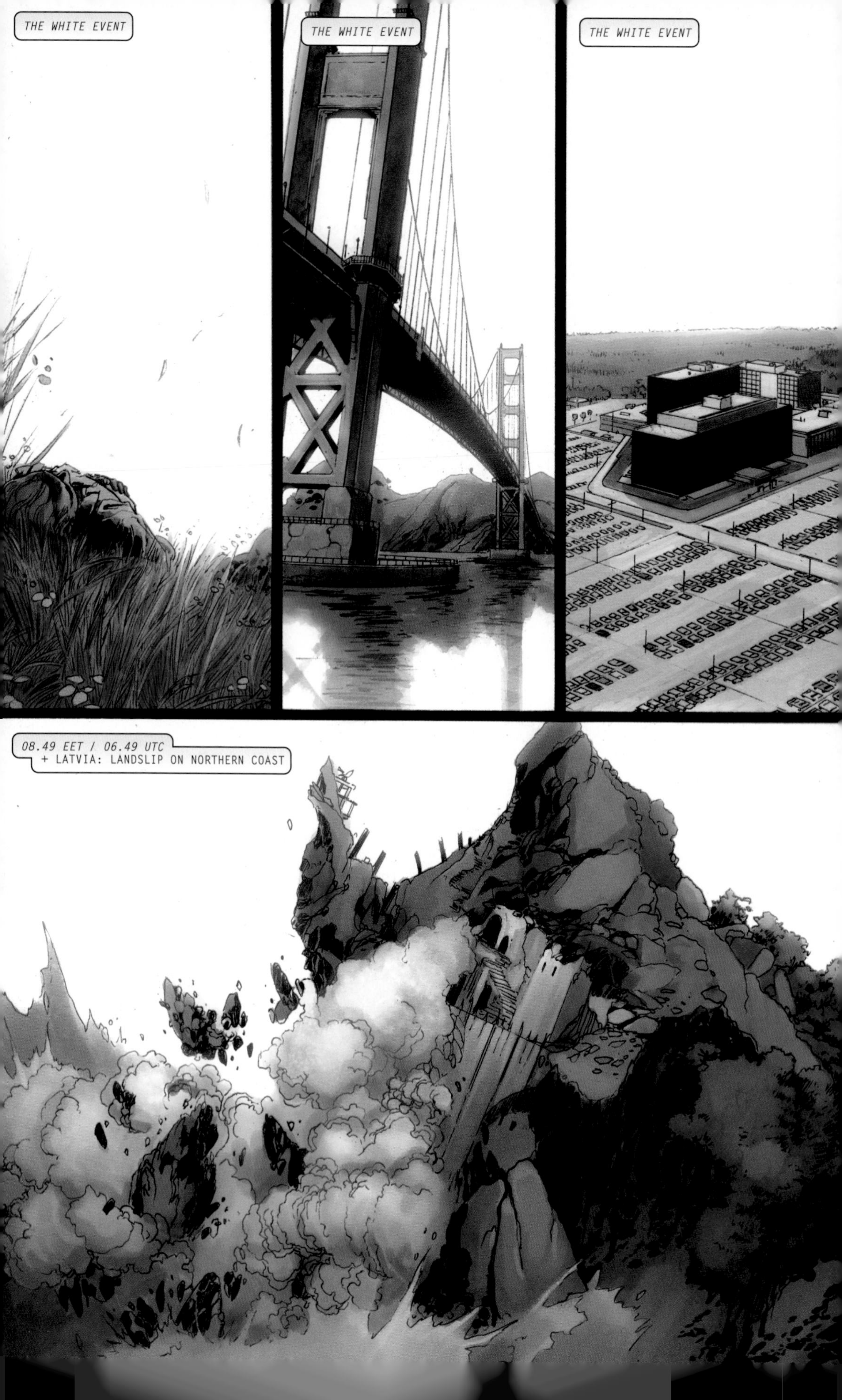
THE WHITE EVENT
THE WHITE EVENT
THE WHITE EVENT
08.49 EET / 06.49 UTC
+ LATVIA: LANDSLIP ON NORTHERN COAST

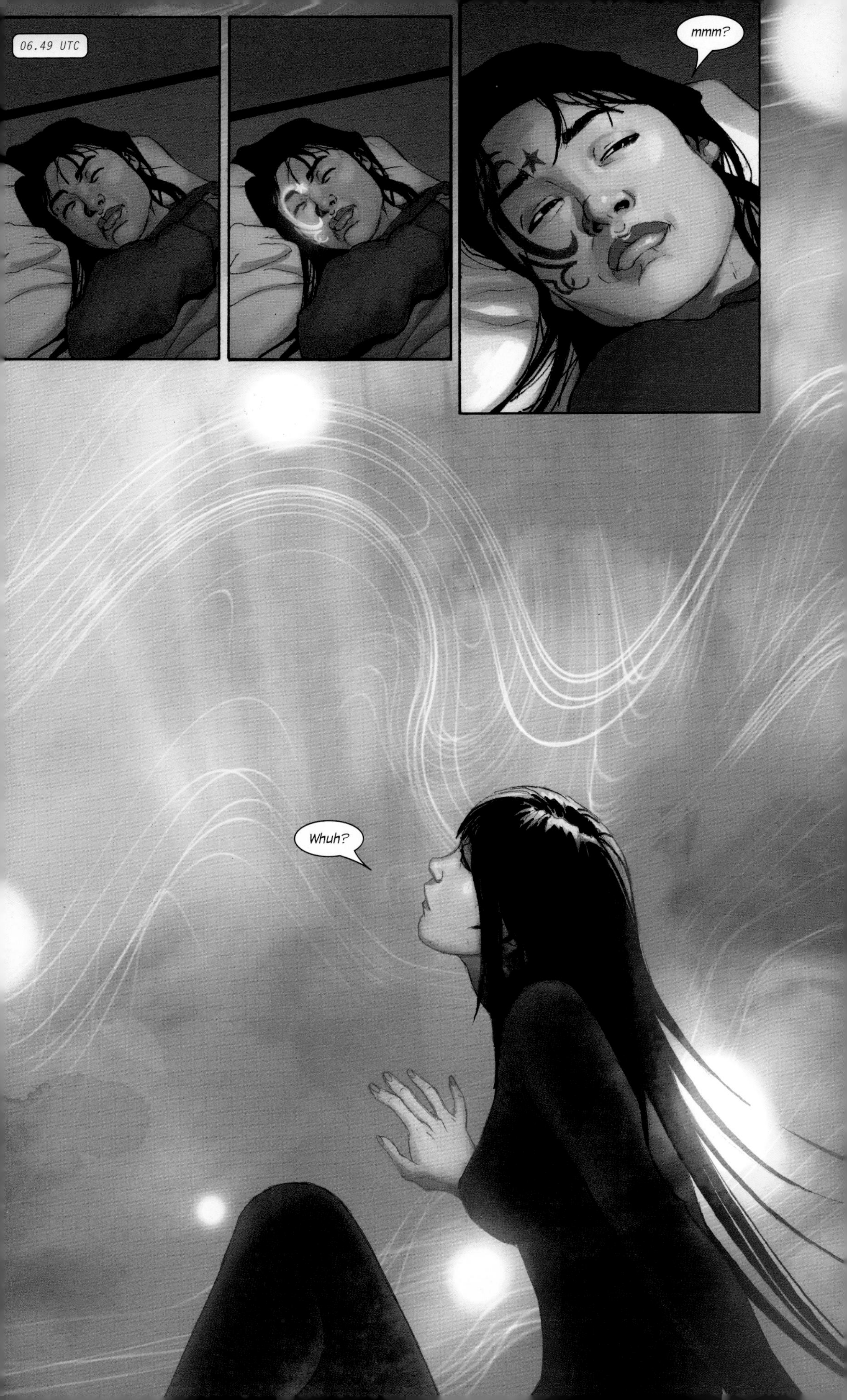
06.49 UTC
mmm?
Whuh?

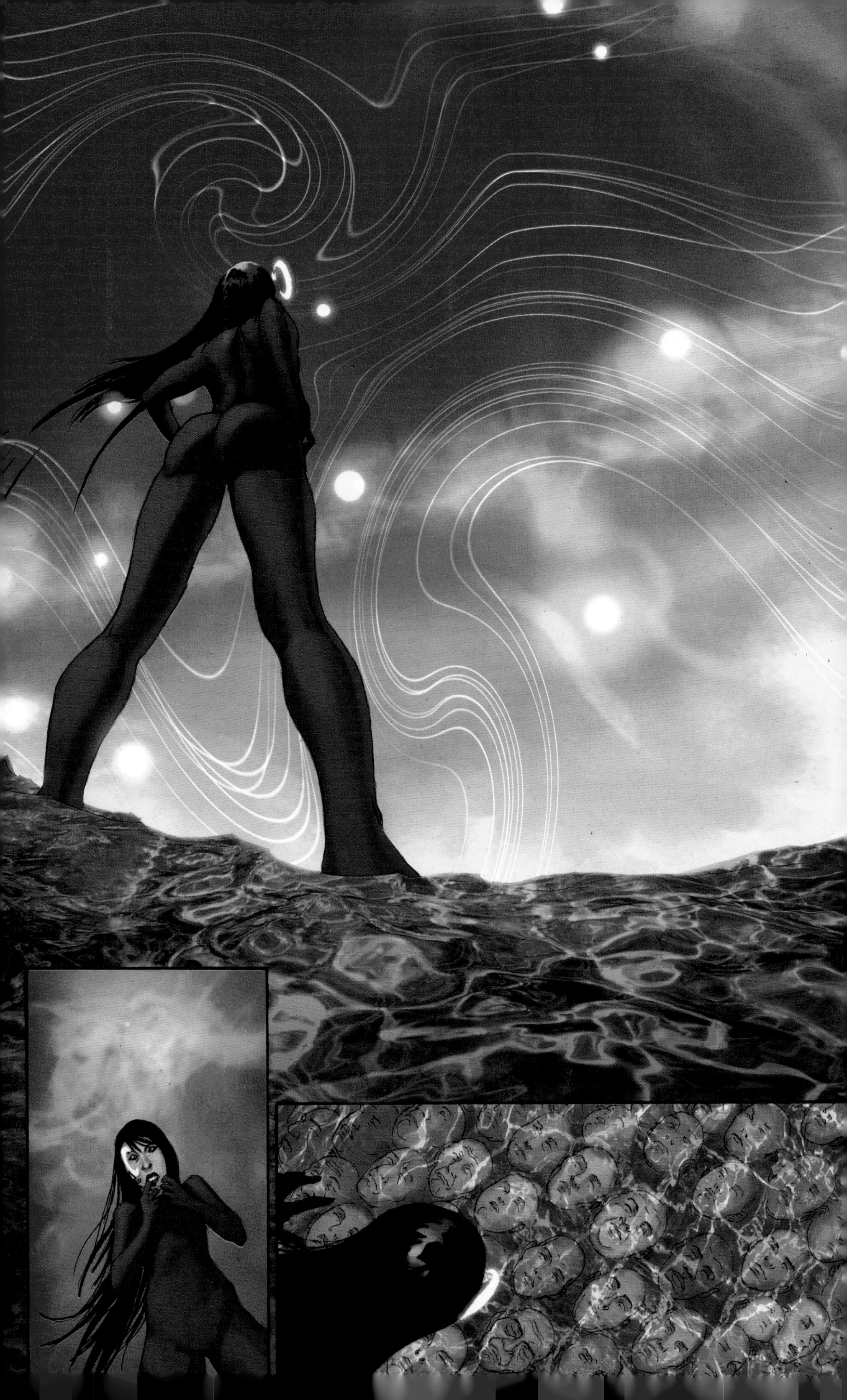

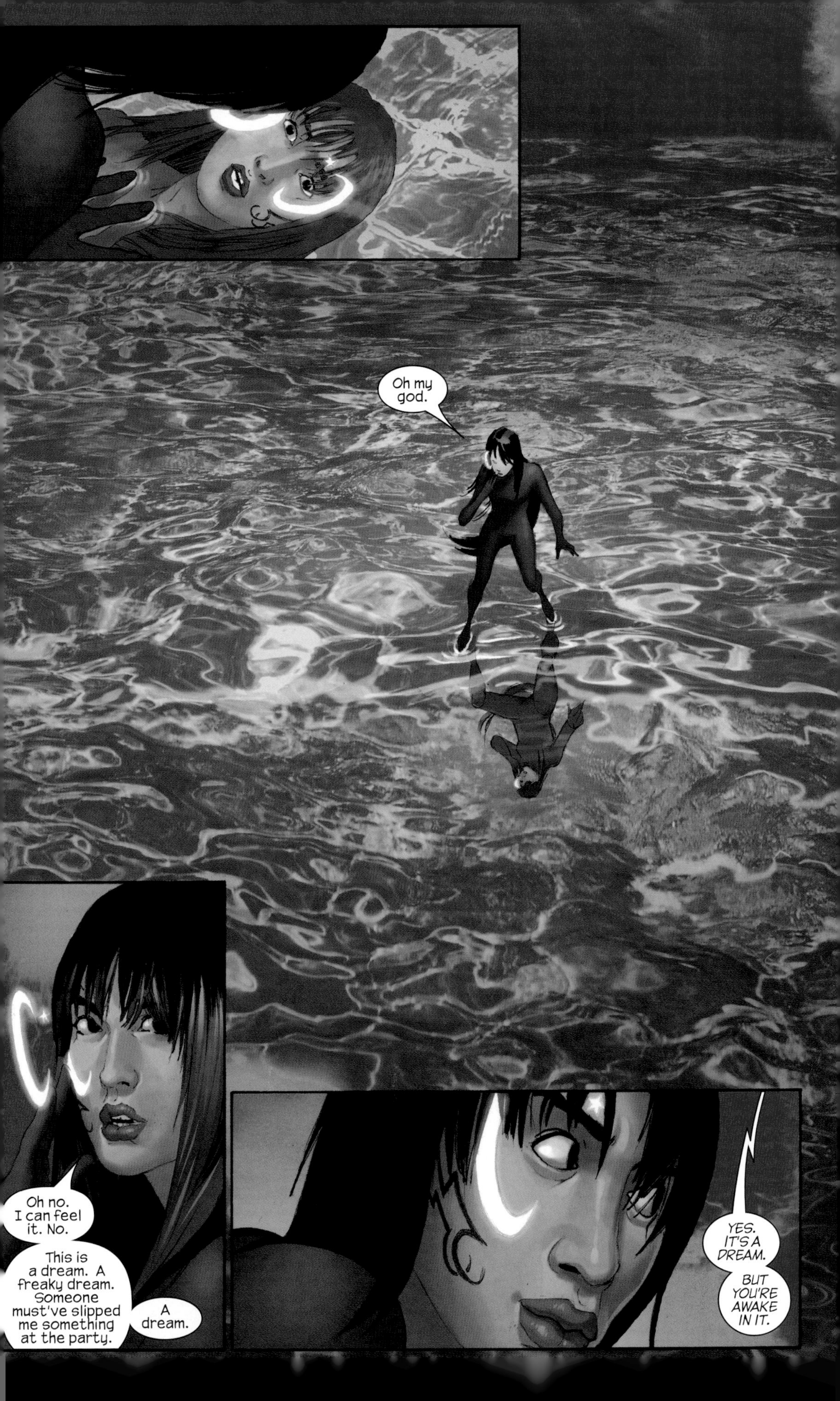
Oh my god.
Oh no. I can feel it. No.
This is a dream. A freaky dream. Someone must've slipped me something at the party.
A dream.
YES. IT'S A DREAM.
BUT YOU'RE AWAKE IN IT.

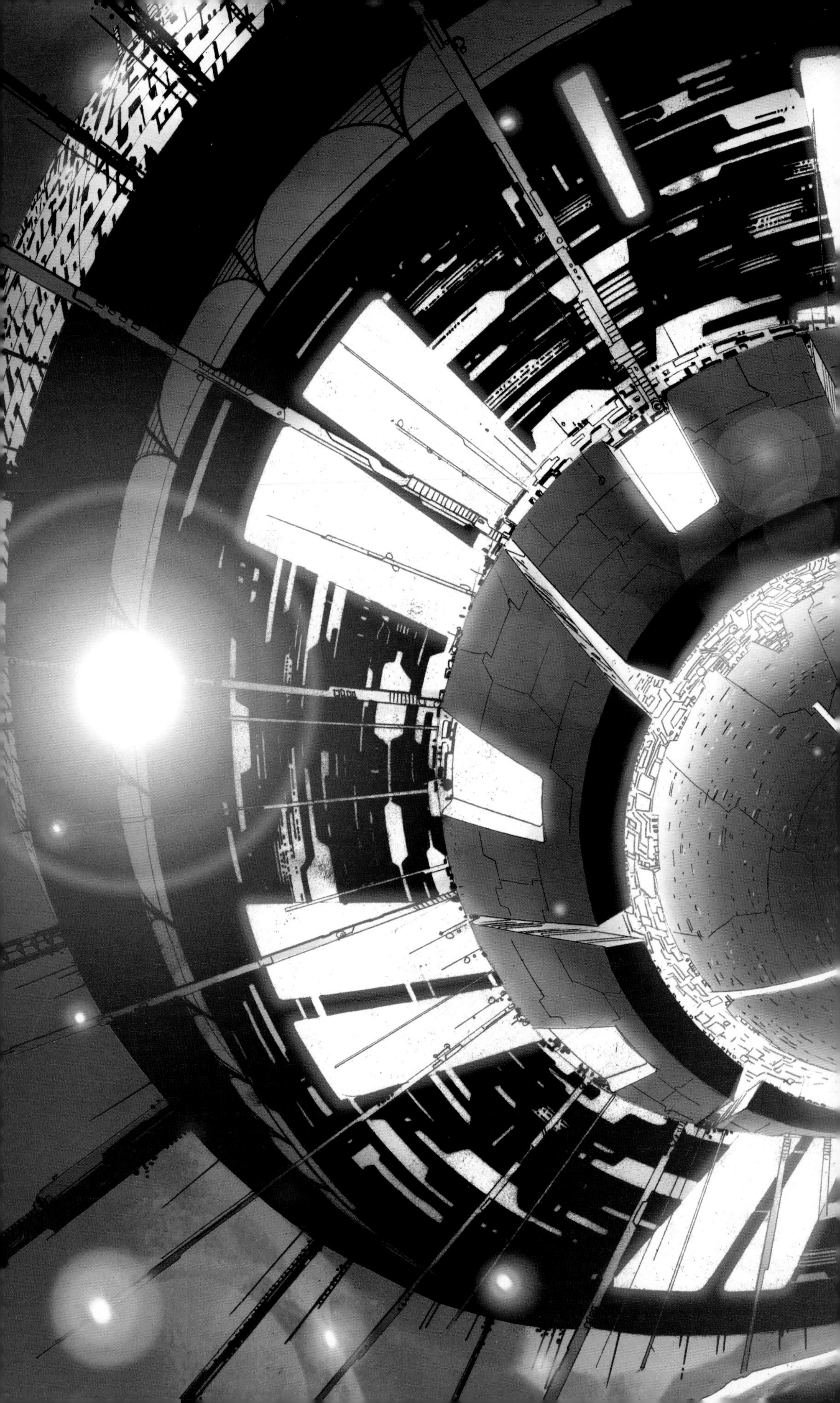

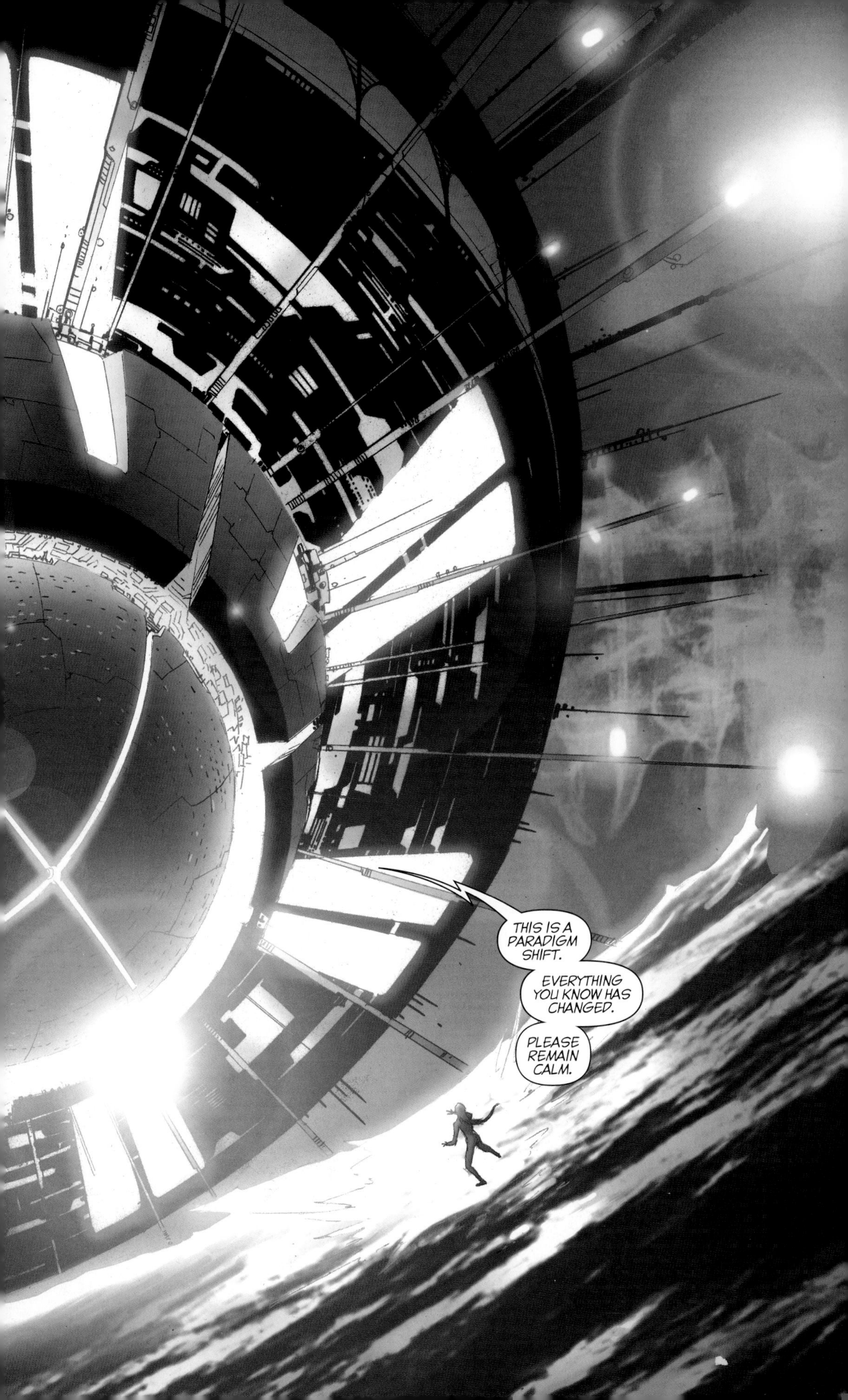
THIS IS A PARADIGM SHIFT.
EVERYTHING YOU KNOW HAS CHANGED.
PLEASE REMAIN CALM.

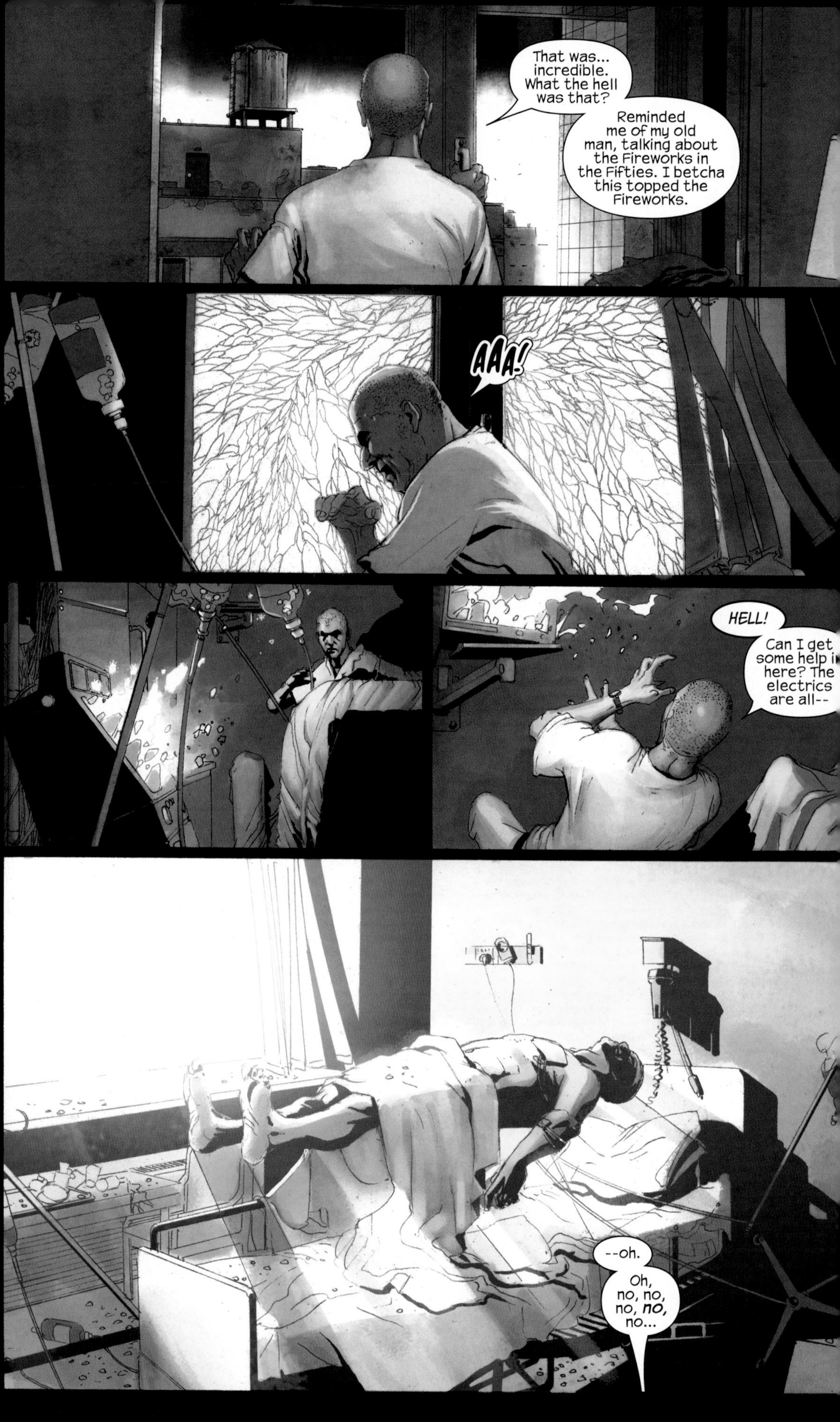

That was... incredible. What the hell was that?
Reminded me of my old man, talking about the Fireworks in the Fifties. I betcha this topped the Fireworks.
AAA!
HELL!
Can I get some help i here? The electrics are all--
--oh.
Oh, no, no, no, NO, no...

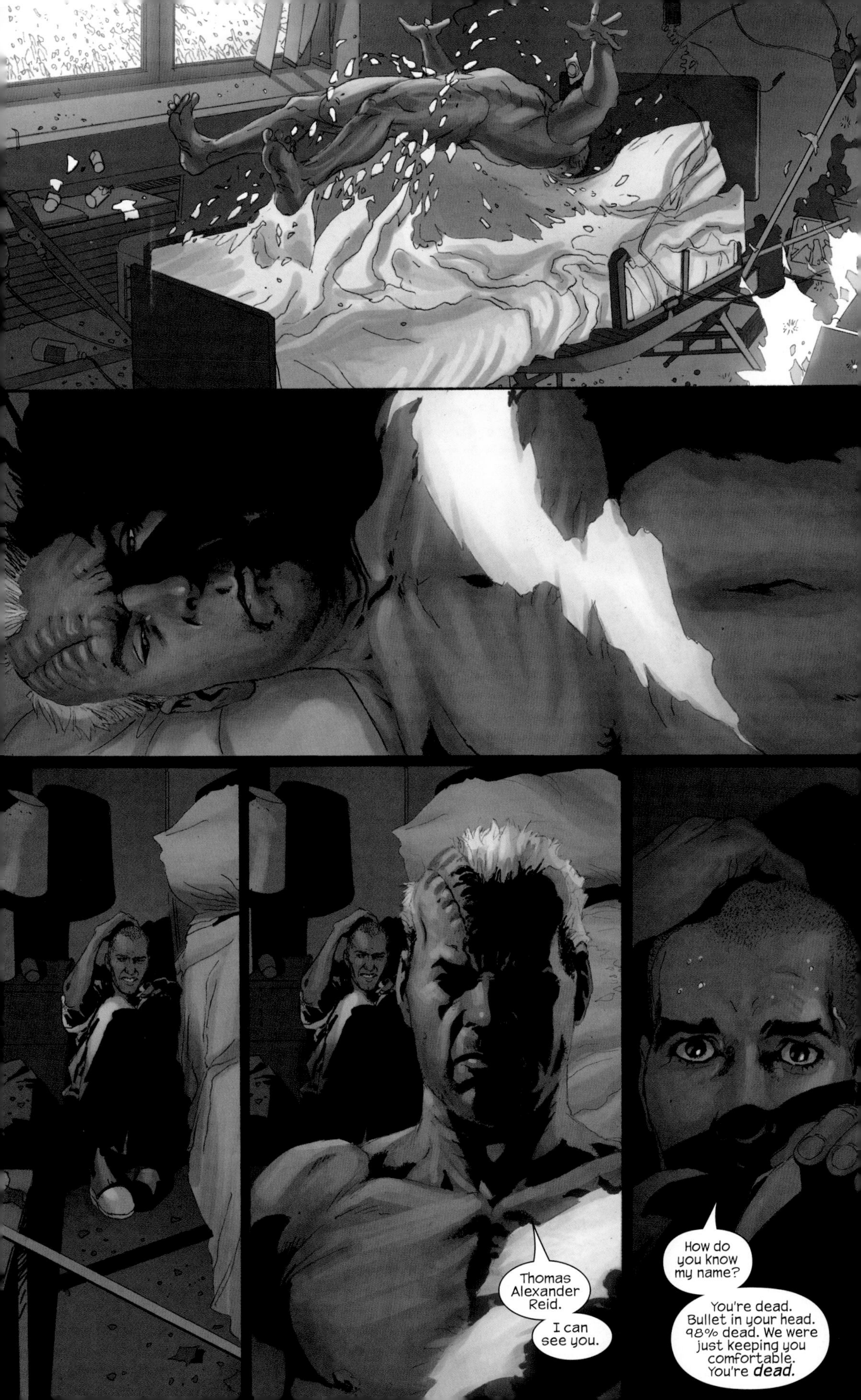
Thomas Alexander Reid.
I can see you.
How do you know my name?
You're dead. Bullet in your head. 98% dead. We were just keeping you comfortable. You're *dead.*

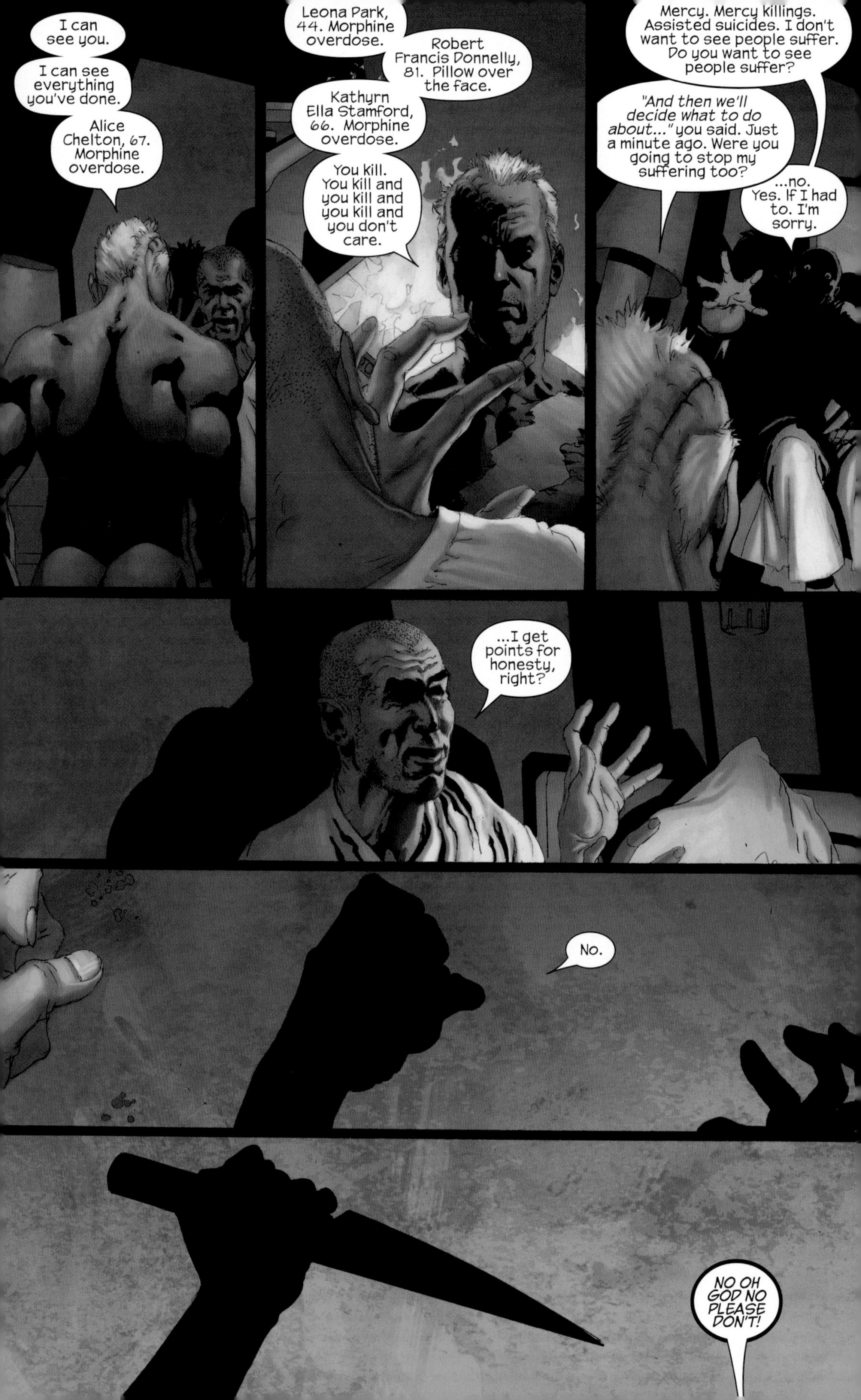
I can see you.
I can see everything you've done.
Alice Chelton, 67. Morphine overdose.
Leona Park, 44. Morphine overdose.
Robert Francis Donnelly, 81. Pillow over the face.
Kathyrn Ella Stamford, 66. Morphine overdose.
You kill. You kill and you kill and you kill and you don't care.
Mercy. Mercy killings. Assisted suicides. I don't want to see people suffer. Do you want to see people suffer?
"And then we'll decide what to do about..." you said. Just a minute ago. Were you going to stop my suffering too?
...no. Yes. If I had to. I'm sorry.
...I get points for honesty, right?
No.
NO OH GOD NO PLEASE DON'T!

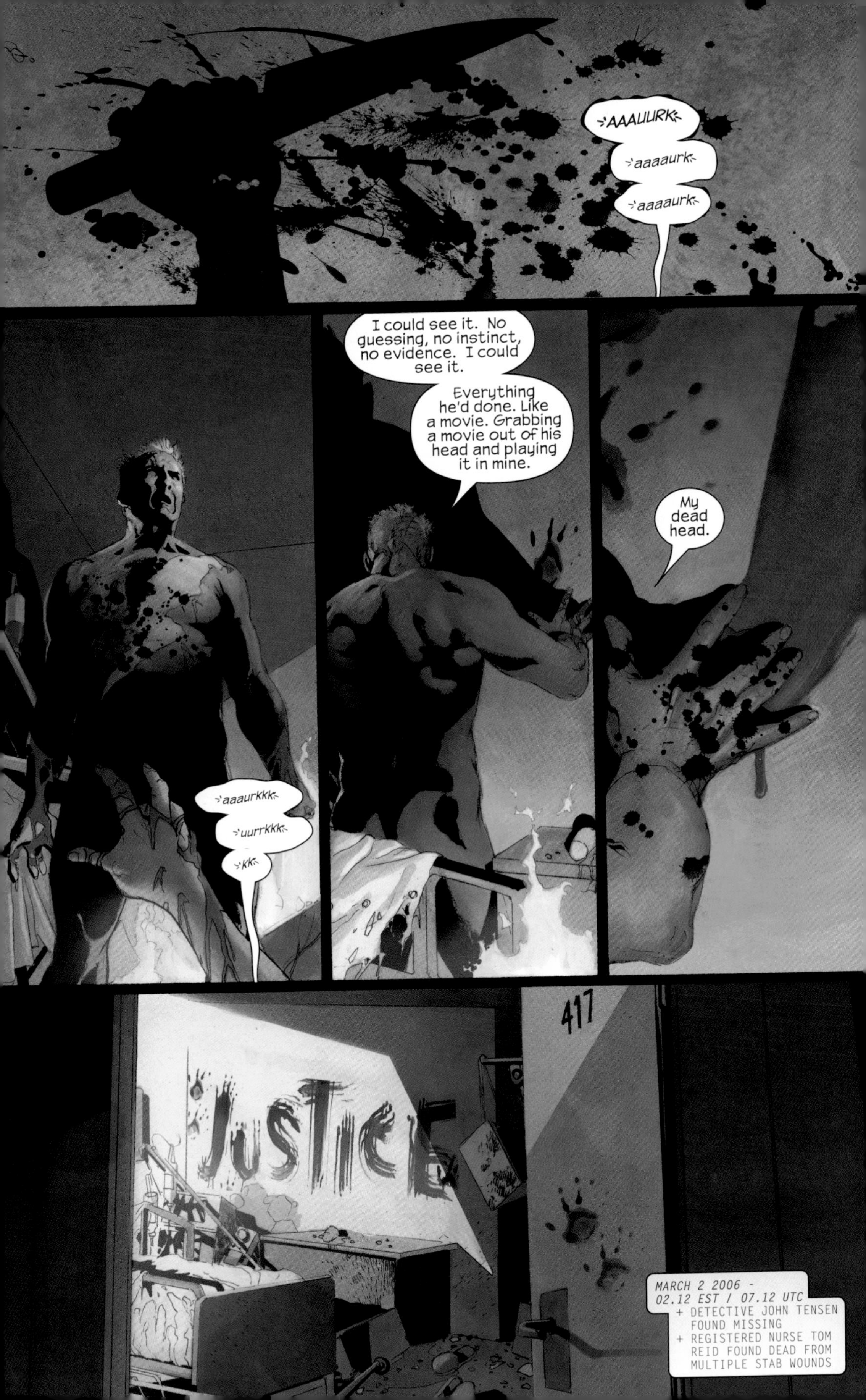
AAAUURK
aaaaurk
aaaaurk
aaaurkkk
uurrkkk
kk
I could see it. No guessing, no instinct, no evidence. I could see it.
Everything he'd done. Like a movie. Grabbing a movie out of his head and playing it in mine.
My dead head.
417
JUSTICE
MARCH 2 2006 -
02.12 EST / 07.12 UTC
+ DETECTIVE JOHN TENSEN FOUND MISSING
+ REGISTERED NURSE TOM REID FOUND DEAD FROM MULTIPLE STAB WOUNDS

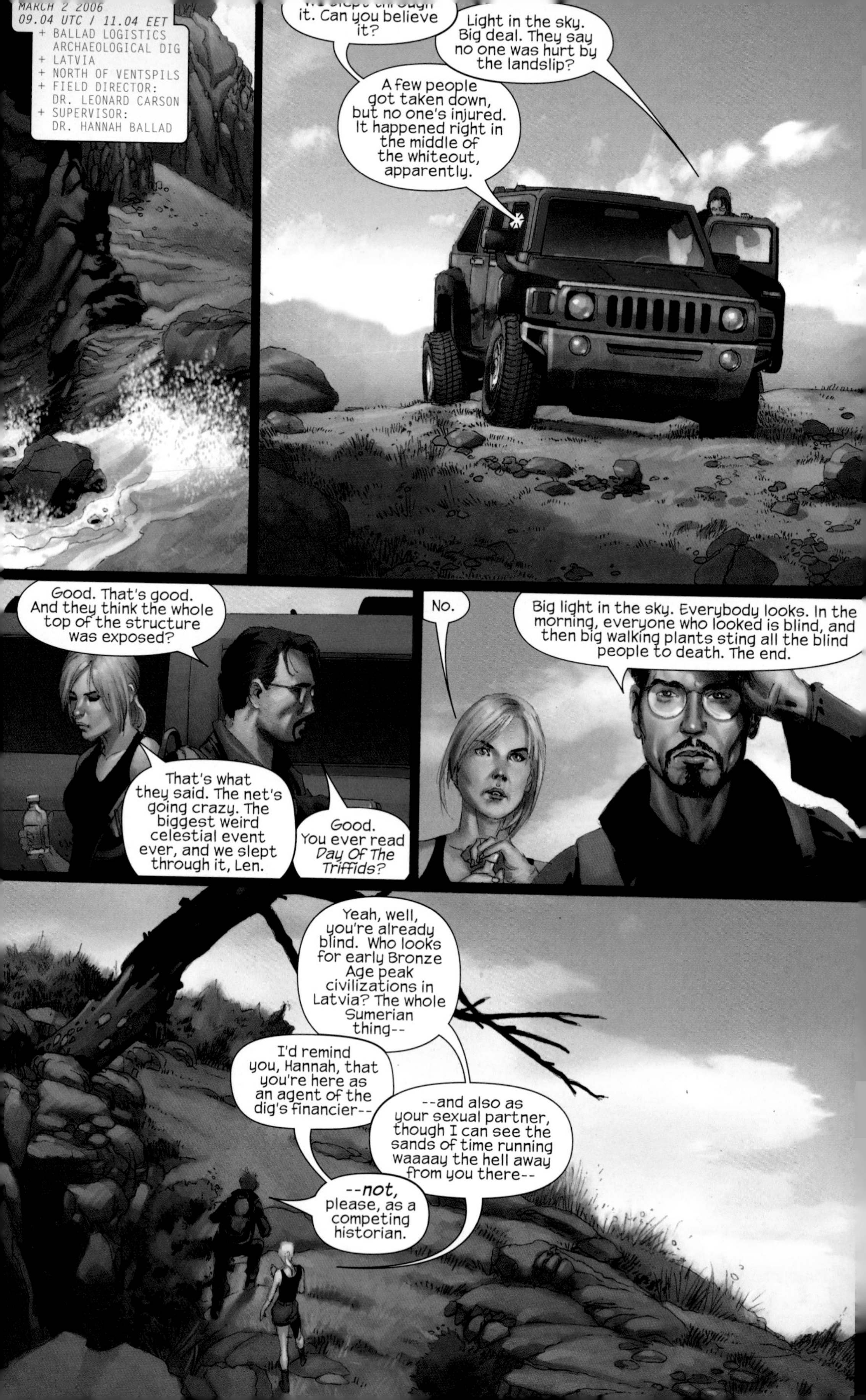
MARCH 2 2006
09.04 UTC / 11.04 EET
+ BALLAD LOGISTICS ARCHAEOLOGICAL DIG
+ LATVIA
+ NORTH OF VENTSPILS
+ FIELD DIRECTOR: DR. LEONARD CARSON
+ SUPERVISOR: DR. HANNAH BALLAD
it. Can you believe it?
Light in the sky. Big deal. They say no one was hurt by the landslip?
A few people got taken down, but no one's injured. It happened right in the middle of the whiteout, apparently.
Good. That's good. And they think the whole top of the structure was exposed?
That's what they said. The net's going crazy. The biggest weird celestial event ever, and we slept through it, Len.
Good. You ever read *Day Of The Triffids?*
No.
Big light in the sky. Everybody looks. In the morning, everyone who looked is blind, and then big walking plants sting all the blind people to death. The end.
Yeah, well, you're already blind. Who looks for early Bronze Age peak civilizations in Latvia? The whole Sumerian thing--
I'd remind you, Hannah, that you're here as an agent of the dig's financier--
--and also as your sexual partner, though I can see the sands of time running waaaay the hell away from you there--
--*not,* please, as a competing historian.

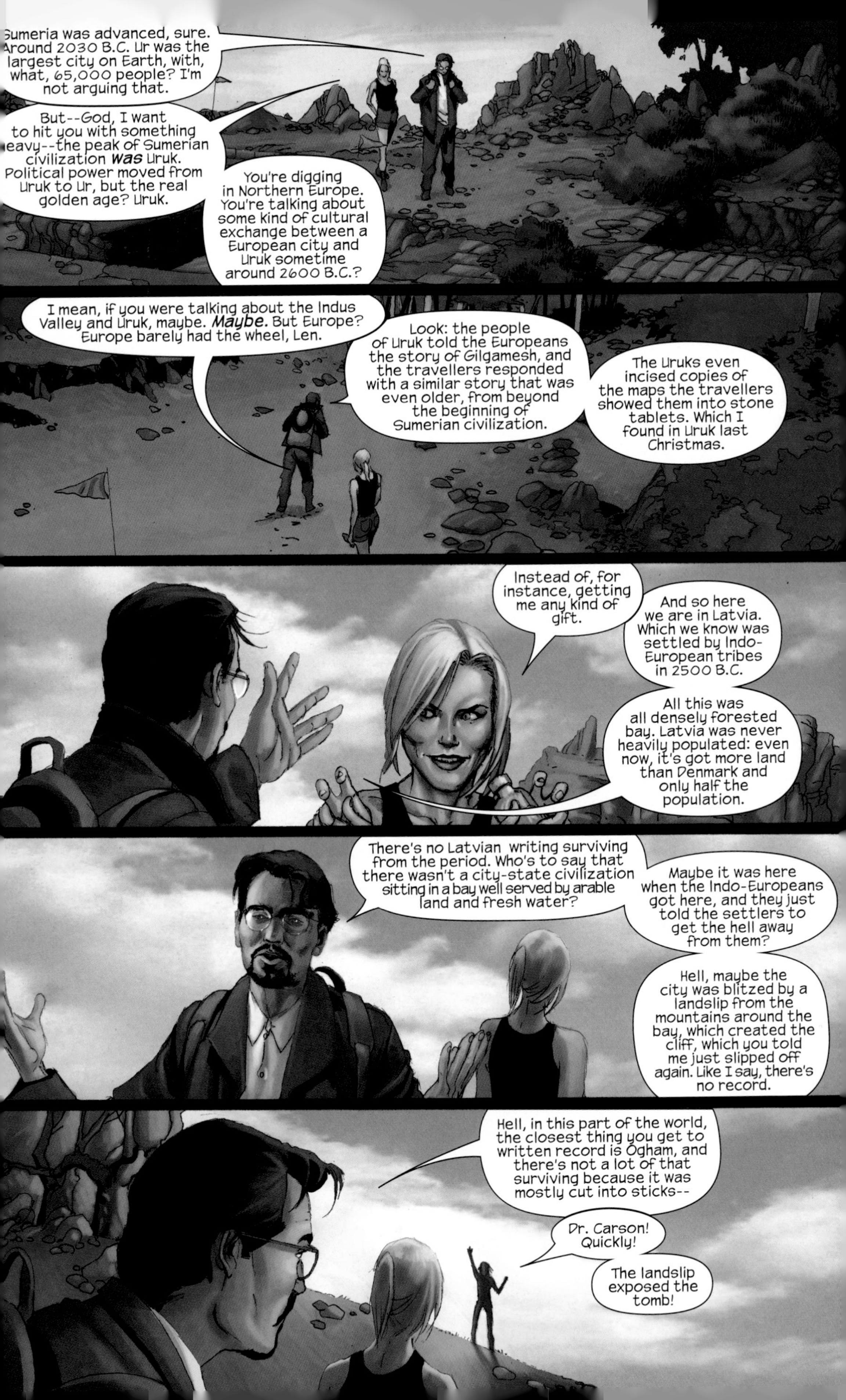

Sumeria was advanced, sure. Around 2030 B.C. Ur was the largest city on Earth, with, what, 65,000 people? I'm not arguing that.
But--God, I want to hit you with something heavy--the peak of Sumerian civilization *was* Uruk. Political power moved from Uruk to Ur, but the real golden age? Uruk.
You're digging in Northern Europe. You're talking about some kind of cultural exchange between a European city and Uruk sometime around 2600 B.C.?
I mean, if you were talking about the Indus Valley and Uruk, maybe. *Maybe.* But Europe? Europe barely had the wheel, Len.
Look: the people of Uruk told the Europeans the story of Gilgamesh, and the travellers responded with a similar story that was even older, from beyond the beginning of Sumerian civilization.
The Uruks even incised copies of the maps the travellers showed them into stone tablets. Which I found in Uruk last Christmas.
Instead of, for instance, getting me any kind of gift.
And so here we are in Latvia. Which we know was settled by Indo-European tribes in 2500 B.C.
All this was all densely forested bay. Latvia was never heavily populated: even now, it's got more land than Denmark and only half the population.
There's no Latvian writing surviving from the period. Who's to say that there wasn't a city-state civilization sitting in a bay well served by arable land and fresh water?
Maybe it was here when the Indo-Europeans got here, and they just told the settlers to get the hell away from them?
Hell, maybe the city was blitzed by a landslip from the mountains around the bay, which created the cliff, which you told me just slipped off again. Like I say, there's no record.
Hell, in this part of the world, the closest thing you get to written record is Ogham, and there's not a lot of that surviving because it was mostly cut into sticks--
Dr. Carson! Quickly!
The landslip exposed the tomb!

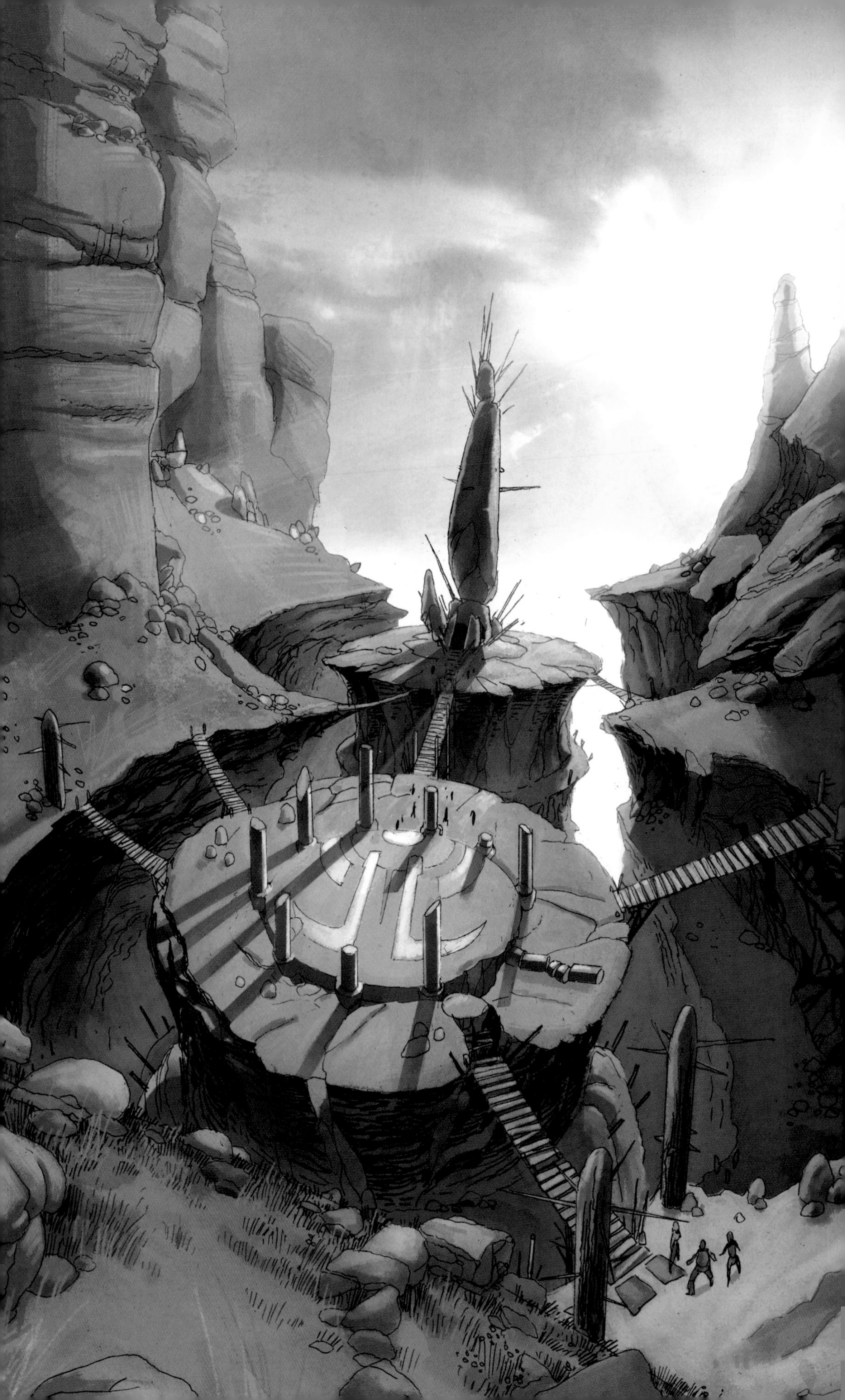

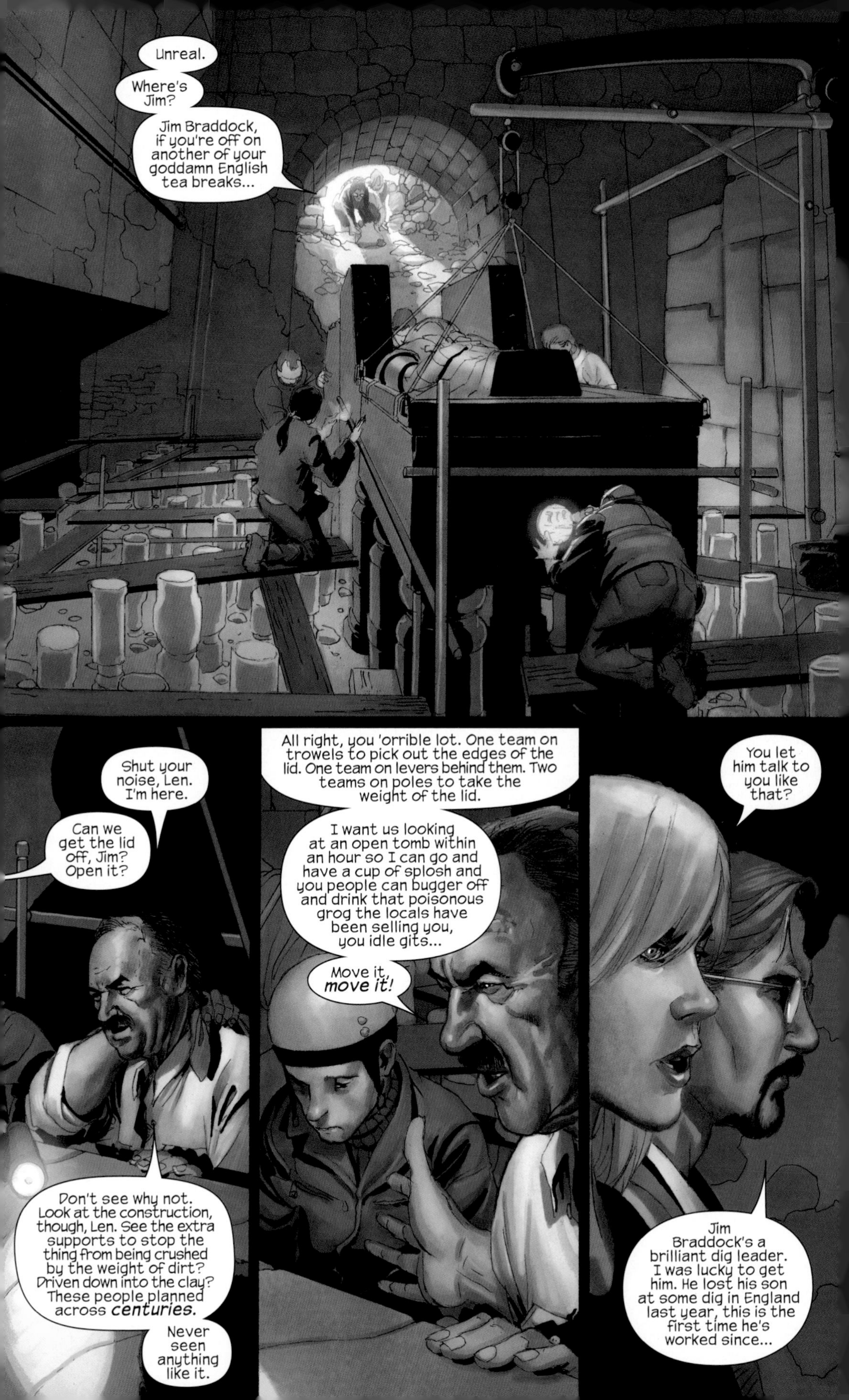

Unreal.
Where's Jim?
Jim Braddock, if you're off on another of your goddamn English tea breaks...
Shut your noise, Len. I'm here.
Can we get the lid off, Jim? Open it?
Don't see why not. Look at the construction, though, Len. See the extra supports to stop the thing from being crushed by the weight of dirt? Driven down into the clay? These people planned across *centuries.*
Never seen anything like it.
All right, you 'orrible lot. One team on trowels to pick out the edges of the lid. One team on levers behind them. Two teams on poles to take the weight of the lid.
I want us looking at an open tomb within an hour so I can go and have a cup of splosh and you people can bugger off and drink that poisonous grog the locals have been selling you, you idle gits...
Move it, *move it!*
You let him talk to you like that?
Jim Braddock's a brilliant dig leader. I was lucky to get him. He lost his son at some dig in England last year, this is the first time he's worked since...

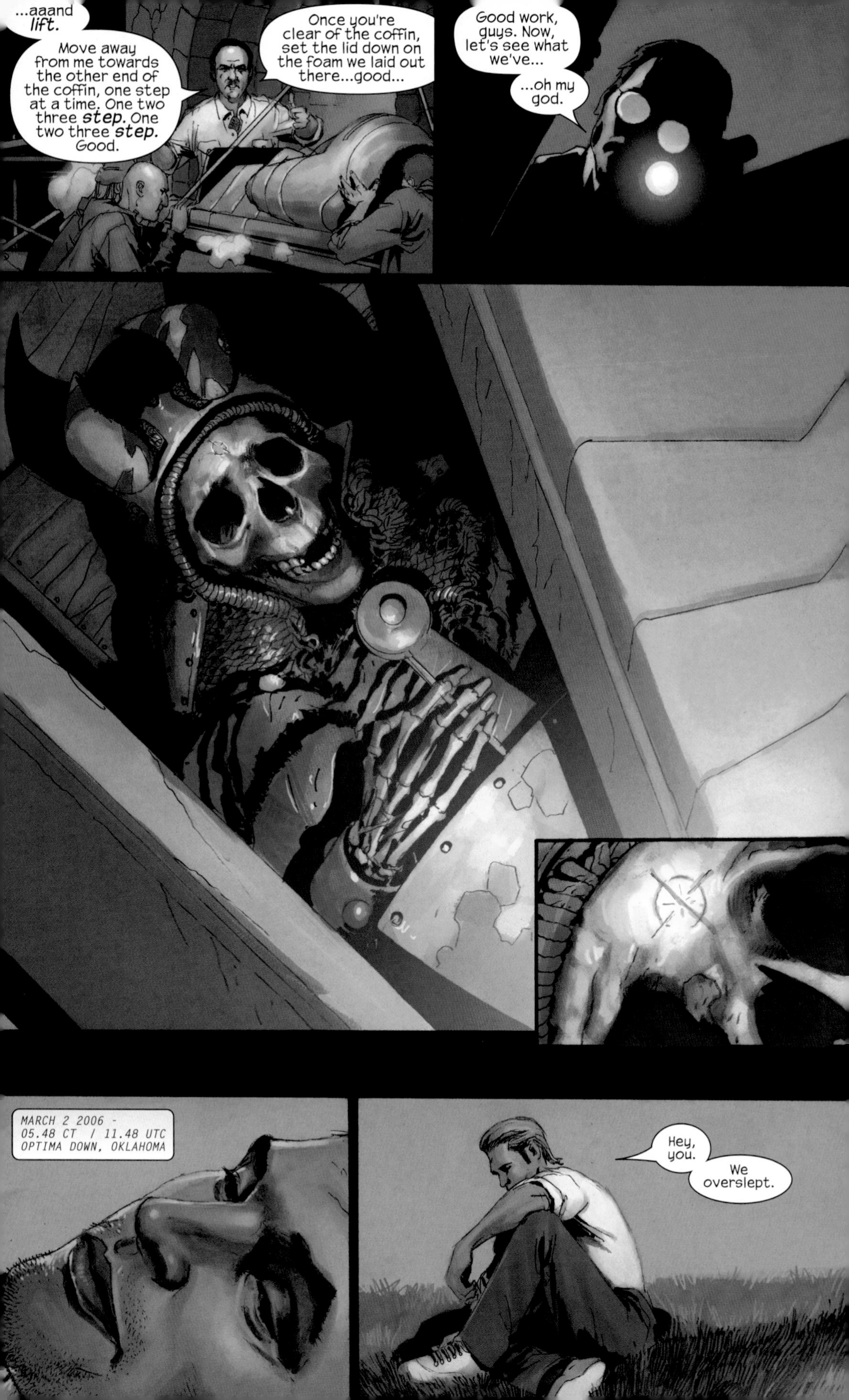
...aaand lift.
Move away from me towards the other end of the coffin, one step at a time. One two three step. One two three step. Good.
Once you're clear of the coffin, set the lid down on the foam we laid out there...good...
Good work, guys. Now, let's see what we've...
...oh my god.
MARCH 2 2006 - 05.48 CT / 11.48 UTC OPTIMA DOWN, OKLAHOMA
Hey, you.
We overslept.

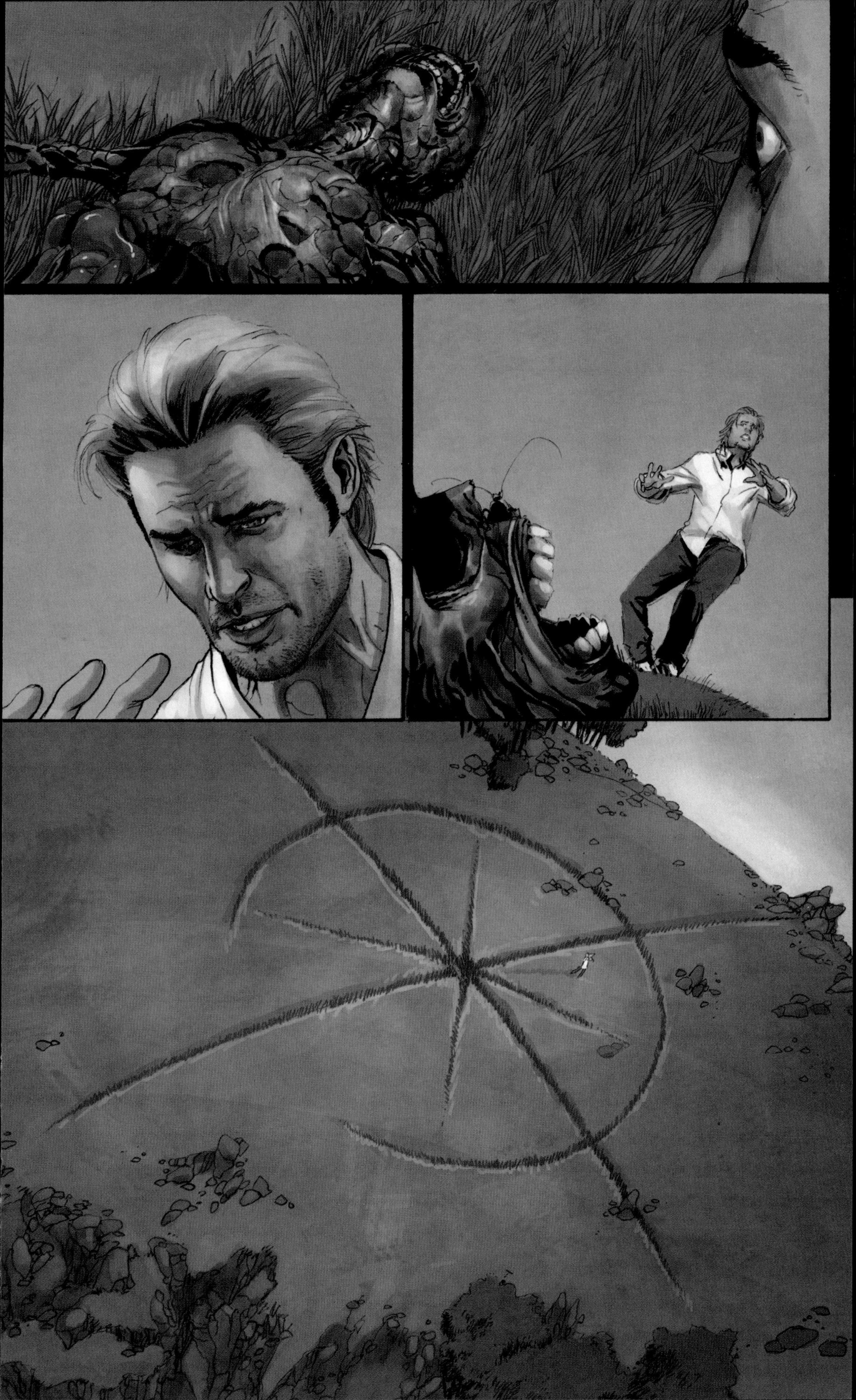

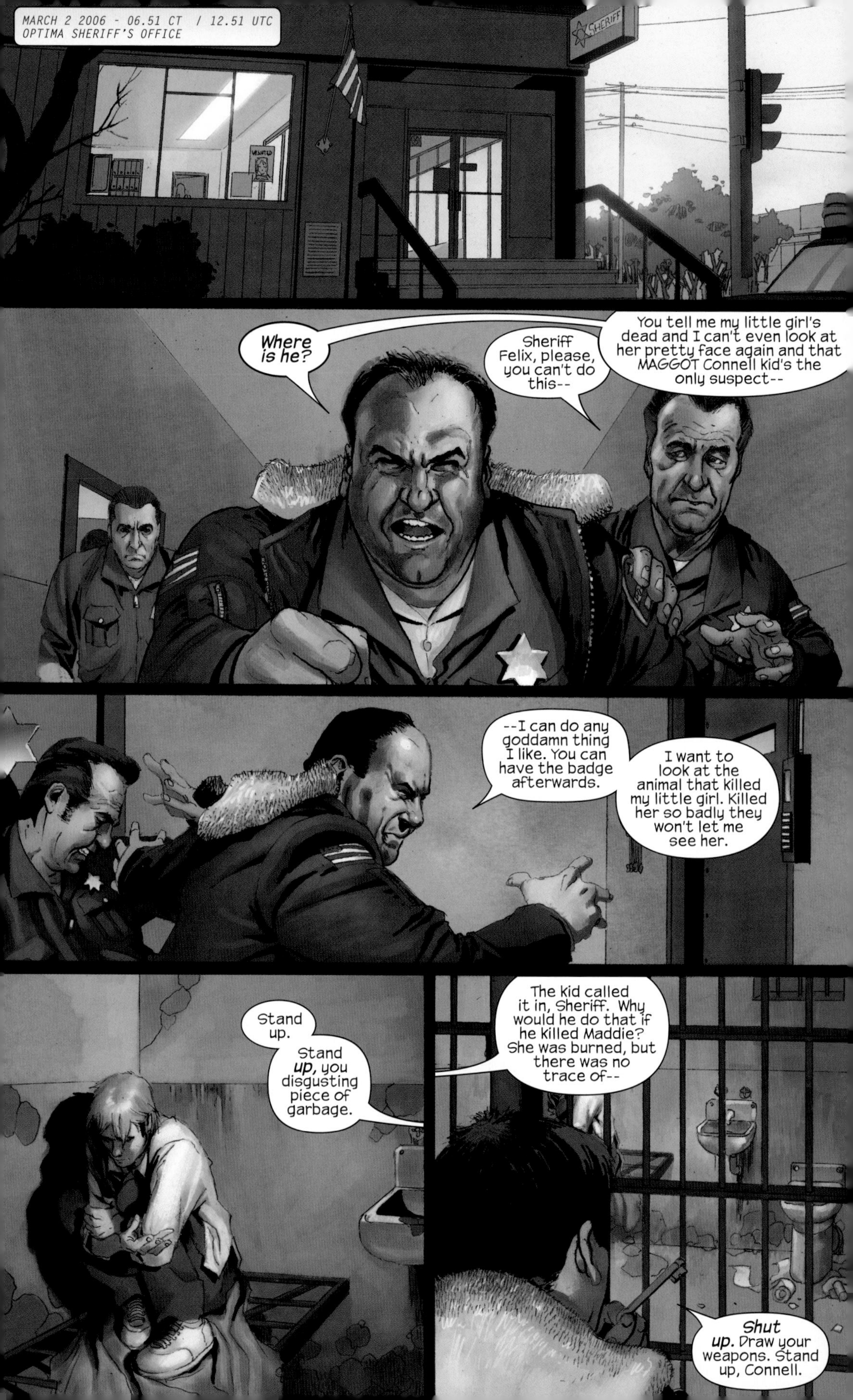
MARCH 2 2006 - 06.51 CT / 12.51 UTC
OPTIMA SHERIFF'S OFFICE
SHERIFF
Where is he?
Sheriff Felix, please, you can't do this--
You tell me my little girl's dead and I can't even look at her pretty face again and that MAGGOT Connell kid's the only suspect--
--I can do any goddamn thing I like. You can have the badge afterwards.
I want to look at the animal that killed my little girl. Killed her so badly they won't let me see her.
Stand up.
Stand up, you disgusting piece of garbage.
The kid called it in, Sheriff. Why would he do that if he killed Maddie? She was burned, but there was no trace of--
Shut up. Draw your weapons. Stand up, Connell.

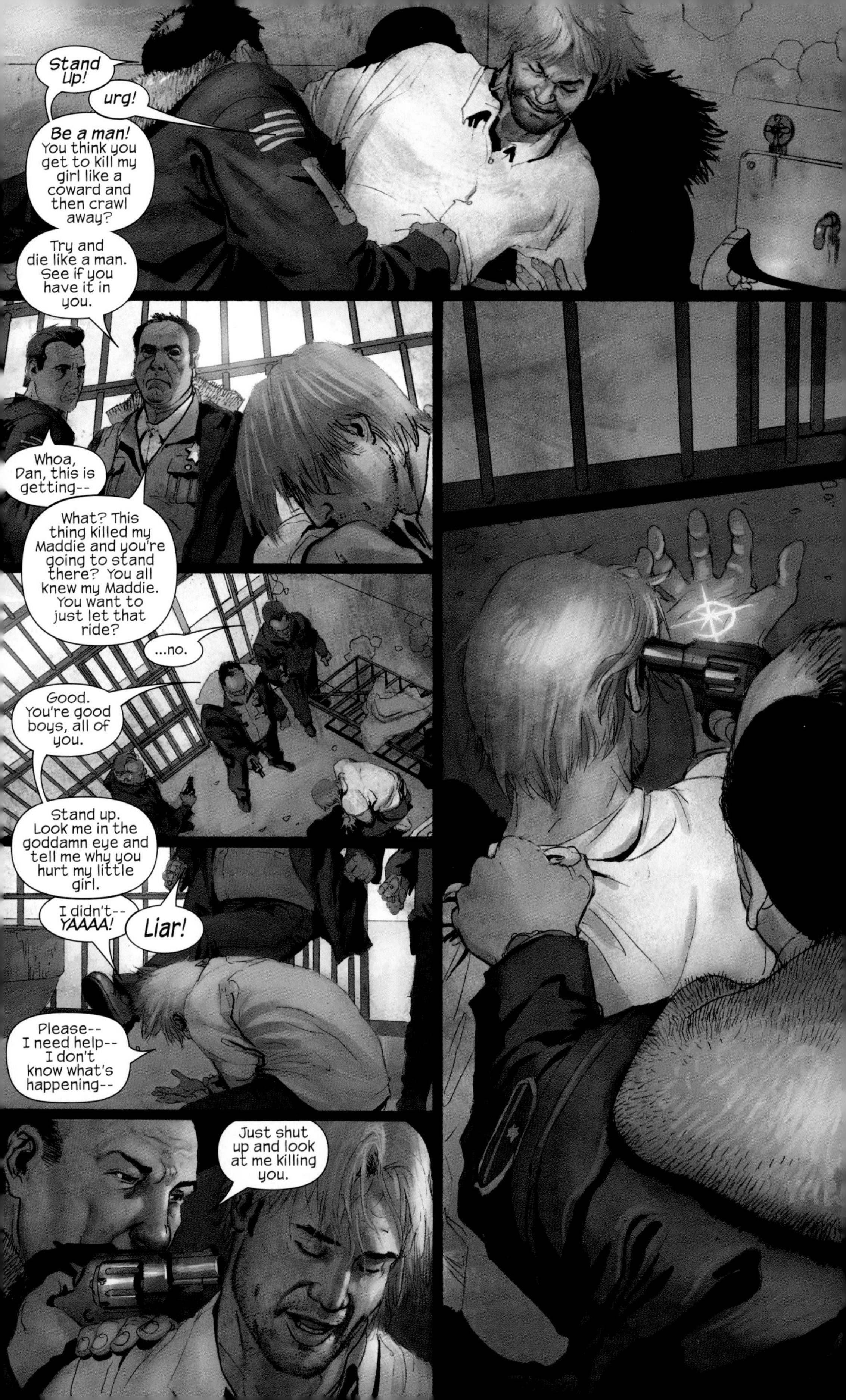
Stand up!
urg!
Be a man! You think you get to kill my girl like a coward and then crawl away?
Try and die like a man. See if you have it in you.
Whoa, Dan, this is getting--
What? This thing killed my Maddie and you're going to stand there? You all knew my Maddie. You want to just let that ride?
...no.
Good. You're good boys, all of you.
Stand up. Look me in the goddamn eye and tell me why you hurt my little girl.
I didn't-- YAAAA!
Liar!
Please-- I need help-- I don't know what's happening--
Just shut up and look at me killing you.

ISSUE #2 VARIANT COVER by ESAD RIBIC

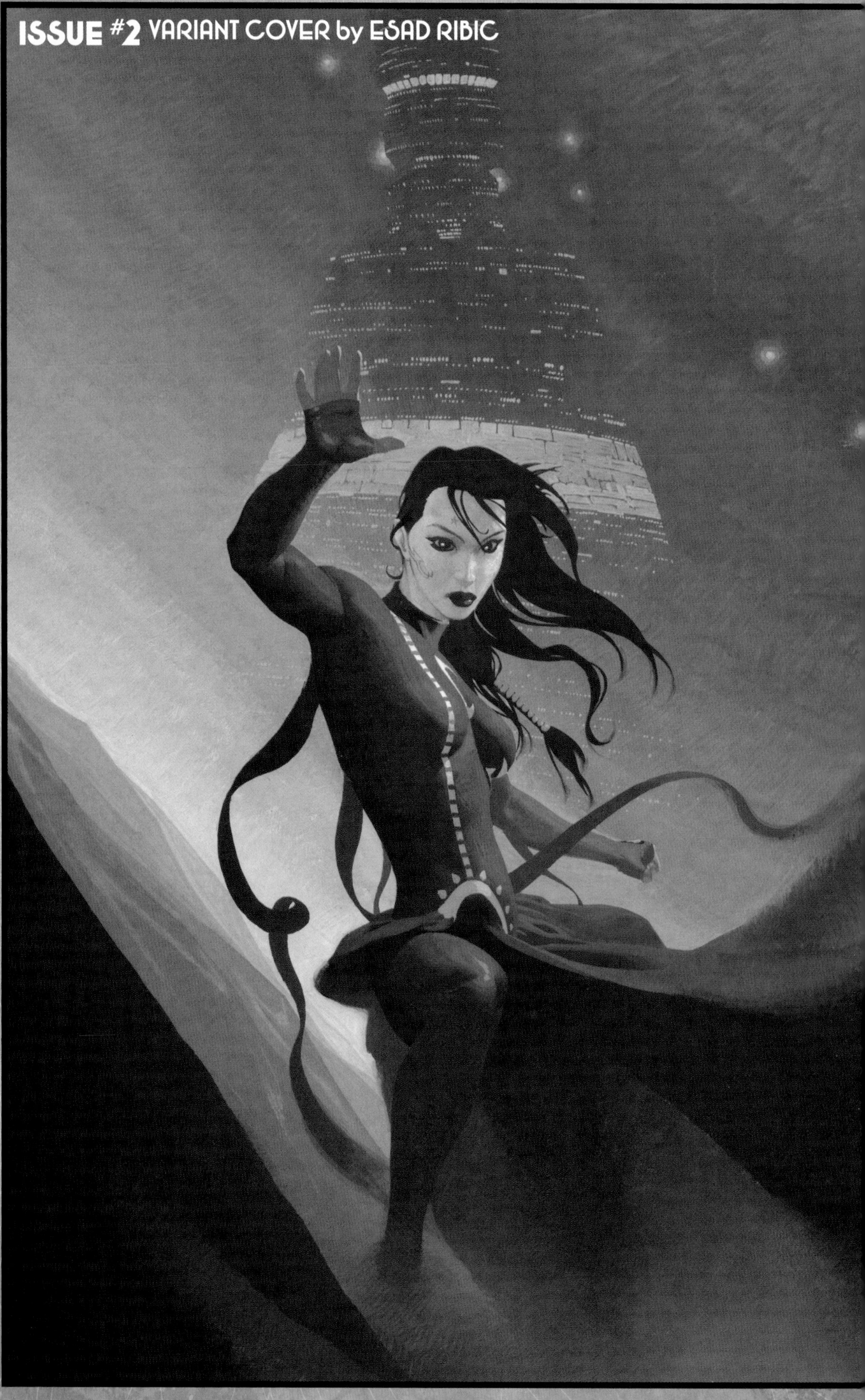

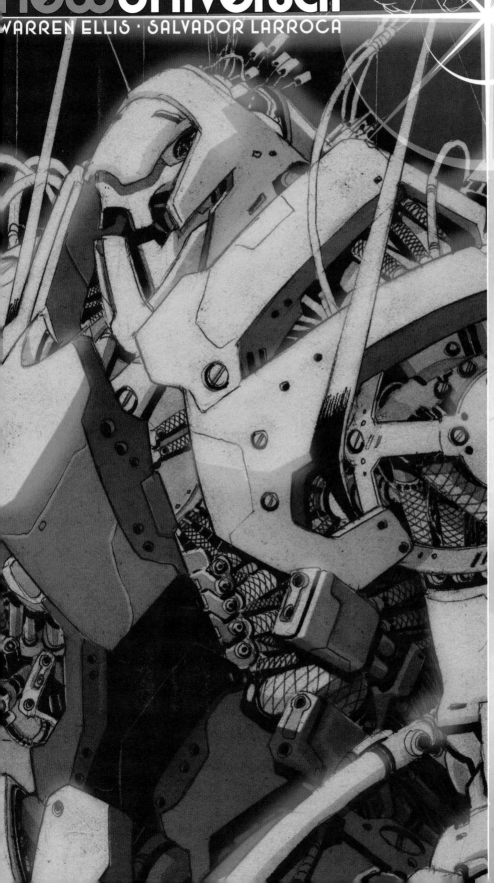

newuniversal

WARREN ELLIS · SALVADOR LARROCA

2

newuniversal
TRAUMA

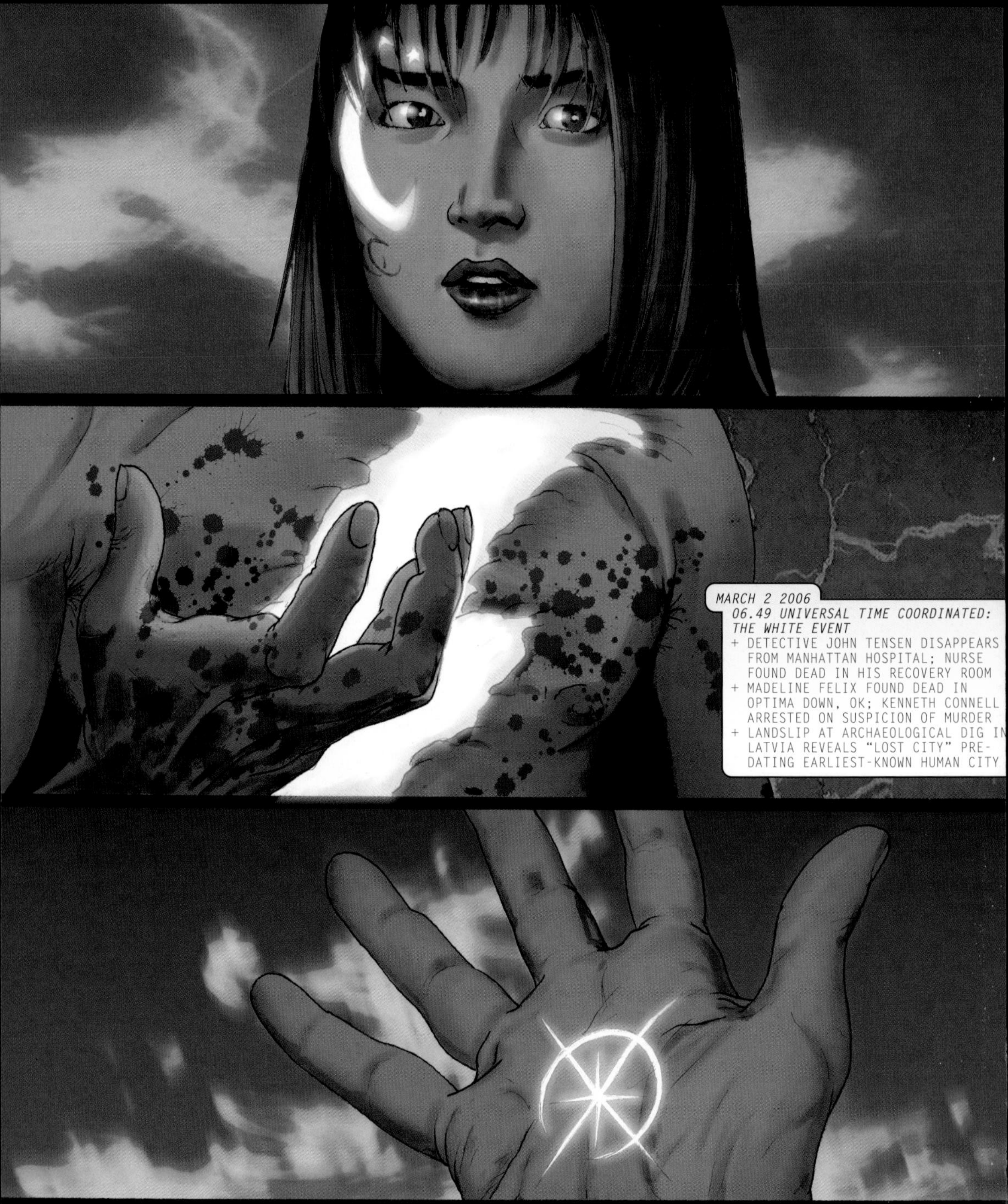

MARCH 2 2006
06.49 UNIVERSAL TIME COORDINATED:
THE WHITE EVENT
+ DETECTIVE JOHN TENSEN DISAPPEARS FROM MANHATTAN HOSPITAL; NURSE FOUND DEAD IN HIS RECOVERY ROOM
+ MADELINE FELIX FOUND DEAD IN OPTIMA DOWN, OK; KENNETH CONNELL ARRESTED ON SUSPICION OF MURDER
+ LANDSLIP AT ARCHAEOLOGICAL DIG IN LATVIA REVEALS "LOST CITY" PRE-DATING EARLIEST-KNOWN HUMAN CITY

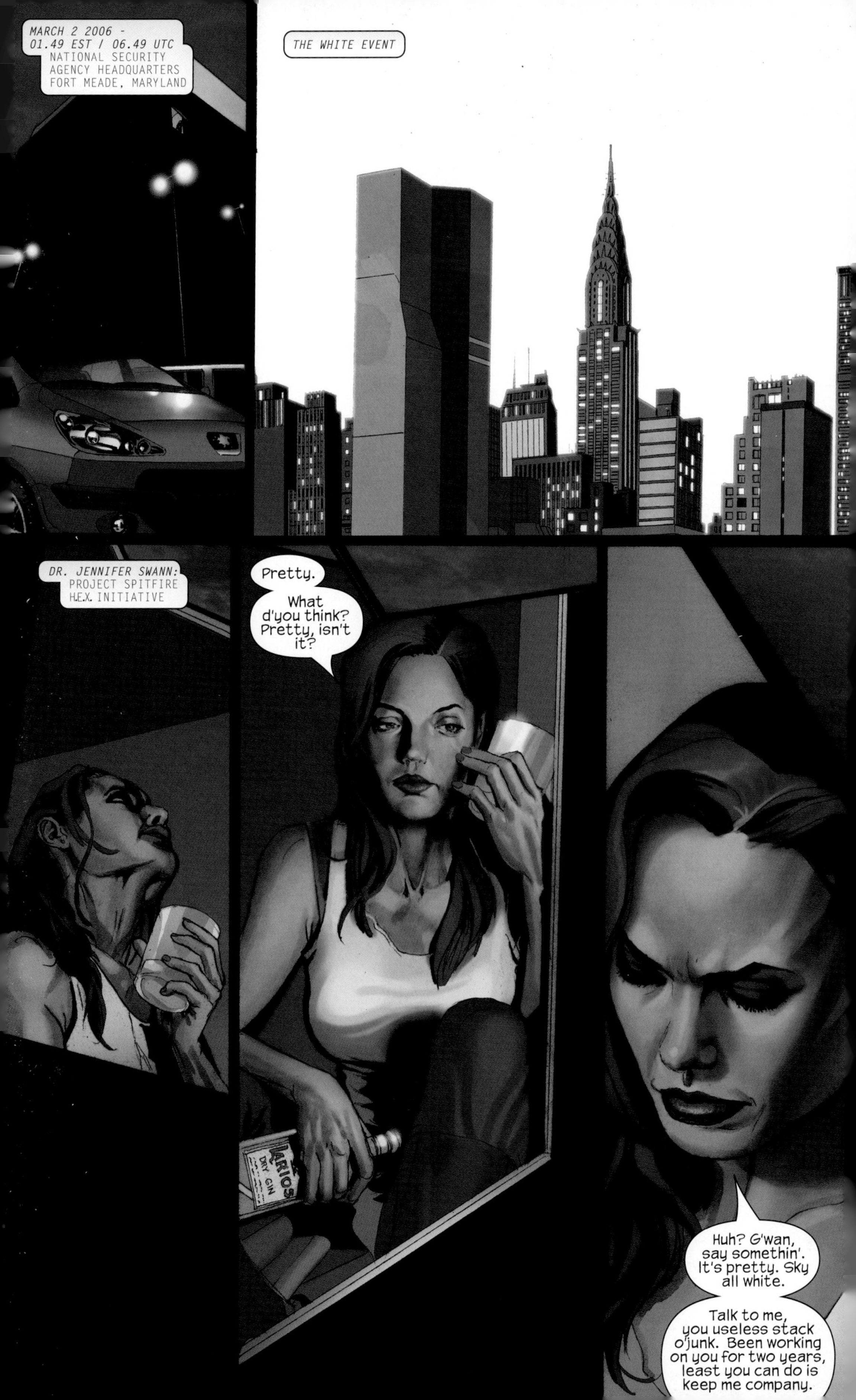
MARCH 2 2006 -
01.49 EST / 06.49 UTC
NATIONAL SECURITY
AGENCY HEADQUARTERS
FORT MEADE, MARYLAND
THE WHITE EVENT
DR. JENNIFER SWANN:
PROJECT SPITFIRE
H.E.X. INITIATIVE
Pretty.
What d'you think? Pretty, isn't it?
LARIOS DRY GIN
Huh? G'wan, say somethin'. It's pretty. Sky all white.
Talk to me, you useless stack o'junk. Been working on you for two years, least you can do is keep me company.

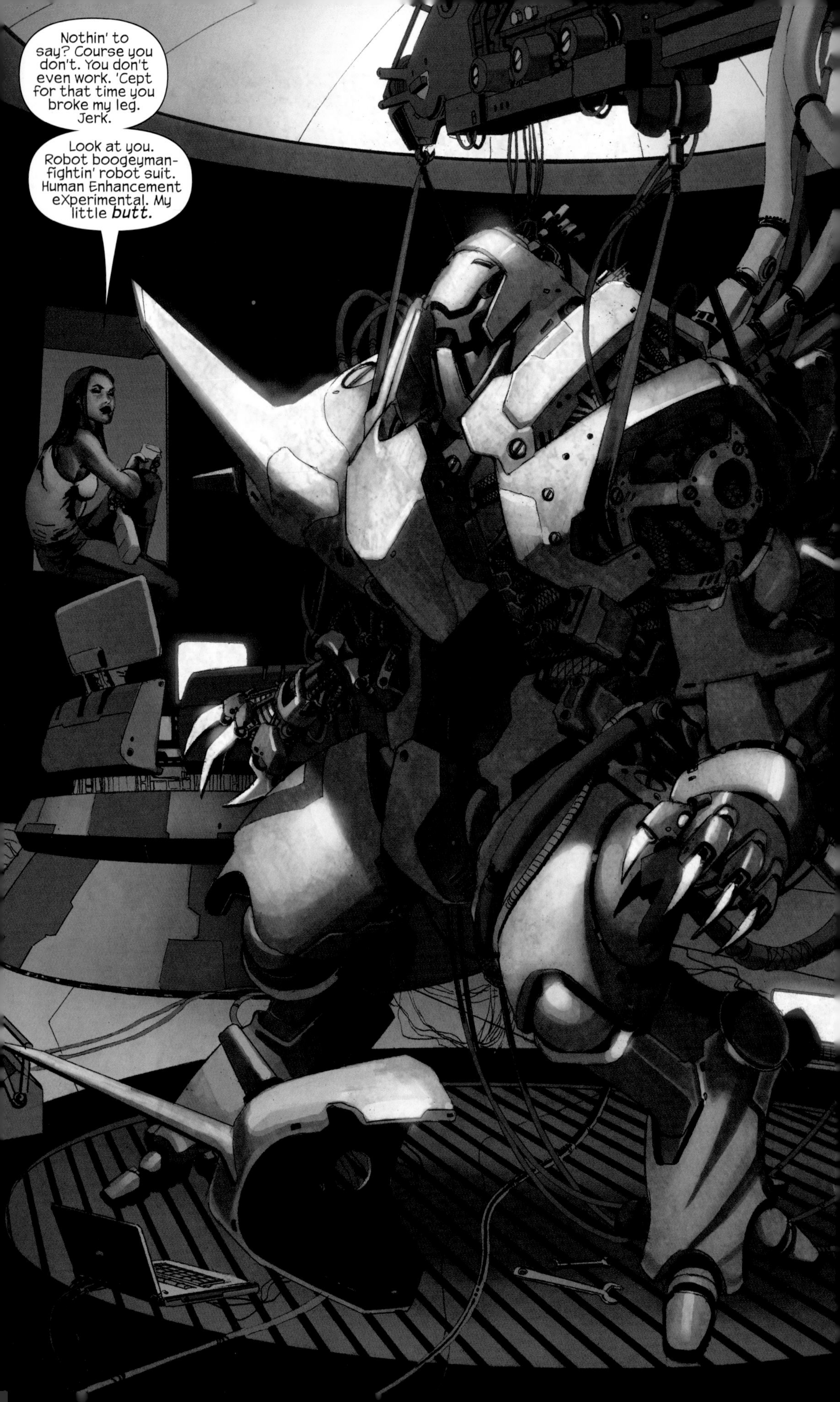
Nothin' to say? Course you don't. You don't even work. 'Cept for that time you broke my leg. Jerk.
Look at you. Robot boogeyman-fightin' robot suit. Human Enhancement eXperimental. My little *butt.*

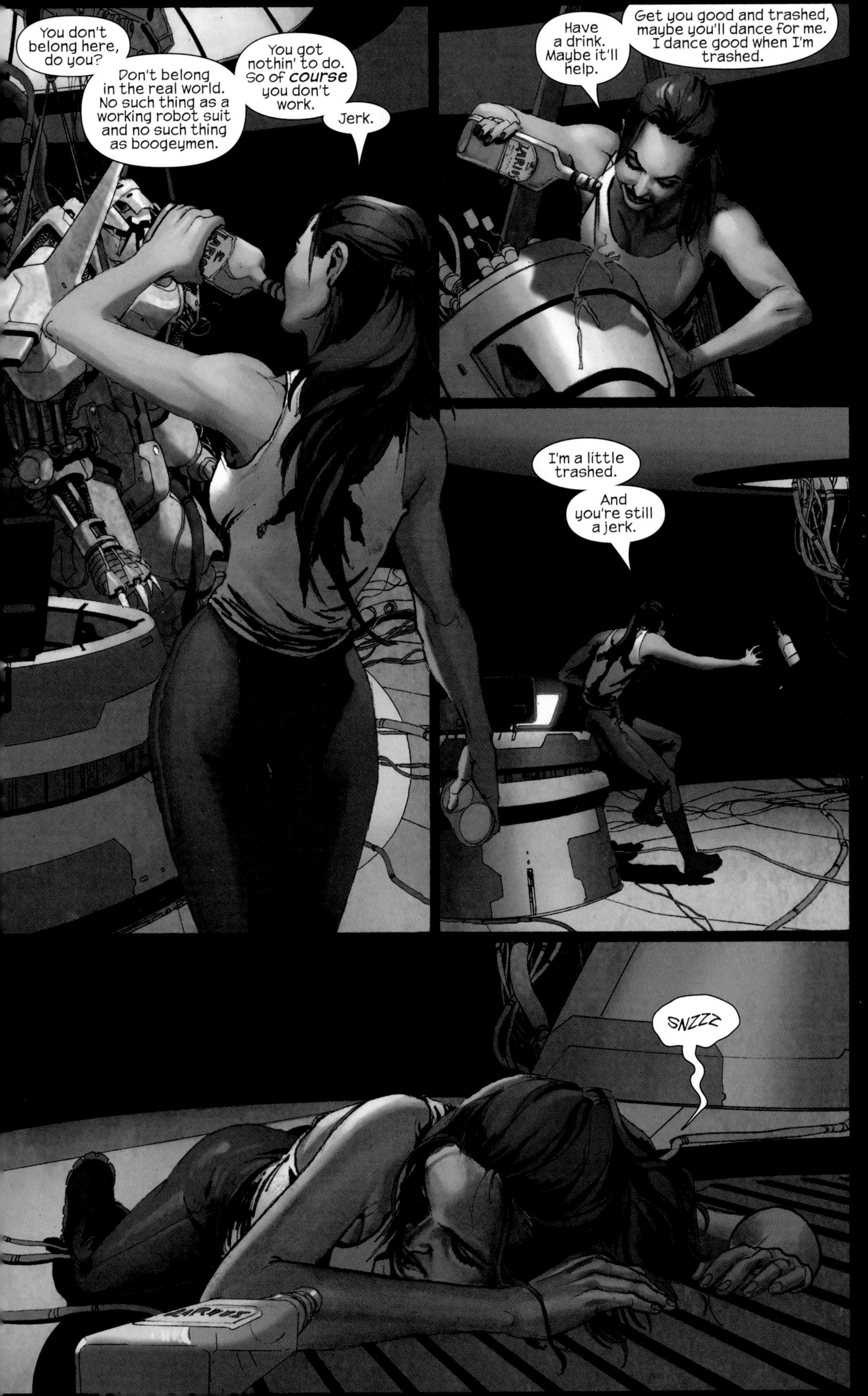
You don't belong here, do you?
Don't belong in the real world. No such thing as a working robot suit and no such thing as boogeymen.
You got nothin' to do. So of *course* you don't work.
Jerk.
Have a drink. Maybe it'll help.
Get you good and trashed, maybe you'll dance for me. I dance good when I'm trashed.
I'm a little trashed.
And you're still a jerk.
SNZZZ

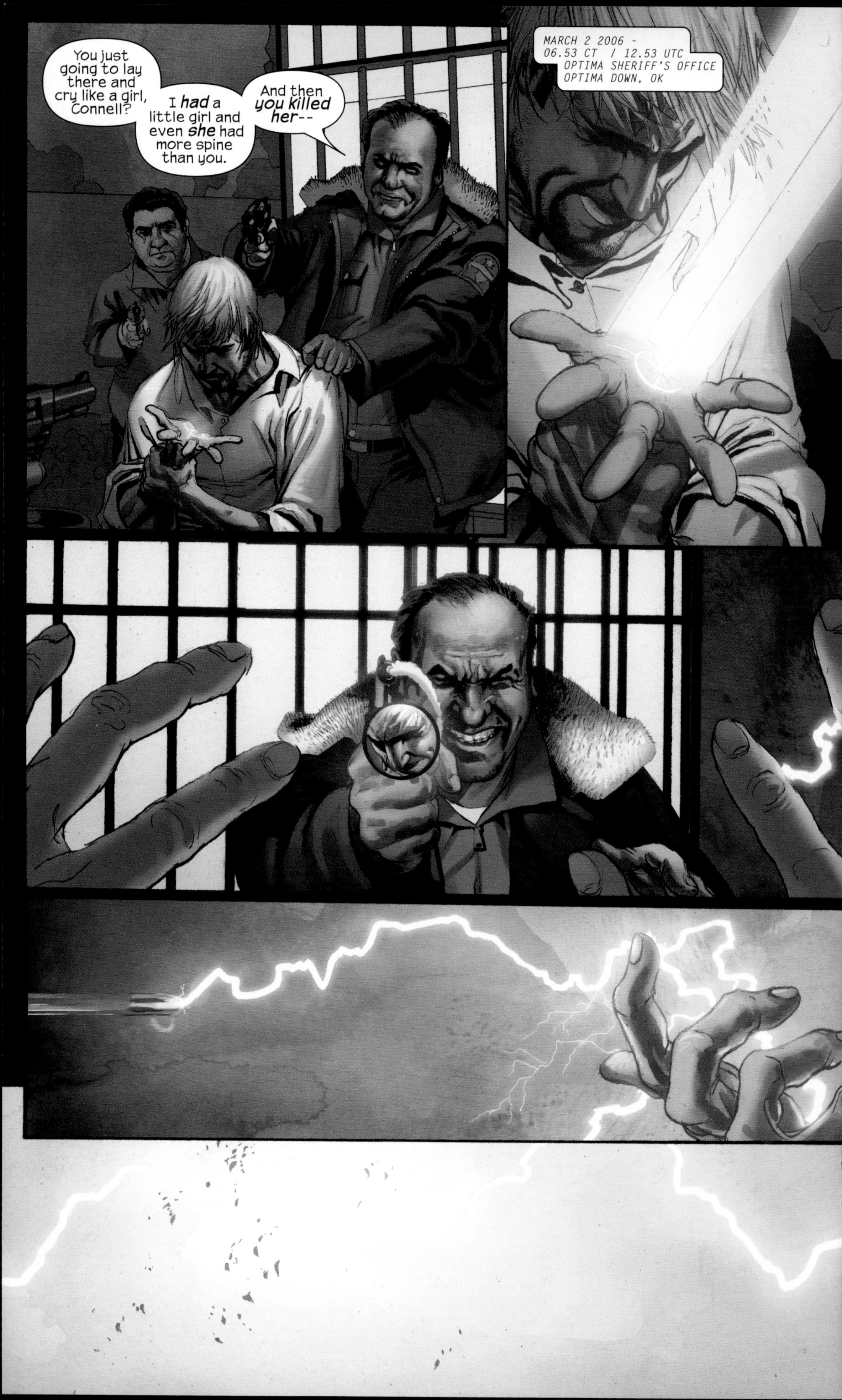

You just going to lay there and cry like a girl, Connell?
I *had* a little girl and even *she* had more spine than you.
And then *you killed her*--
MARCH 2 2006 - 06.53 CT / 12.53 UTC OPTIMA SHERIFF'S OFFICE OPTIMA DOWN, OK

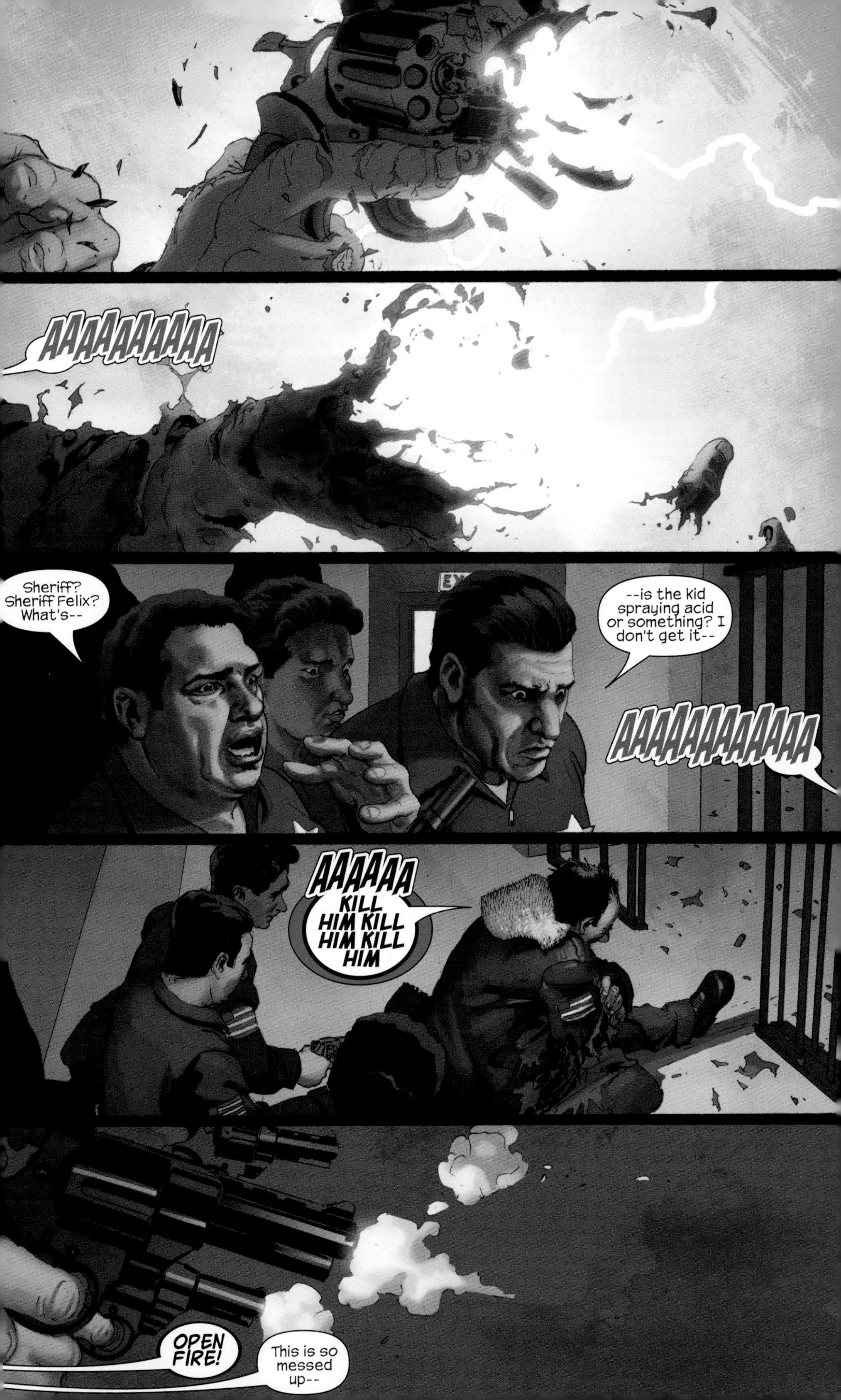

AAAAAAAAAA
Sheriff? Sheriff Felix? What's--
--is the kid spraying acid or something? I don't get it--
AAAAAAAAAAA
AAAAAA KILL HIM KILL HIM KILL HIM
OPEN FIRE!
This is so messed up--

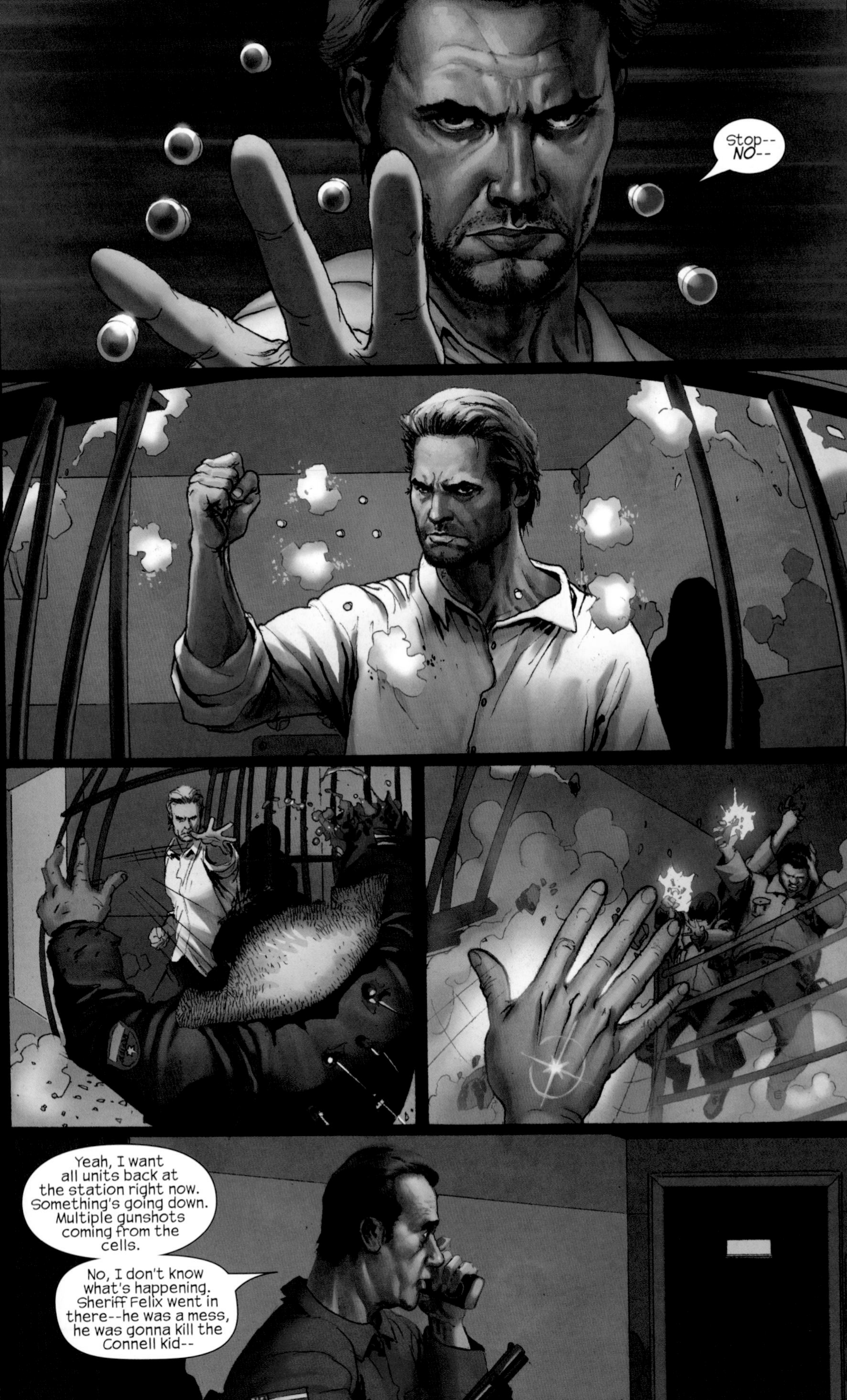
Stop--
NO--
Yeah, I want all units back at the station right now. Something's going down. Multiple gunshots coming from the cells.
No, I don't know what's happening. Sheriff Felix went in there--he was a mess, he was gonna kill the Connell kid--

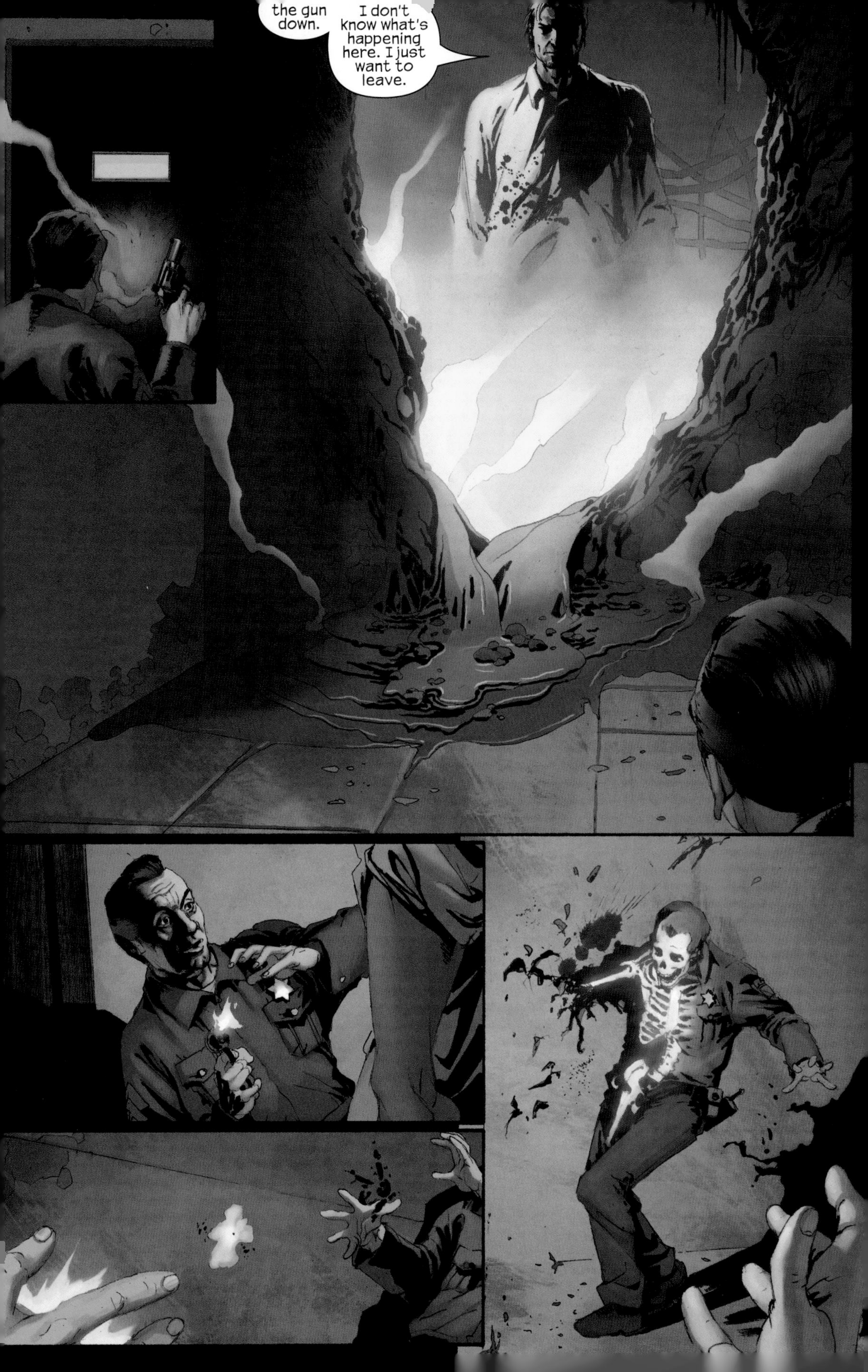
the gun down.
I don't know what's happening here. I just want to leave.

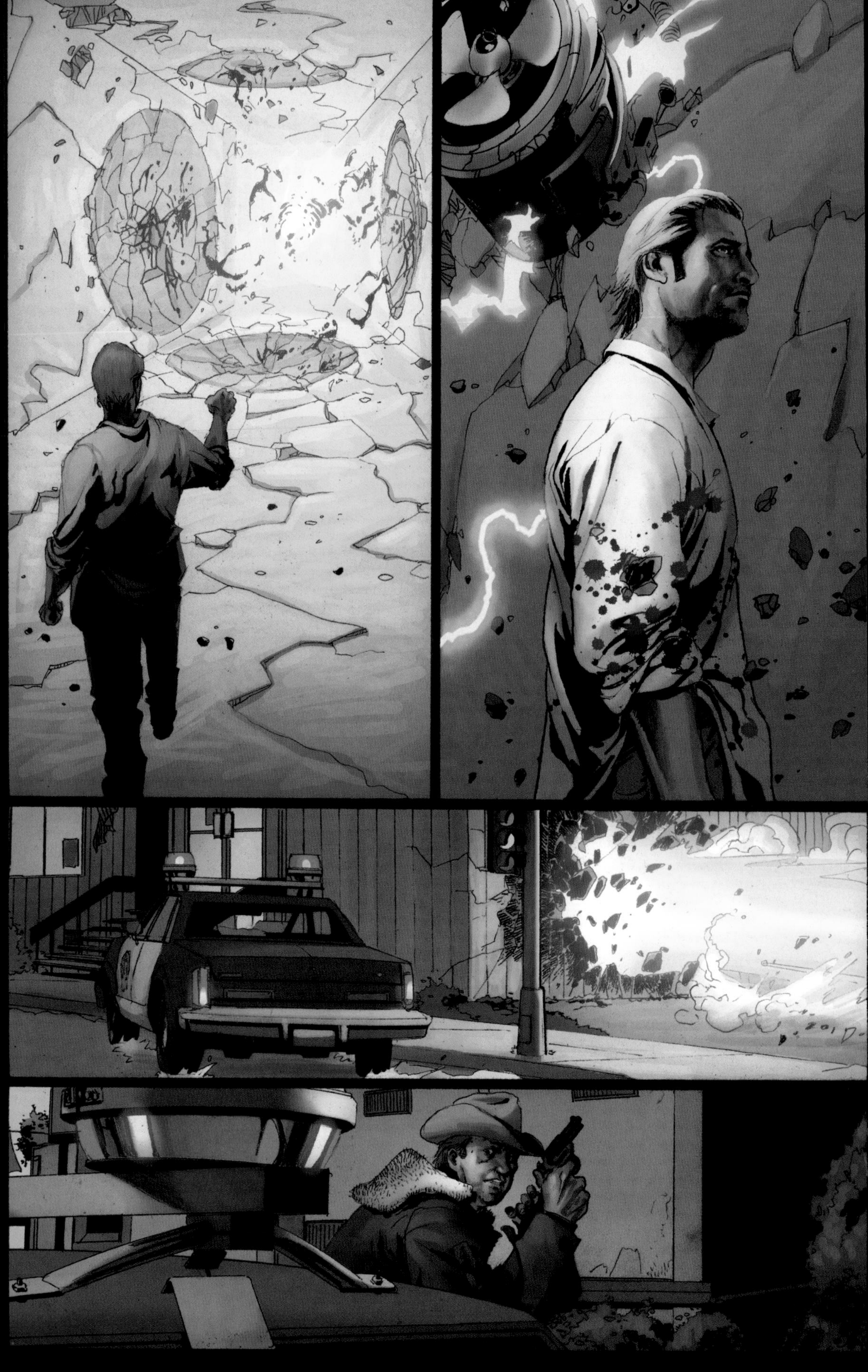

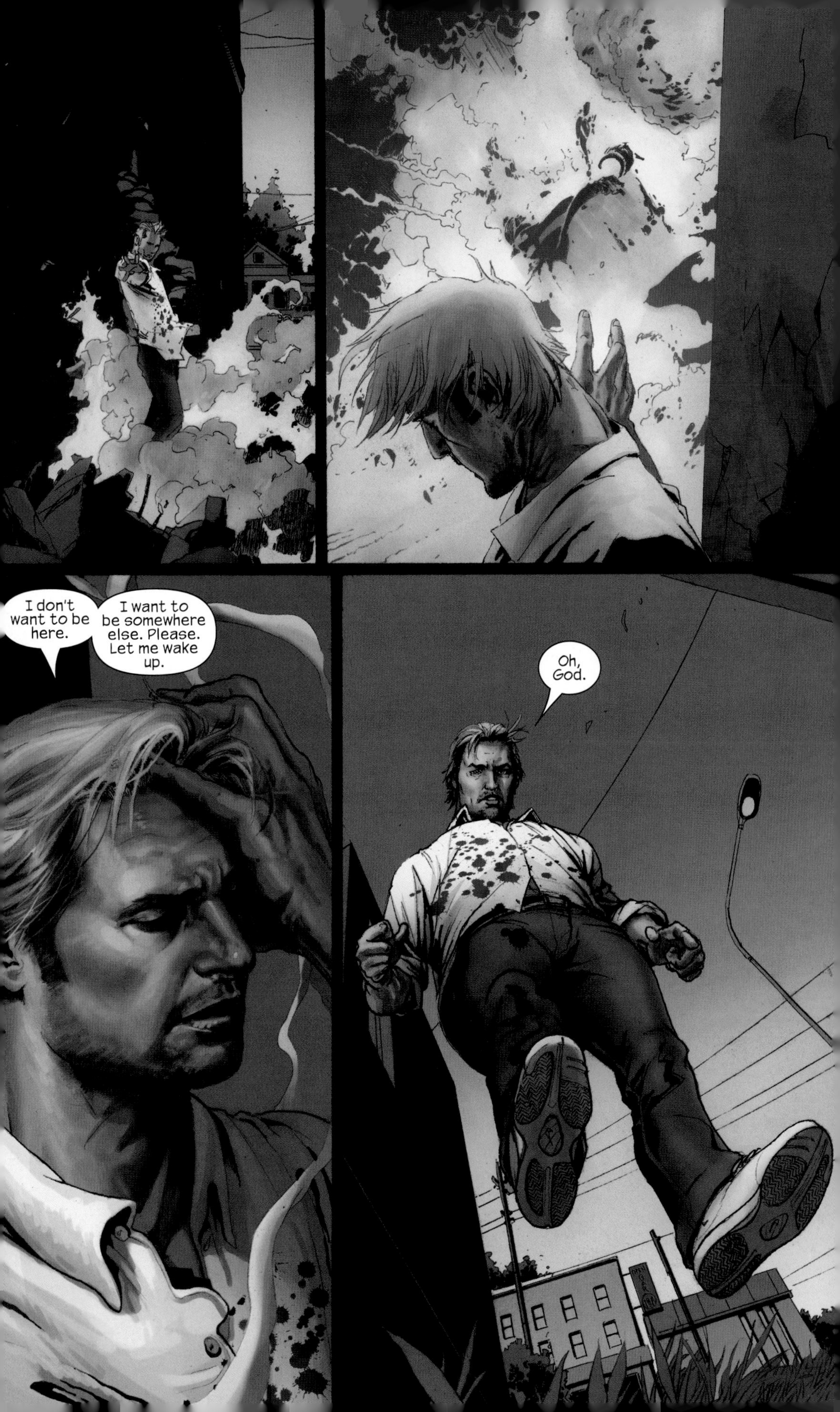
I don't want to be here.
I want to be somewhere else. Please. Let me wake up.
Oh, God.

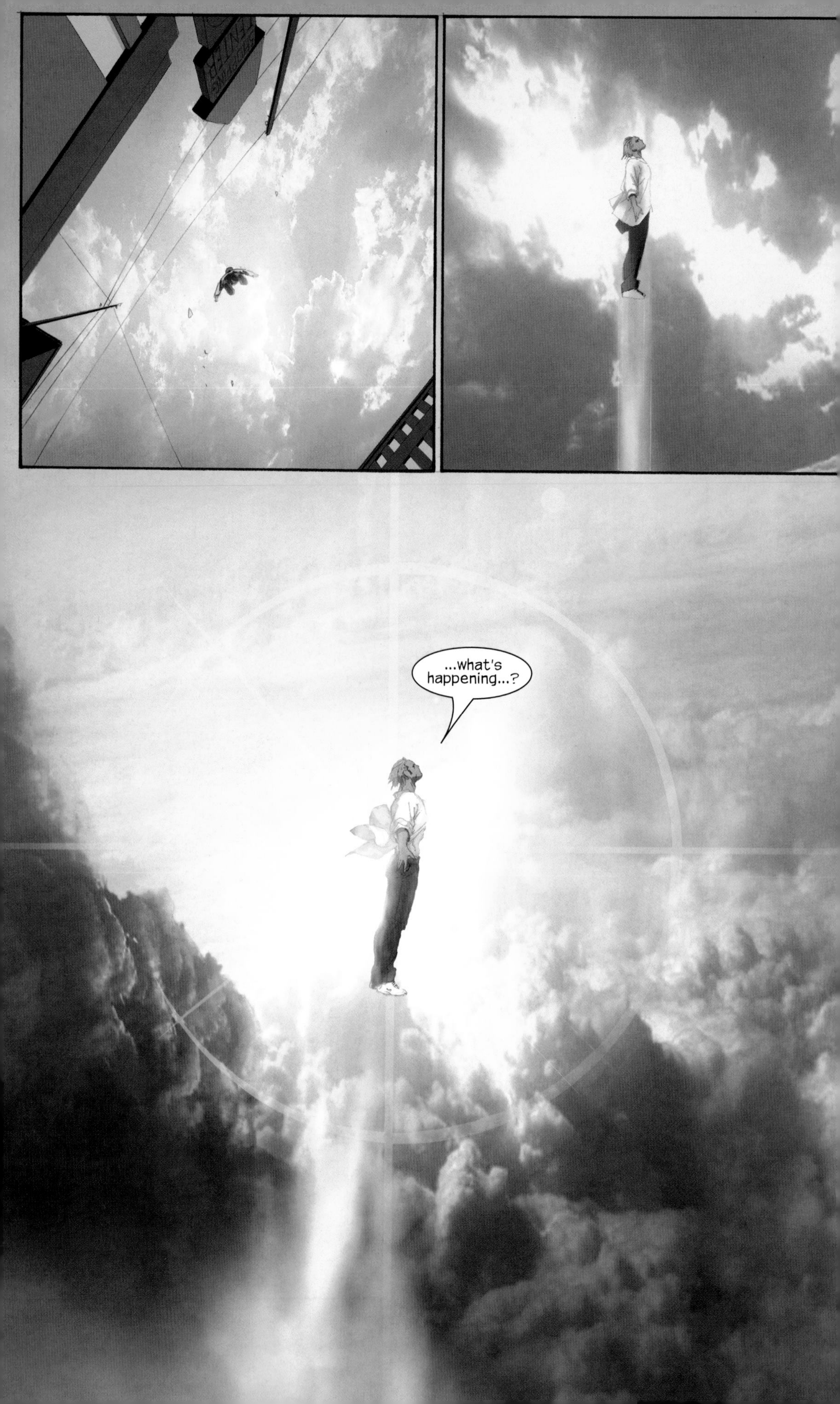
...what's happening...?

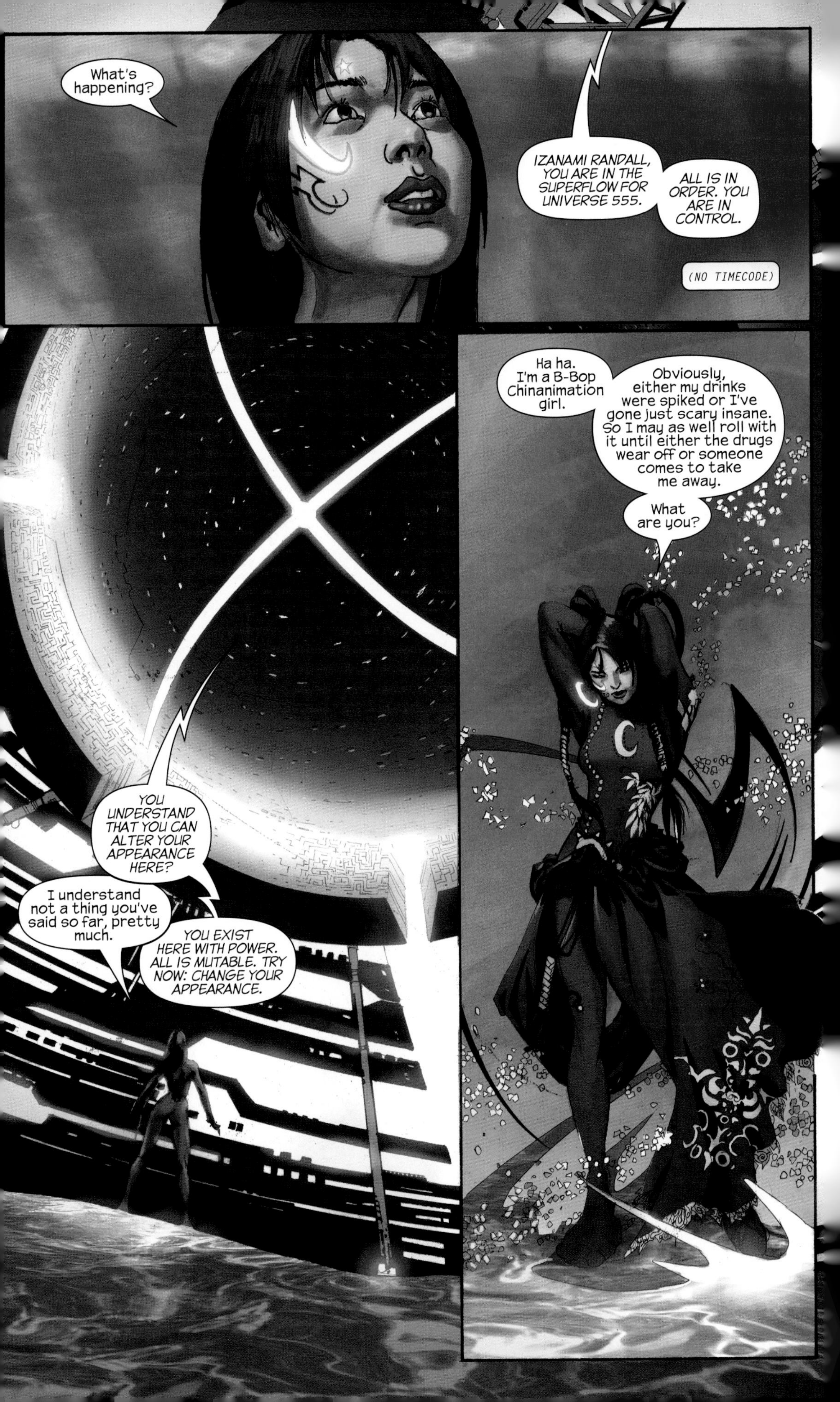
What's happening?
IZANAMI RANDALL, YOU ARE IN THE SUPERFLOW FOR UNIVERSE 555.
ALL IS IN ORDER. YOU ARE IN CONTROL.
(NO TIMECODE)
YOU UNDERSTAND THAT YOU CAN ALTER YOUR APPEARANCE HERE?
I understand not a thing you've said so far, pretty much.
YOU EXIST HERE WITH POWER. ALL IS MUTABLE. TRY NOW: CHANGE YOUR APPEARANCE.
Ha ha. I'm a B-Bop Chinanimation girl.
Obviously, either my drinks were spiked or I've gone just scary insane. So I may as well roll with it until either the drugs wear off or someone comes to take me away.
What are you?

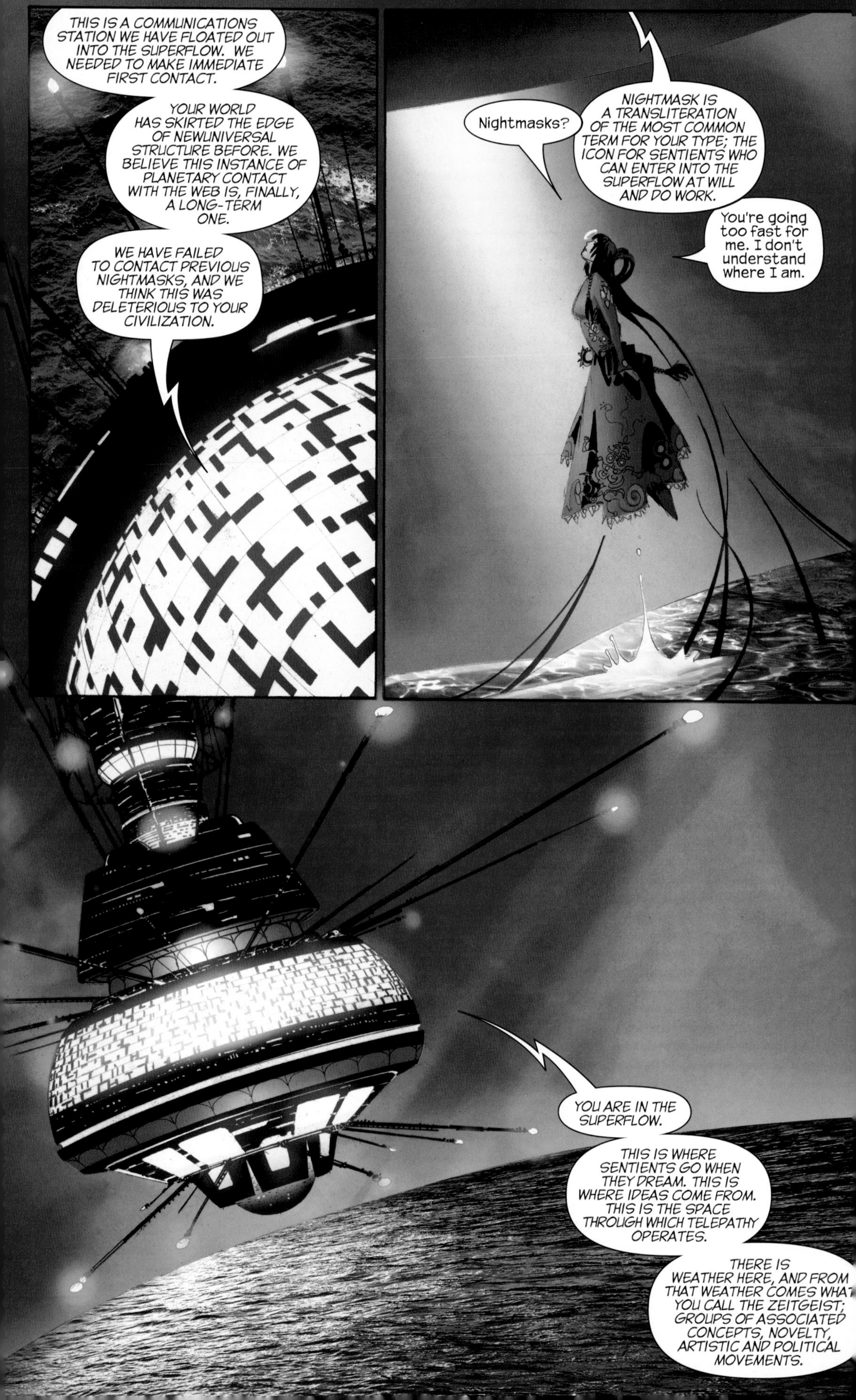
THIS IS A COMMUNICATIONS STATION WE HAVE FLOATED OUT INTO THE SUPERFLOW. WE NEEDED TO MAKE IMMEDIATE FIRST CONTACT.
YOUR WORLD HAS SKIRTED THE EDGE OF NEWUNIVERSAL STRUCTURE BEFORE. WE BELIEVE THIS INSTANCE OF PLANETARY CONTACT WITH THE WEB IS, FINALLY, A LONG-TERM ONE.
WE HAVE FAILED TO CONTACT PREVIOUS NIGHTMASKS, AND WE THINK THIS WAS DELETERIOUS TO YOUR CIVILIZATION.
Nightmasks?
NIGHTMASK IS A TRANSLITERATION OF THE MOST COMMON TERM FOR YOUR TYPE; THE ICON FOR SENTIENTS WHO CAN ENTER INTO THE SUPERFLOW AT WILL AND DO WORK.
You're going too fast for me. I don't understand where I am.
YOU ARE IN THE SUPERFLOW.
THIS IS WHERE SENTIENTS GO WHEN THEY DREAM. THIS IS WHERE IDEAS COME FROM. THIS IS THE SPACE THROUGH WHICH TELEPATHY OPERATES.
THERE IS WEATHER HERE, AND FROM THAT WEATHER COMES WHAT YOU CALL THE ZEITGEIST; GROUPS OF ASSOCIATED CONCEPTS, NOVELTY, ARTISTIC AND POLITICAL MOVEMENTS.

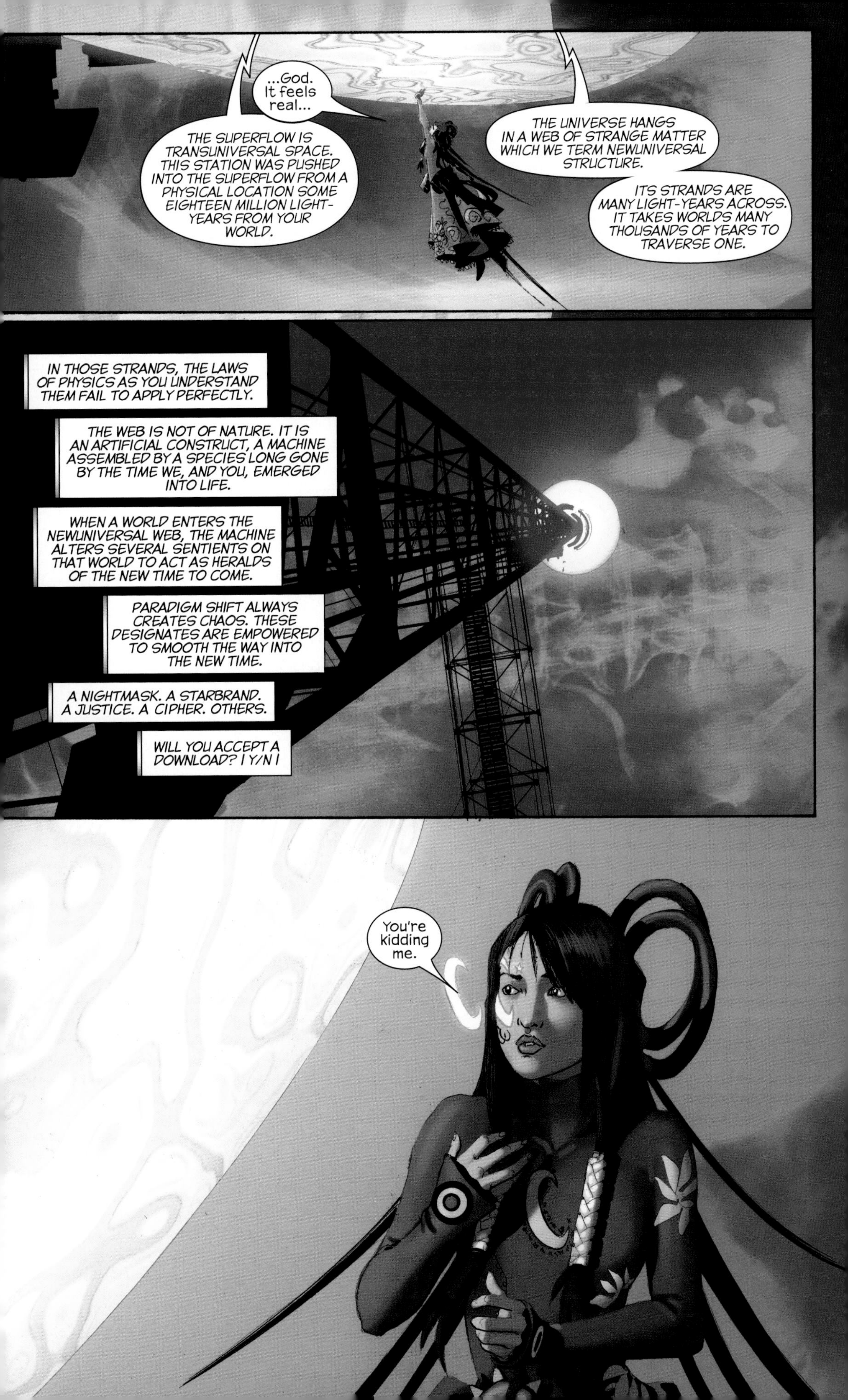
...God. It feels real...
THE SUPERFLOW IS TRANSUNIVERSAL SPACE. THIS STATION WAS PUSHED INTO THE SUPERFLOW FROM A PHYSICAL LOCATION SOME EIGHTEEN MILLION LIGHT-YEARS FROM YOUR WORLD.
THE UNIVERSE HANGS IN A WEB OF STRANGE MATTER WHICH WE TERM NEWUNIVERSAL STRUCTURE.
ITS STRANDS ARE MANY LIGHT-YEARS ACROSS. IT TAKES WORLDS MANY THOUSANDS OF YEARS TO TRAVERSE ONE.
IN THOSE STRANDS, THE LAWS OF PHYSICS AS YOU UNDERSTAND THEM FAIL TO APPLY PERFECTLY.
THE WEB IS NOT OF NATURE. IT IS AN ARTIFICIAL CONSTRUCT, A MACHINE ASSEMBLED BY A SPECIES LONG GONE BY THE TIME WE, AND YOU, EMERGED INTO LIFE.
WHEN A WORLD ENTERS THE NEWUNIVERSAL WEB, THE MACHINE ALTERS SEVERAL SENTIENTS ON THAT WORLD TO ACT AS HERALDS OF THE NEW TIME TO COME.
PARADIGM SHIFT ALWAYS CREATES CHAOS. THESE DESIGNATES ARE EMPOWERED TO SMOOTH THE WAY INTO THE NEW TIME.
A NIGHTMASK. A STARBRAND. A JUSTICE. A CIPHER. OTHERS.
WILL YOU ACCEPT A DOWNLOAD? | Y/N |
You're kidding me.

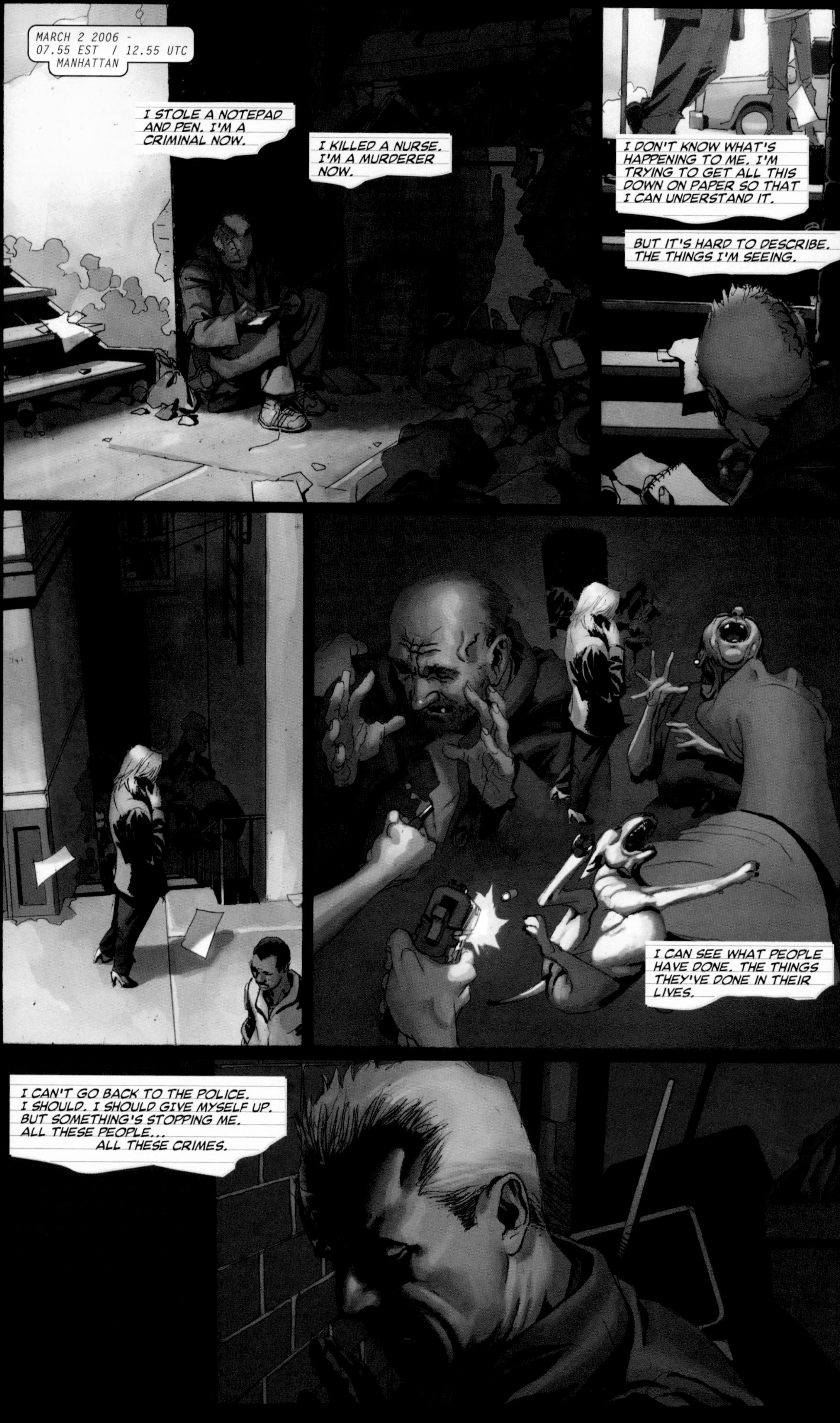
MARCH 2 2006 - 07.55 EST / 12.55 UTC MANHATTAN
I STOLE A NOTEPAD AND PEN. I'M A CRIMINAL NOW.
I KILLED A NURSE. I'M A MURDERER NOW.
I DON'T KNOW WHAT'S HAPPENING TO ME. I'M TRYING TO GET ALL THIS DOWN ON PAPER SO THAT I CAN UNDERSTAND IT.
BUT IT'S HARD TO DESCRIBE. THE THINGS I'M SEEING.
I CAN SEE WHAT PEOPLE HAVE DONE. THE THINGS THEY'VE DONE IN THEIR LIVES.
I CAN'T GO BACK TO THE POLICE. I SHOULD. I SHOULD GIVE MYSELF UP. BUT SOMETHING'S STOPPING ME. ALL THESE PEOPLE... ALL THESE CRIMES.

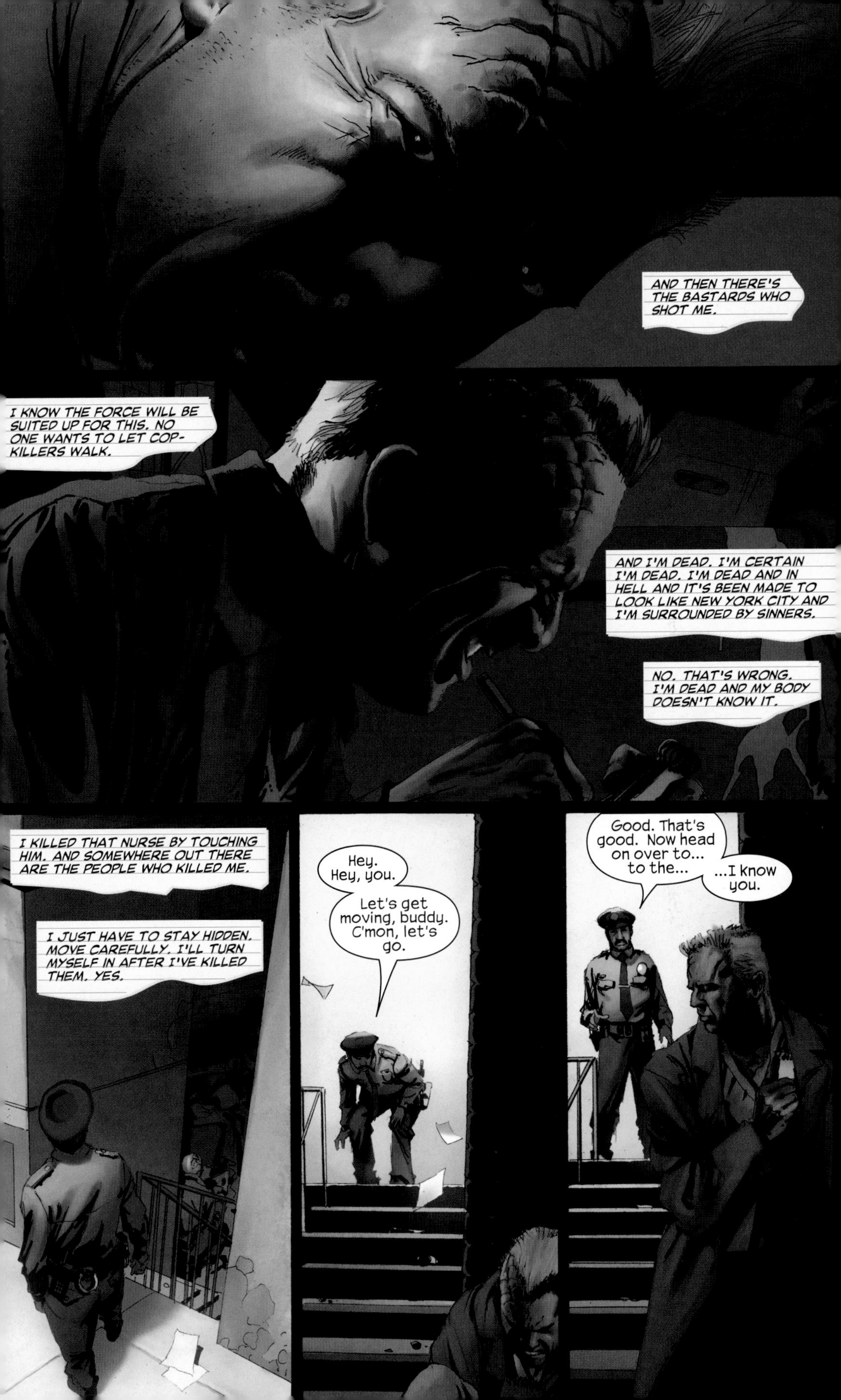
AND THEN THERE'S THE BASTARDS WHO SHOT ME.
I KNOW THE FORCE WILL BE SUITED UP FOR THIS. NO ONE WANTS TO LET COP-KILLERS WALK.
AND I'M DEAD. I'M CERTAIN I'M DEAD. I'M DEAD AND IN HELL AND IT'S BEEN MADE TO LOOK LIKE NEW YORK CITY AND I'M SURROUNDED BY SINNERS.
NO. THAT'S WRONG. I'M DEAD AND MY BODY DOESN'T KNOW IT.
I KILLED THAT NURSE BY TOUCHING HIM. AND SOMEWHERE OUT THERE ARE THE PEOPLE WHO KILLED ME.
I JUST HAVE TO STAY HIDDEN. MOVE CAREFULLY. I'LL TURN MYSELF IN AFTER I'VE KILLED THEM. YES.
Hey. Hey, you.
Let's get moving, buddy. C'mon, let's go.
Good. That's good. Now head on over to... to the...
...I know you.

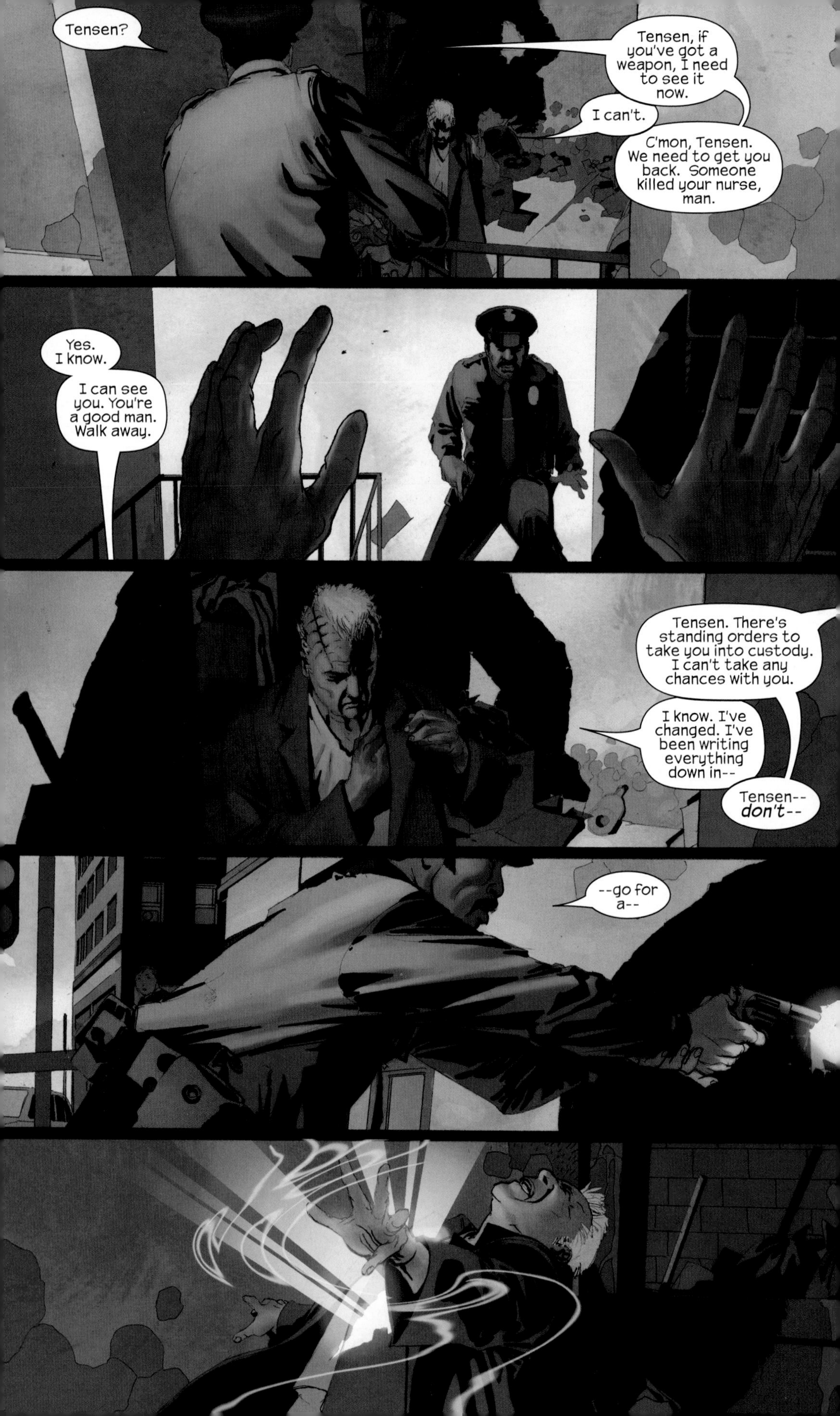
Tensen?
Tensen, if you've got a weapon, I need to see it now.
I can't.
C'mon, Tensen. We need to get you back. Someone killed your nurse, man.
Yes. I know.
I can see you. You're a good man. Walk away.
Tensen. There's standing orders to take you into custody. I can't take any chances with you.
I know. I've changed. I've been writing everything down in--
Tensen-- *don't*--
--go for a--

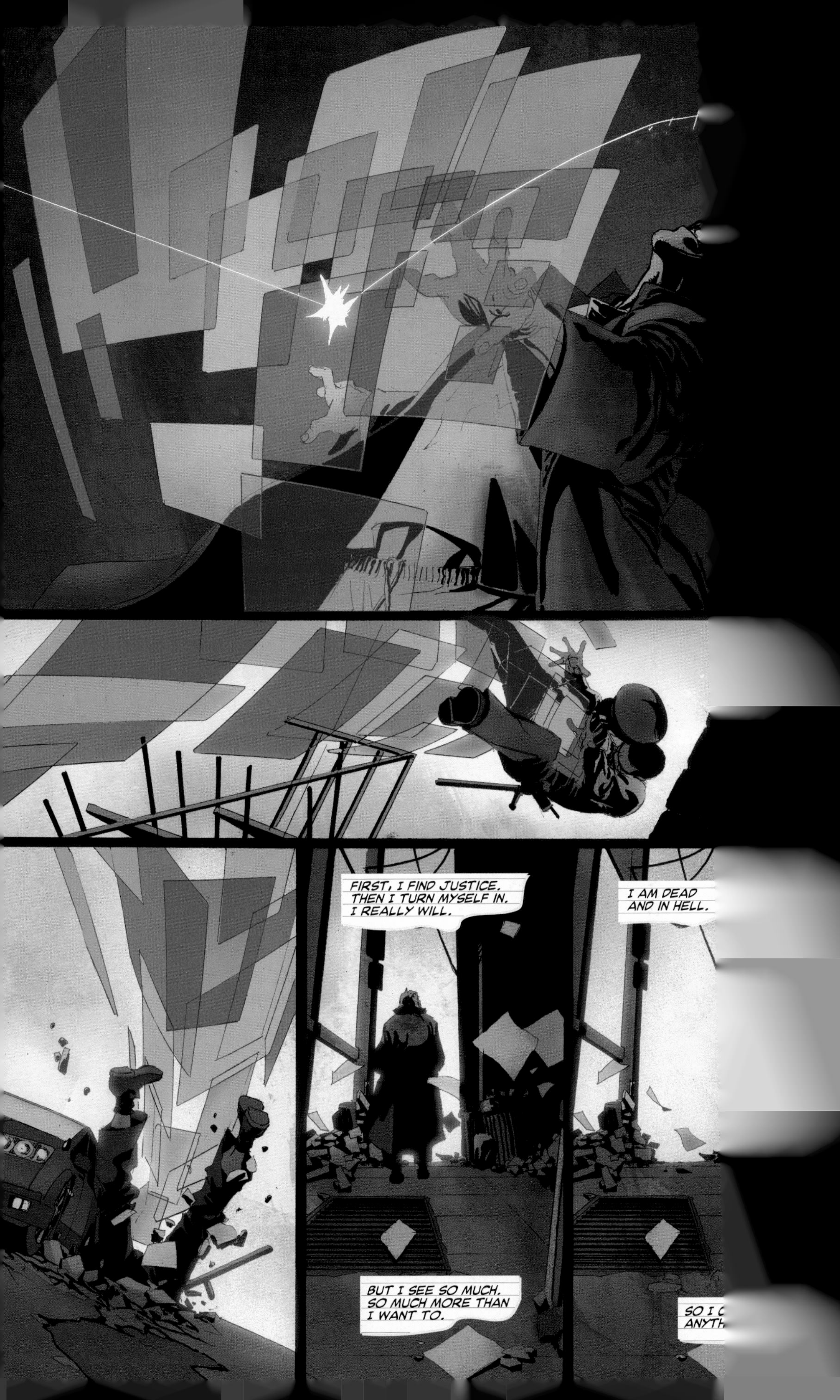
FIRST, I FIND JUSTICE. THEN I TURN MYSELF IN. I REALLY WILL.
BUT I SEE SO MUCH. SO MUCH MORE THAN I WANT TO.
I AM DEAD AND IN HELL.

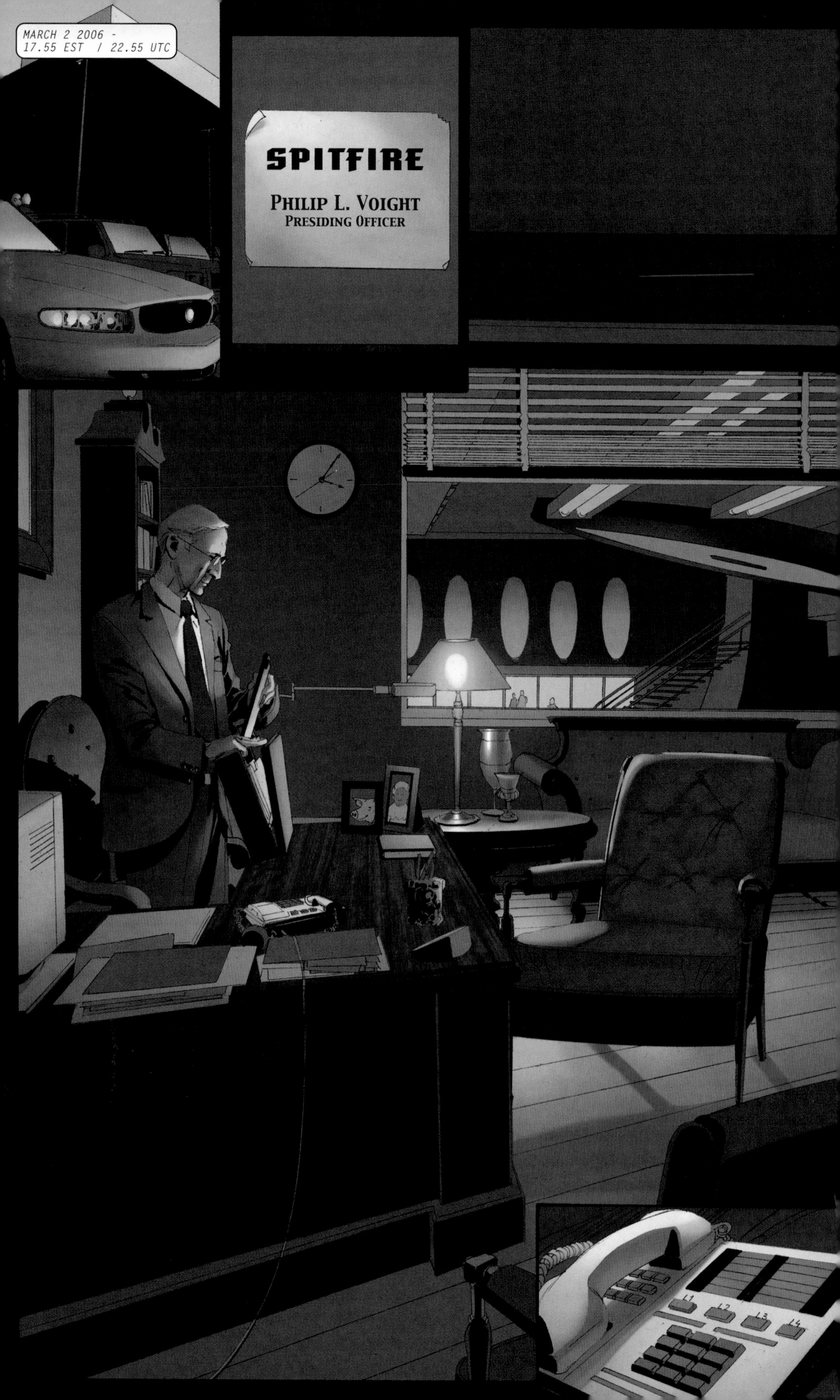
MARCH 2 2006 -
17.55 EST / 22.55 UTC
SPITFIRE
PHILIP L. VOIGHT
PRESIDING OFFICER
L1
L2
L3
L4

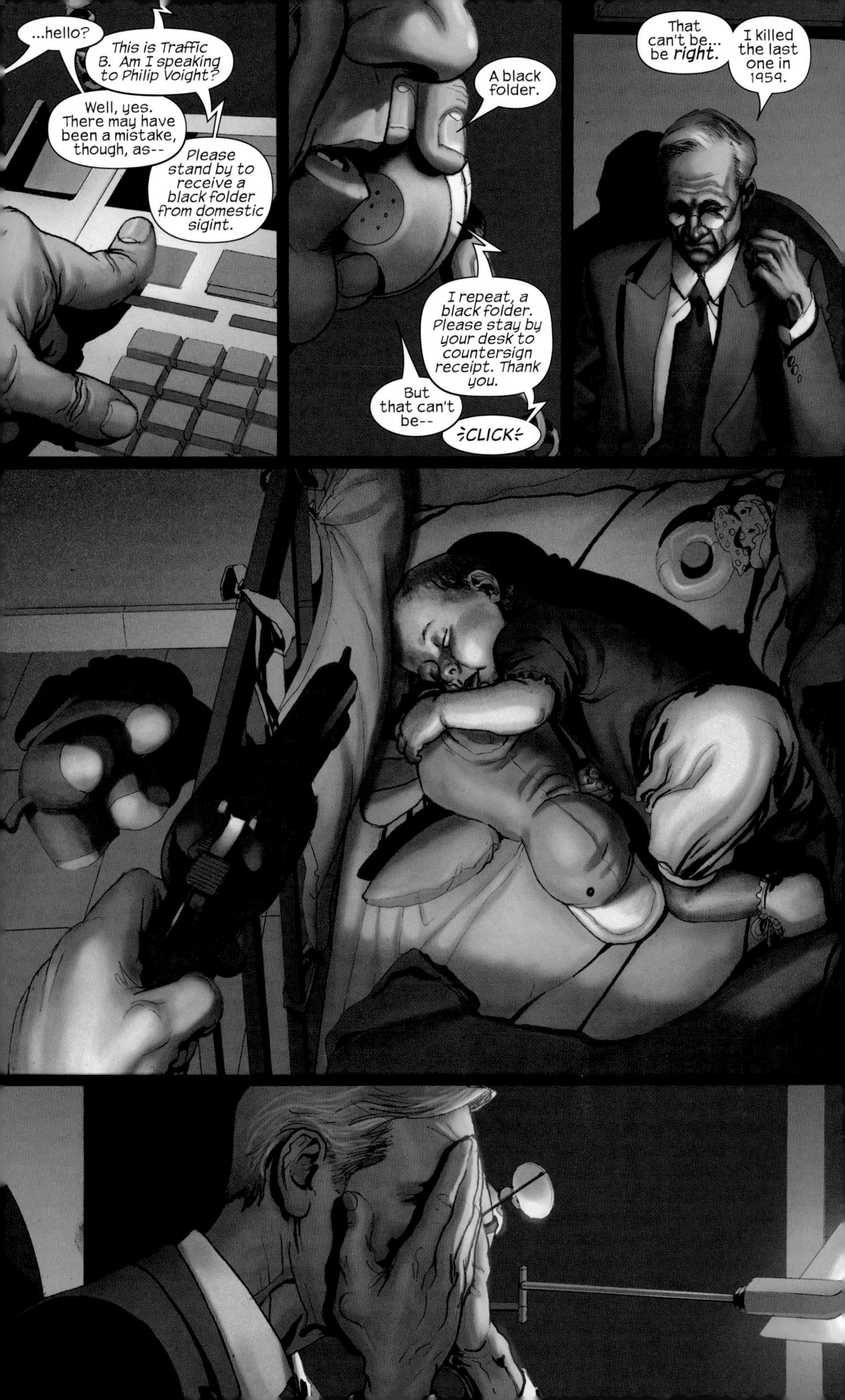
...hello?
This is Traffic B. Am I speaking to Philip Voight?
Well, yes. There may have been a mistake, though, as--
Please stand by to receive a black folder from domestic sigint.
A black folder.
I repeat, a black folder. Please stay by your desk to countersign receipt. Thank you.
But that can't be--
CLICK
That can't be... be *right.*
I killed the last one in 1959.

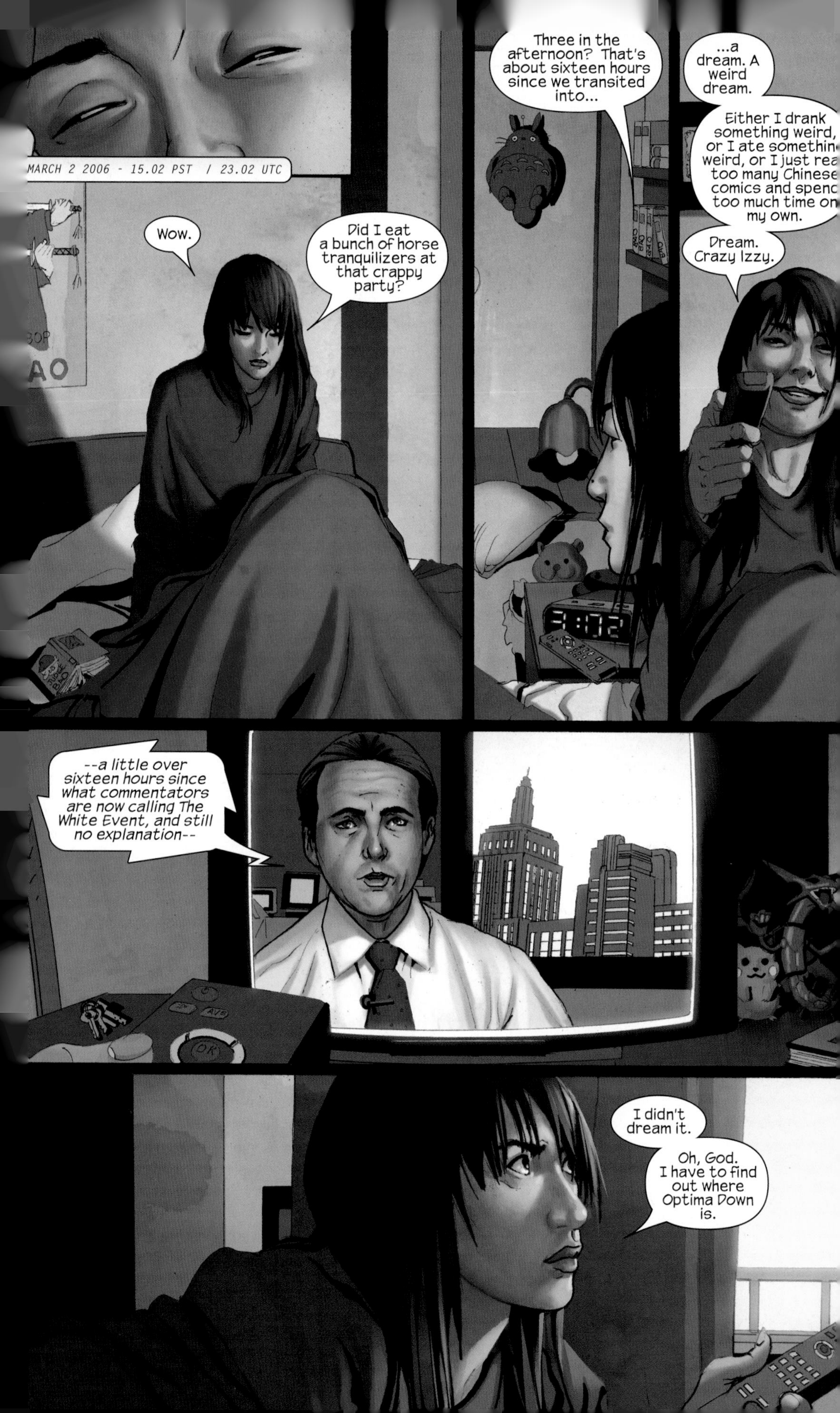
MARCH 2 2006 - 15.02 PST / 23.02 UTC
Wow.
Did I eat a bunch of horse tranquilizers at that crappy party?
Three in the afternoon? That's about sixteen hours since we transited into...
...a dream. A weird dream.
Either I drank something weird, or I ate somethin weird, or I just rea too many Chinese comics and spenc too much time on my own.
Dream. Crazy Izzy.
--a little over sixteen hours since what commentators are now calling The White Event, and still no explanation--
I didn't dream it.
Oh, God. I have to find out where Optima Down is.

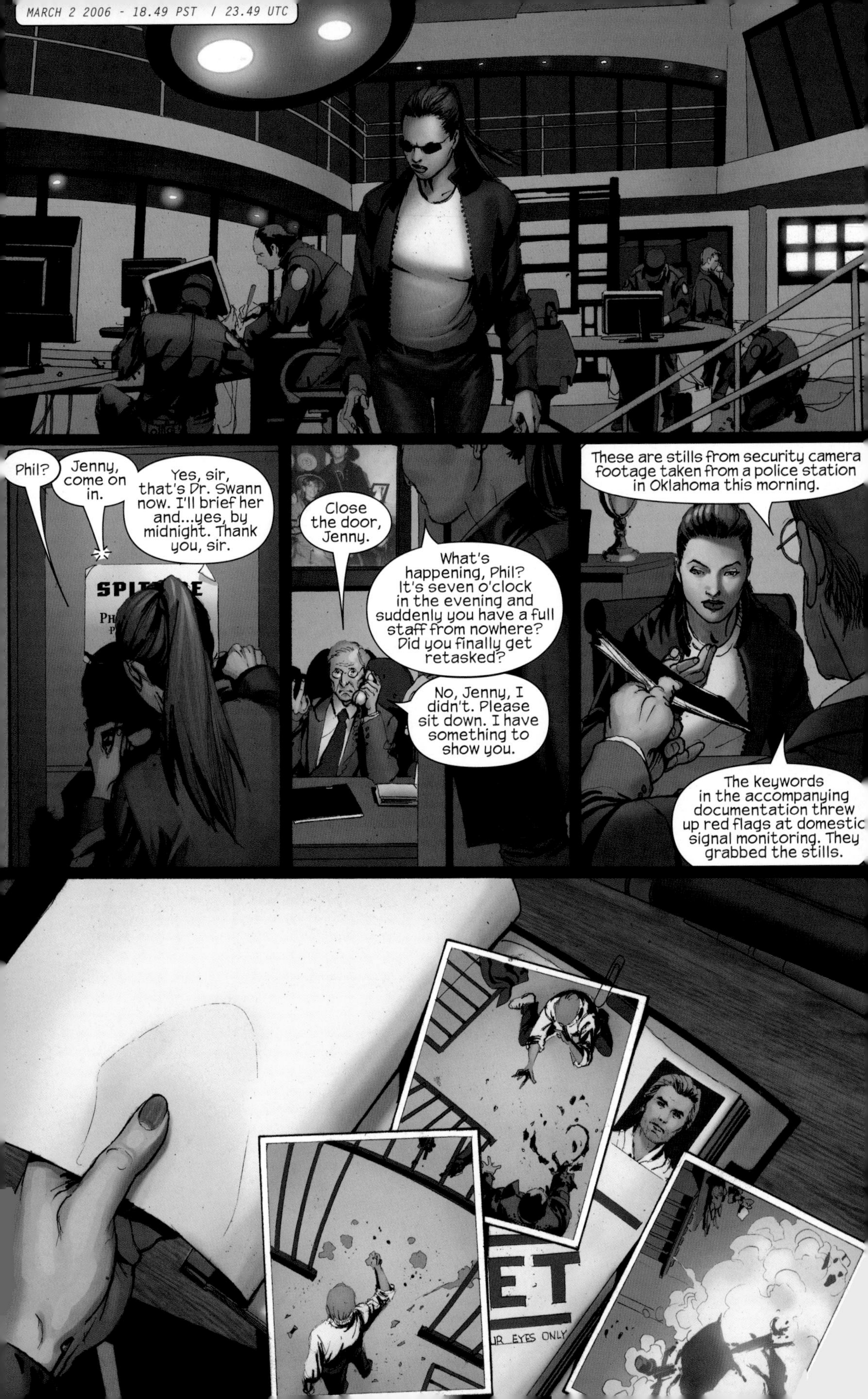
MARCH 2 2006 - 18.49 PST / 23.49 UTC
Phil?
Jenny, come on in.
Yes, sir, that's Dr. Swann now. I'll brief her and...yes, by midnight. Thank you, sir.
SPIT
Close the door, Jenny.
What's happening, Phil? It's seven o'clock in the evening and suddenly you have a full staff from nowhere? Did you finally get retasked?
No, Jenny, I didn't. Please sit down. I have something to show you.
These are stills from security camera footage taken from a police station in Oklahoma this morning.
The keywords in the accompanying documentation threw up red flags at domestic signal monitoring. They grabbed the stills.
ET
UR EYES ONLY

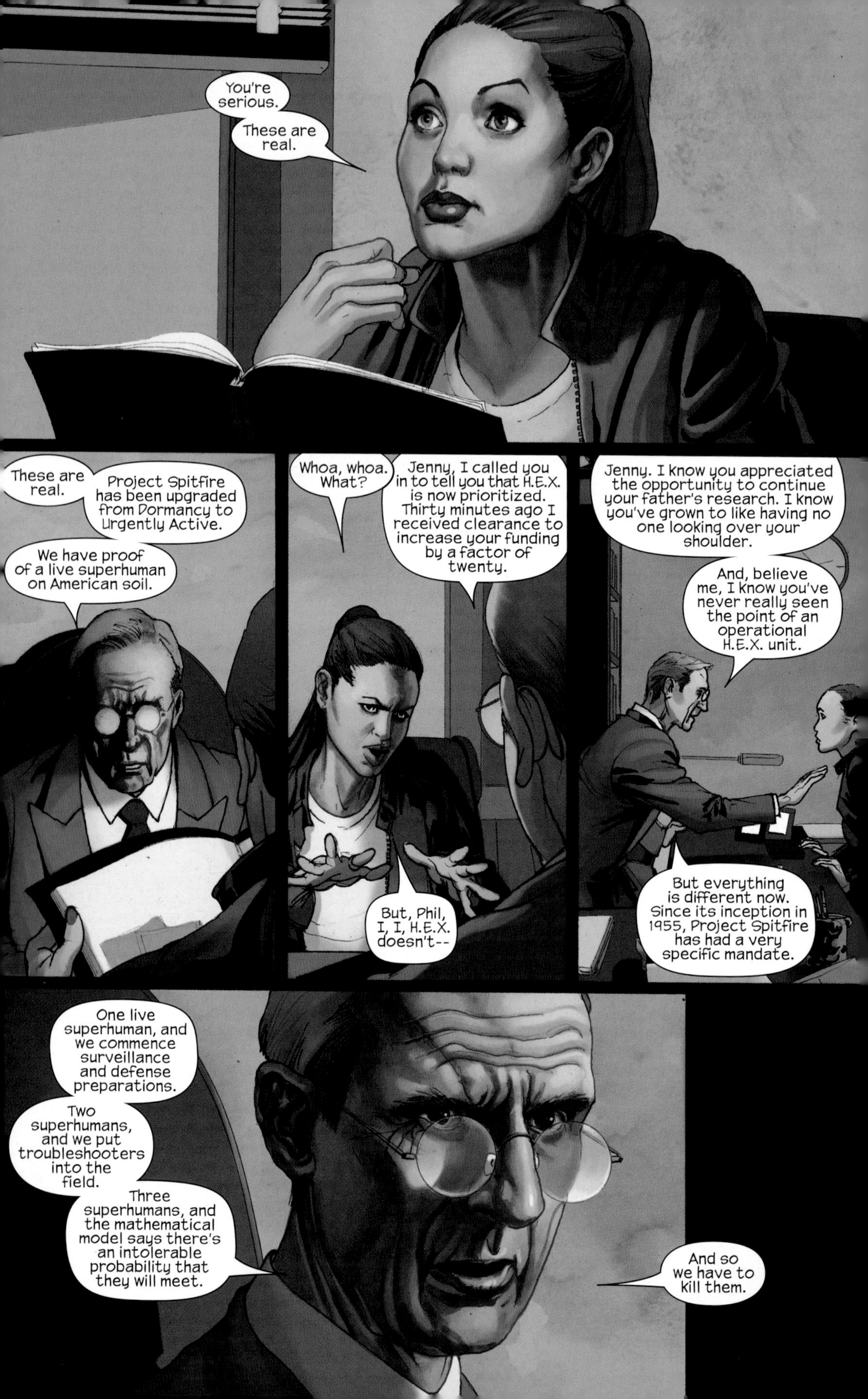
You're serious.
These are real.
These are real.
Project Spitfire has been upgraded from Dormancy to Urgently Active.
We have proof of a live superhuman on American soil.
Whoa, whoa. What?
Jenny, I called you in to tell you that H.E.X. is now prioritized. Thirty minutes ago I received clearance to increase your funding by a factor of twenty.
But, Phil, I, I, H.E.X. doesn't--
Jenny. I know you appreciated the opportunity to continue your father's research. I know you've grown to like having no one looking over your shoulder.
And, believe me, I know you've never really seen the point of an operational H.E.X. unit.
But everything is different now. Since its inception in 1955, Project Spitfire has had a very specific mandate.
One live superhuman, and we commence surveillance and defense preparations.
Two superhumans, and we put troubleshooters into the field.
Three superhumans, and the mathematical model says there's an intolerable probability that they will meet.
And so we have to kill them.

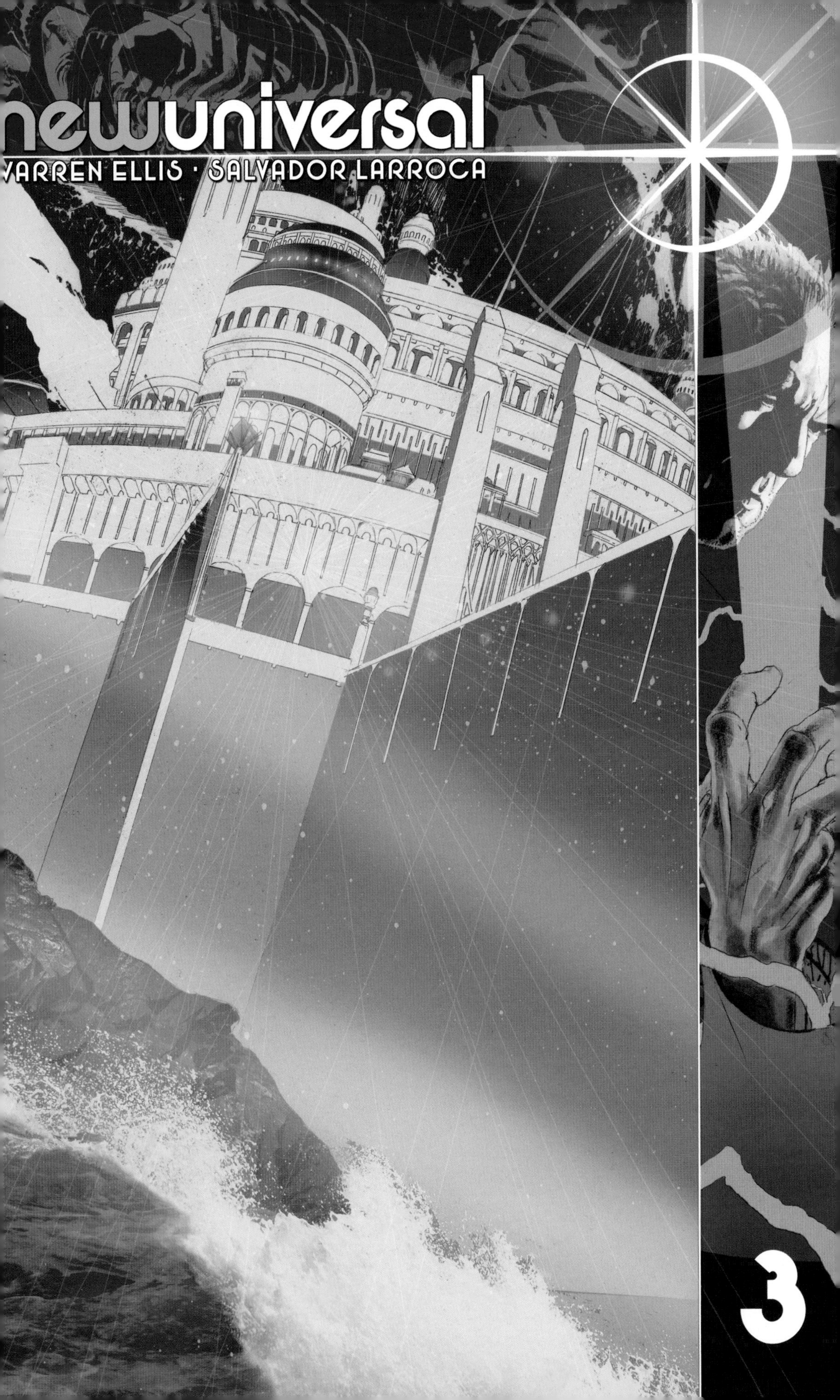
newuniversal
WARREN ELLIS · SALVADOR LARROCA
3

newuniversal MATHEMATICS

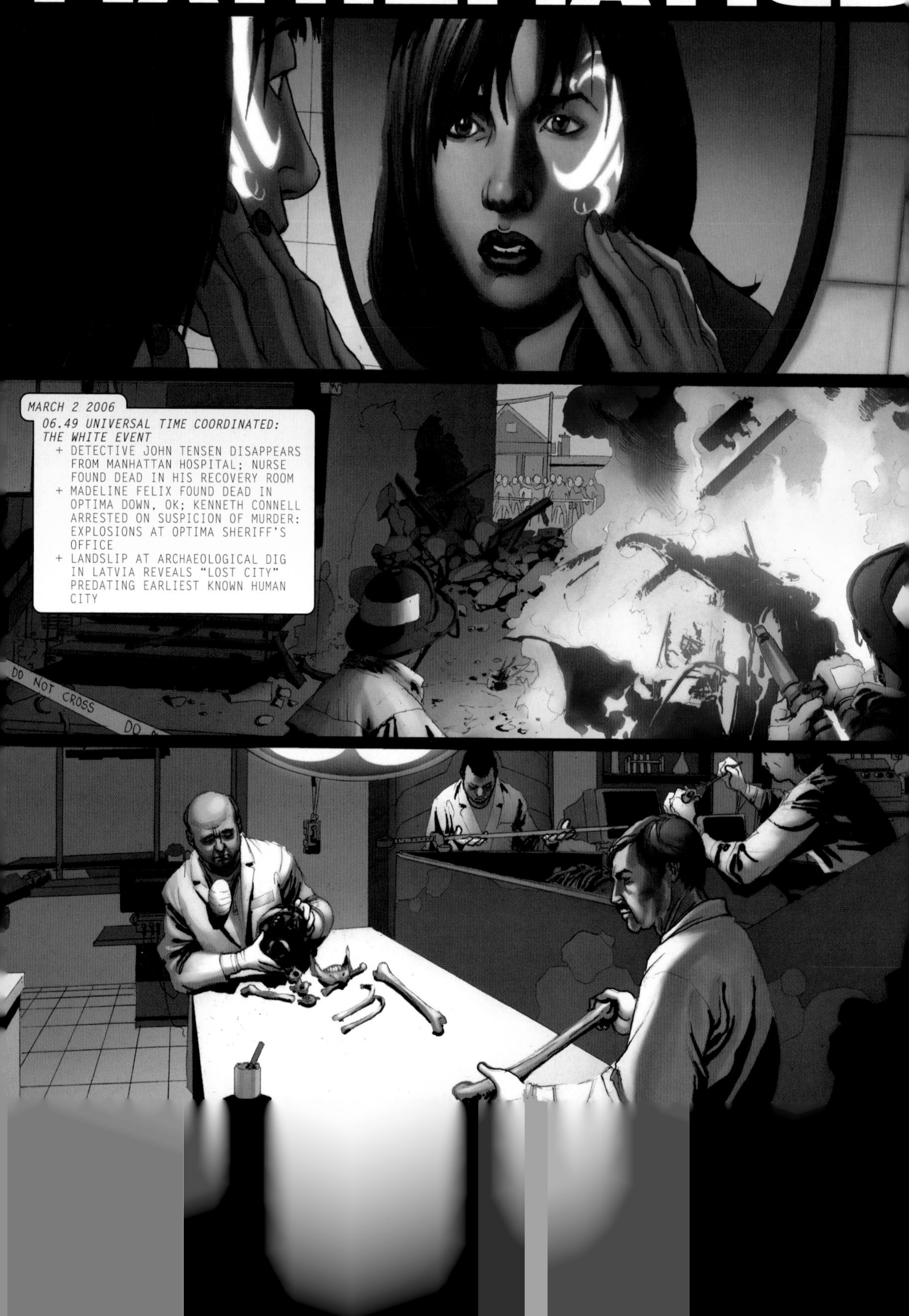

MARCH 2 2006
06.49 UNIVERSAL TIME COORDINATED:
THE WHITE EVENT
+ DETECTIVE JOHN TENSEN DISAPPEARS FROM MANHATTAN HOSPITAL; NURSE FOUND DEAD IN HIS RECOVERY ROOM
+ MADELINE FELIX FOUND DEAD IN OPTIMA DOWN, OK; KENNETH CONNELL ARRESTED ON SUSPICION OF MURDER: EXPLOSIONS AT OPTIMA SHERIFF'S OFFICE
+ LANDSLIP AT ARCHAEOLOGICAL DIG IN LATVIA REVEALS "LOST CITY" PREDATING EARLIEST KNOWN HUMAN CITY
DO NOT CROSS

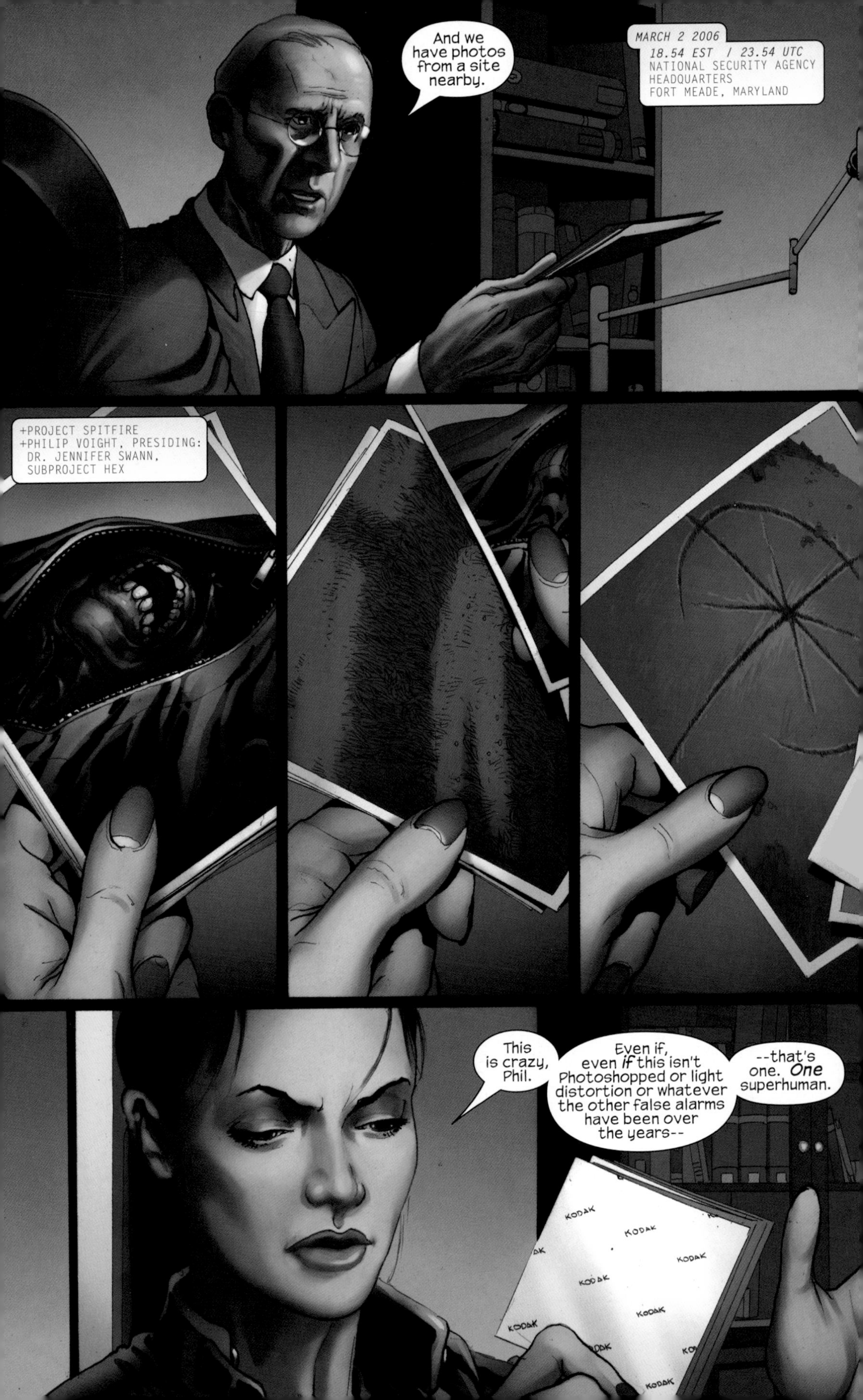
And we have photos from a site nearby.
MARCH 2 2006
18.54 EST / 23.54 UTC
NATIONAL SECURITY AGENCY HEADQUARTERS
FORT MEADE, MARYLAND
+PROJECT SPITFIRE
+PHILIP VOIGHT, PRESIDING:
DR. JENNIFER SWANN, SUBPROJECT HEX
This is crazy, Phil.
Even if, even *if* this isn't Photoshopped or light distortion or whatever the other false alarms have been over the years--
--that's one. *One* superhuman.

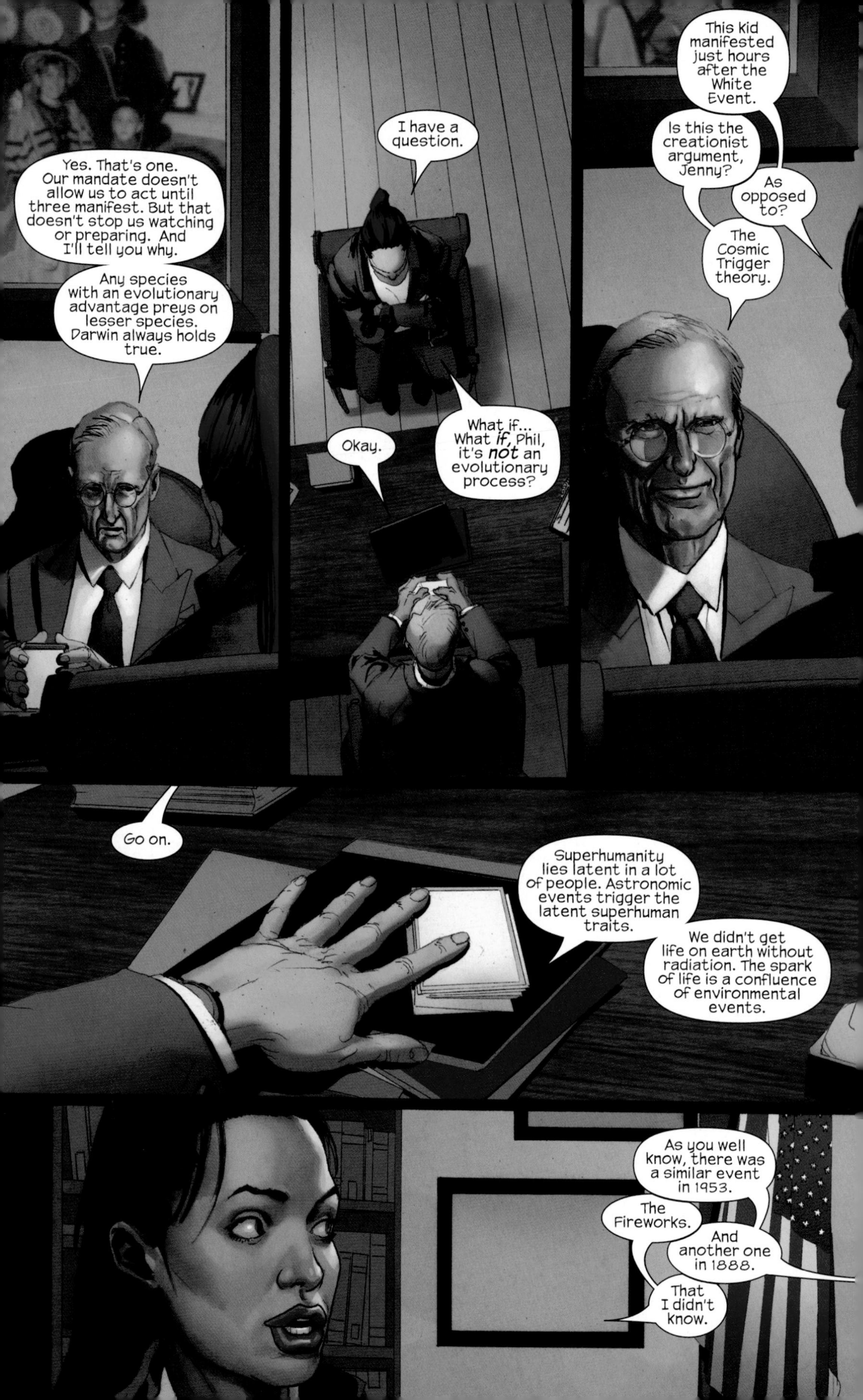
Yes. That's one. Our mandate doesn't allow us to act until three manifest. But that doesn't stop us watching or preparing. And I'll tell you why.
Any species with an evolutionary advantage preys on lesser species. Darwin always holds true.
I have a question.
Okay.
What if... What *if*, Phil, it's ***not*** an evolutionary process?
This kid manifested just hours after the White Event.
Is this the creationist argument, Jenny?
As opposed to?
The Cosmic Trigger theory.
Go on.
Superhumanity lies latent in a lot of people. Astronomic events trigger the latent superhuman traits.
We didn't get life on earth without radiation. The spark of life is a confluence of environmental events.
As you well know, there was a similar event in 1953.
The Fireworks.
And another one in 1888.
That I didn't know.

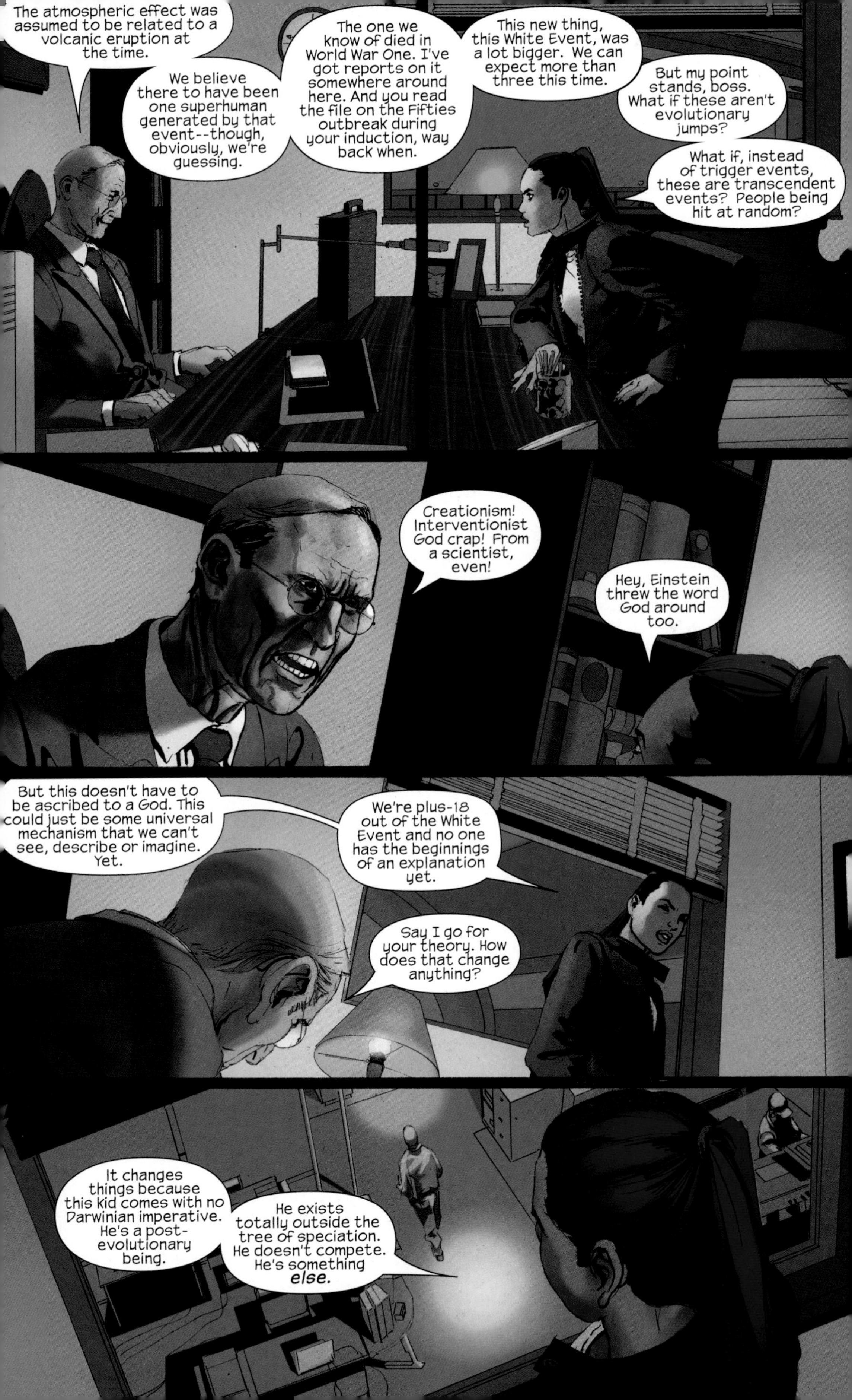
The atmospheric effect was assumed to be related to a volcanic eruption at the time.
We believe there to have been one superhuman generated by that event--though, obviously, we're guessing.
The one we know of died in World War One. I've got reports on it somewhere around here. And you read the file on the Fifties outbreak during your induction, way back when.
This new thing, this White Event, was a lot bigger. We can expect more than three this time.
But my point stands, boss. What if these aren't evolutionary jumps?
What if, instead of trigger events, these are transcendent events? People being hit at random?
Creationism! Interventionist God crap! From a scientist, even!
Hey, Einstein threw the word God around too.
But this doesn't have to be ascribed to a God. This could just be some universal mechanism that we can't see, describe or imagine. Yet.
We're plus-18 out of the White Event and no one has the beginnings of an explanation yet.
Say I go for your theory. How does that change anything?
It changes things because this kid comes with no Darwinian imperative. He's a post-evolutionary being.
He exists totally outside the tree of speciation. He doesn't compete. He's something *else.*

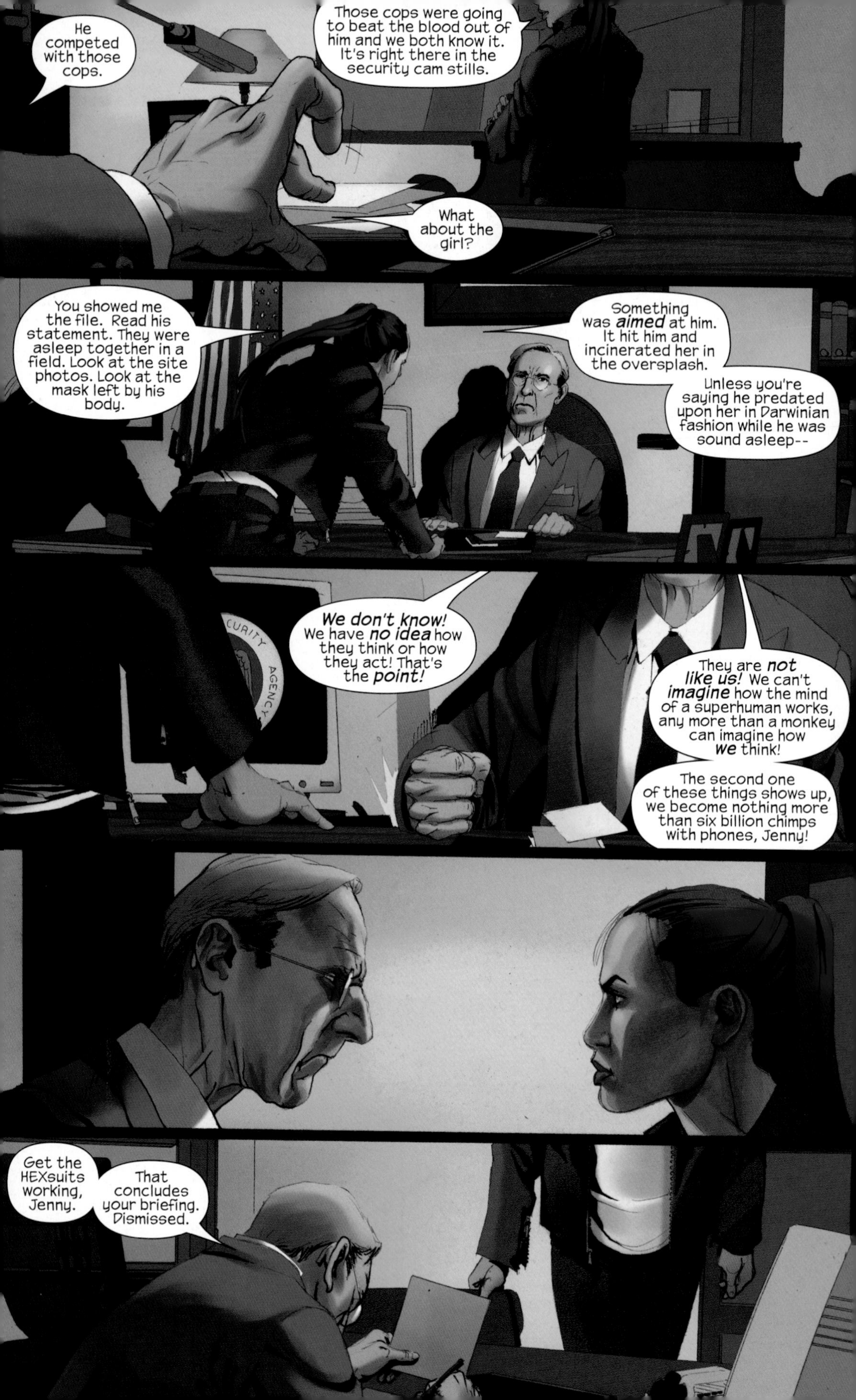
He competed with those cops.
Those cops were going to beat the blood out of him and we both know it. It's right there in the security cam stills.
What about the girl?
You showed me the file. Read his statement. They were asleep together in a field. Look at the site photos. Look at the mask left by his body.
Something was *aimed* at him. It hit him and incinerated her in the oversplash.
Unless you're saying he predated upon her in Darwinian fashion while he was sound asleep--
CURITY AGENCY
We don't know! We have *no idea* how they think or how they act! That's the *point!*
They are *not like us!* We can't *imagine* how the mind of a superhuman works, any more than a monkey can imagine how *we* think!
The second one of these things shows up, we become nothing more than six billion chimps with phones, Jenny!
Get the HEXsuits working, Jenny.
That concludes your briefing. Dismissed.

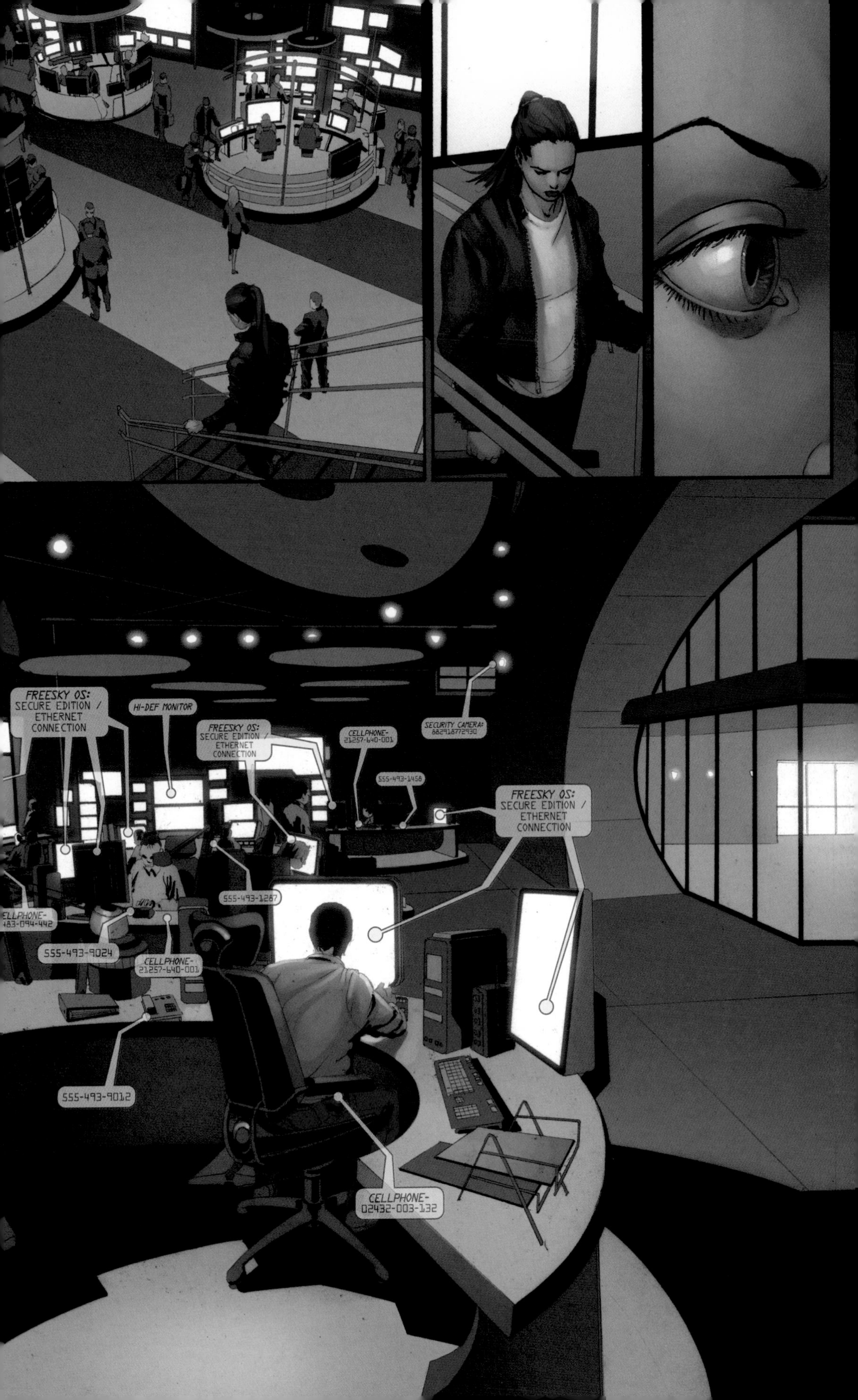
FREESKY OS: SECURE EDITION / ETHERNET CONNECTION
HI-DEF MONITOR
FREESKY OS: SECURE EDITION / ETHERNET CONNECTION
CELLPHONE- 21257-640-001
SECURITY CAMERA: 882918772930
555-493-1458
FREESKY OS: SECURE EDITION / ETHERNET CONNECTION
555-493-1287
ELLPHONE- 483-094-442
555-493-9024
CELLPHONE- 21257-640-001
555-493-9012
CELLPHONE- 02432-003-132

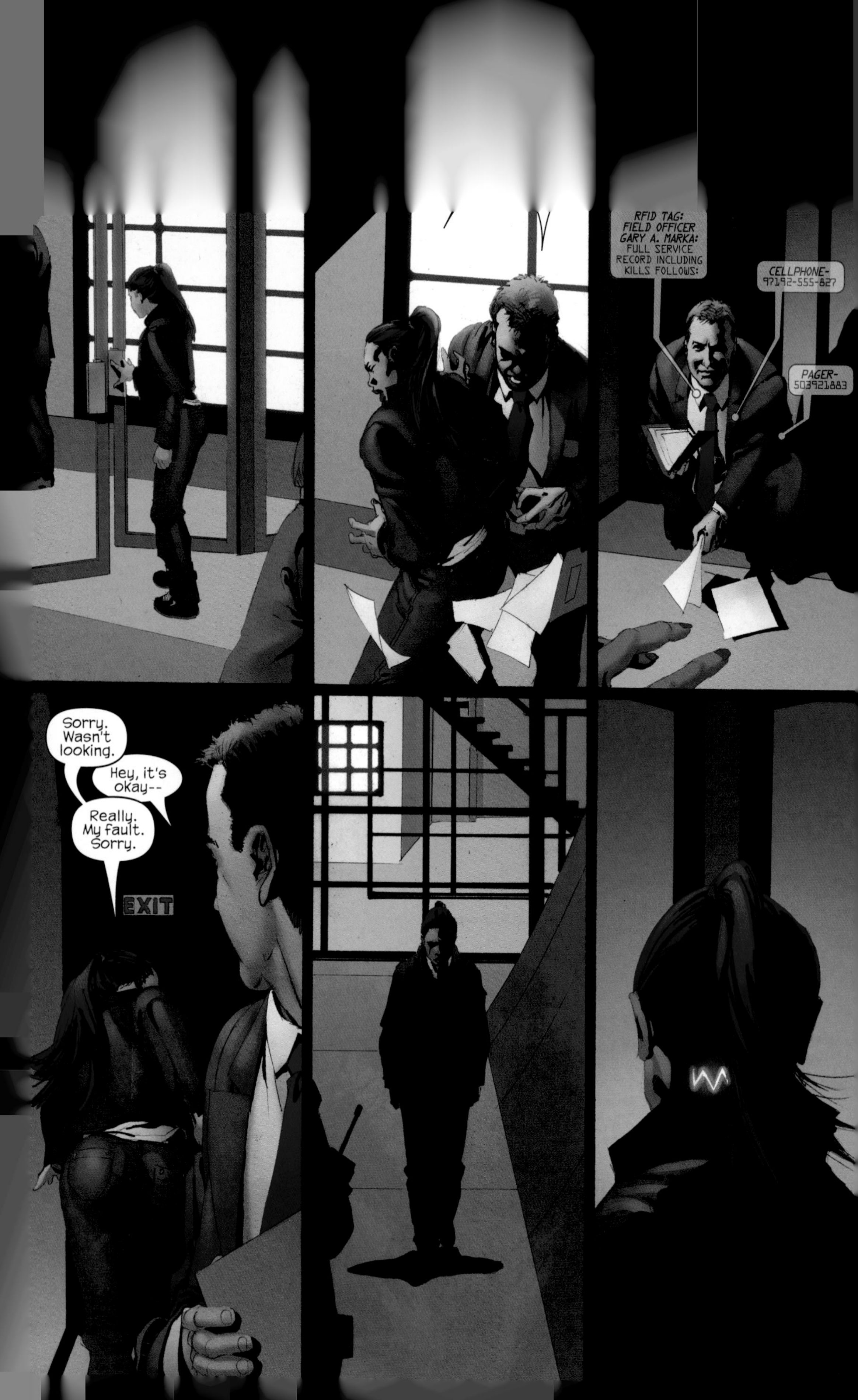
RFID TAG:
FIELD OFFICER
GARY A. MARKA:
FULL SERVICE
RECORD INCLUDING
KILLS FOLLOWS:
CELLPHONE-
97192-555-827
PAGER-
503921883
Sorry. Wasn't looking.
Hey, it's okay--
Really. My fault. Sorry.
EXIT

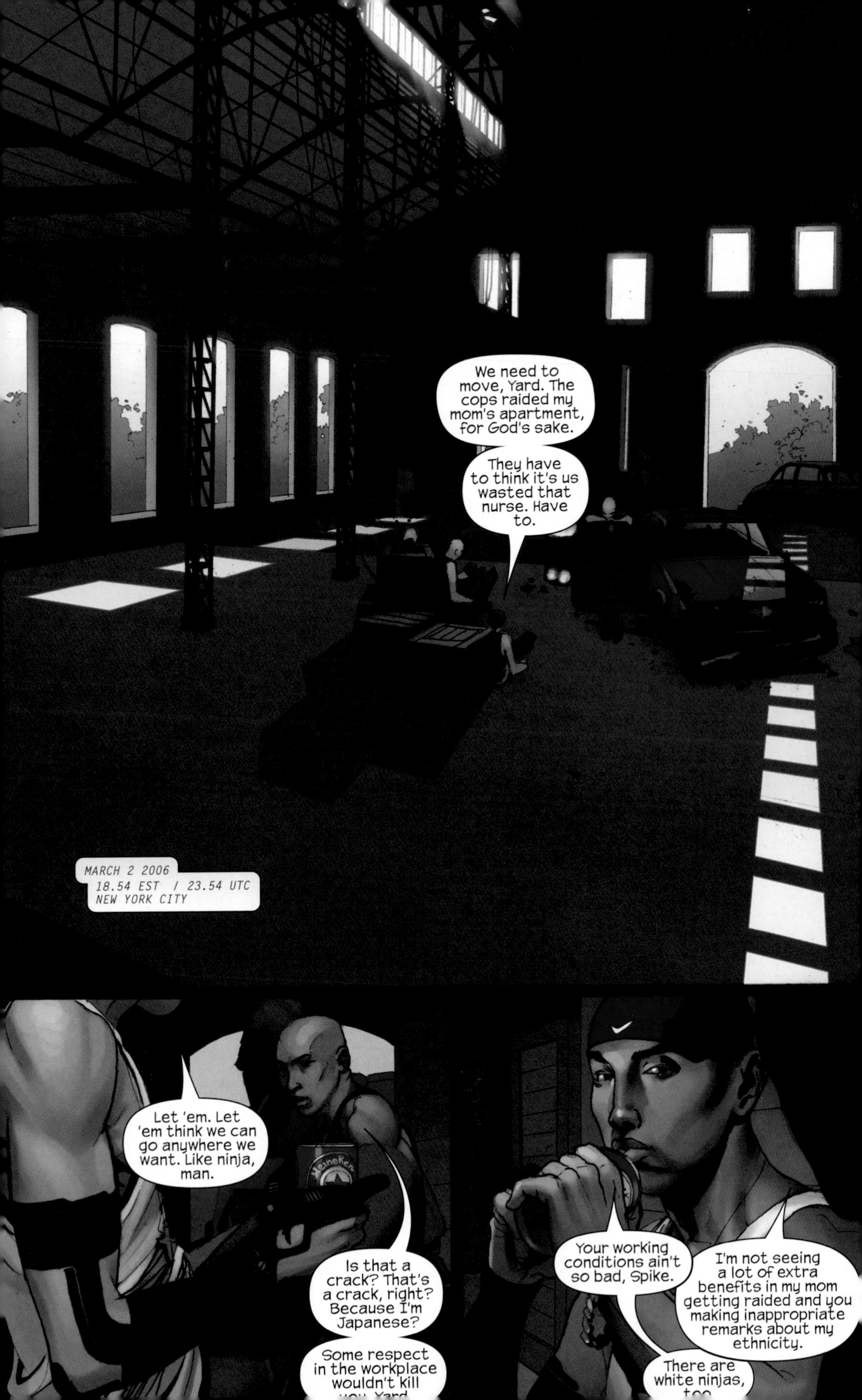
We need to move, Yard. The cops raided my mom's apartment, for God's sake.
They have to think it's us wasted that nurse. Have to.
MARCH 2 2006
18.54 EST / 23.54 UTC
NEW YORK CITY
Let 'em. Let 'em think we can go anywhere we want. Like ninja, man.
Is that a crack? That's a crack, right? Because I'm Japanese?
Some respect in the workplace wouldn't kill
Your working conditions ain't so bad, Spike.
I'm not seeing a lot of extra benefits in my mom getting raided and you making inappropriate remarks about my ethnicity.
There are white ninjas,

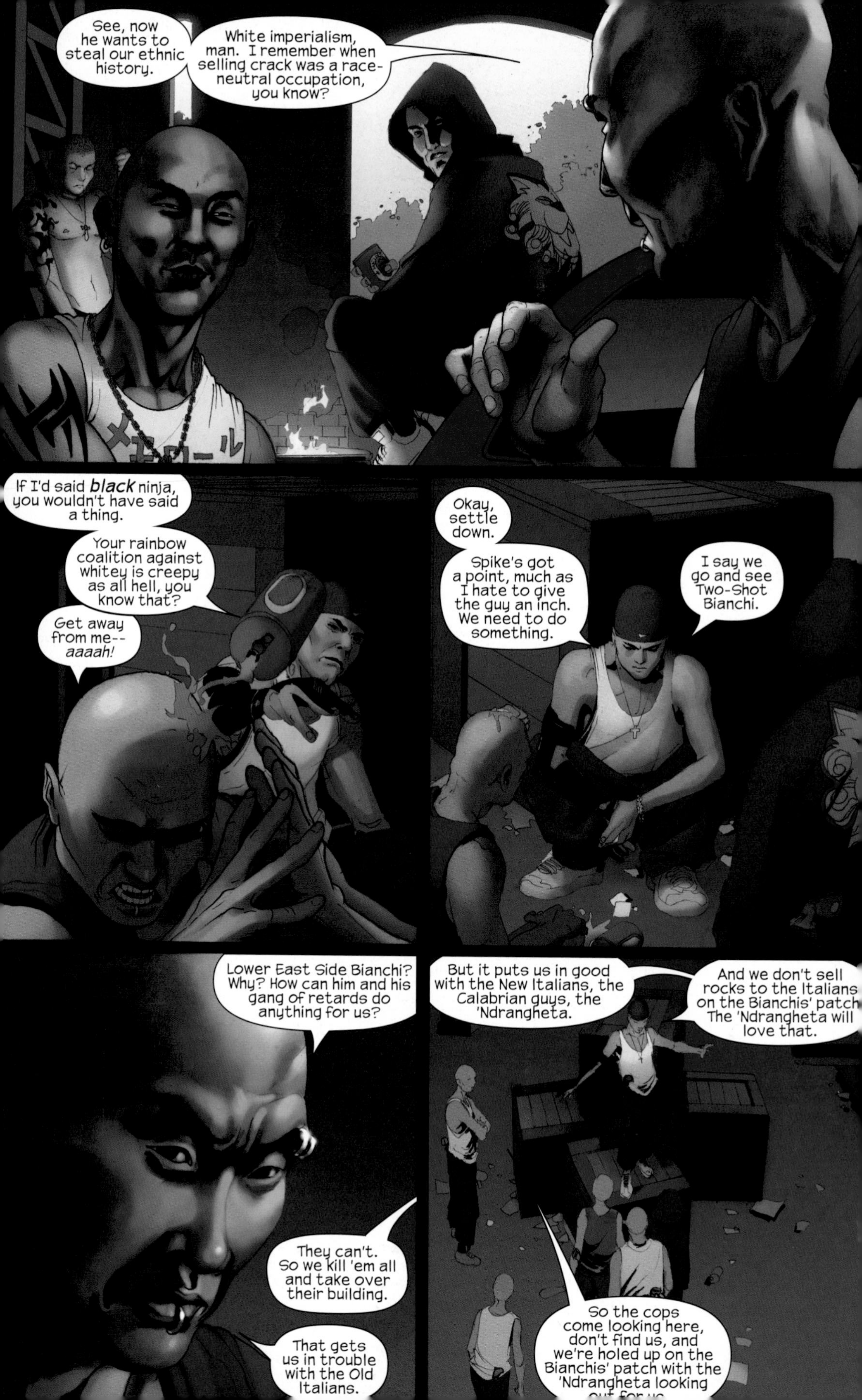
See, now he wants to steal our ethnic history.
White imperialism, man. I remember when selling crack was a race-neutral occupation, you know?
If I'd said *black* ninja, you wouldn't have said a thing.
Your rainbow coalition against whitey is creepy as all hell, you know that?
Get away from me-- *aaaah!*
Okay, settle down.
Spike's got a point, much as I hate to give the guy an inch. We need to do something.
I say we go and see Two-Shot Bianchi.
Lower East Side Bianchi? Why? How can him and his gang of retards do anything for us?
They can't. So we kill 'em all and take over their building.
That gets us in trouble with the Old Italians.
But it puts us in good with the New Italians, the Calabrian guys, the 'Ndrangheta.
And we don't sell rocks to the Italians on the Bianchis' patch. The 'Ndrangheta will love that.
So the cops come looking here, don't find us, and we're holed up on the Bianchis' patch with the 'Ndrangheta looking

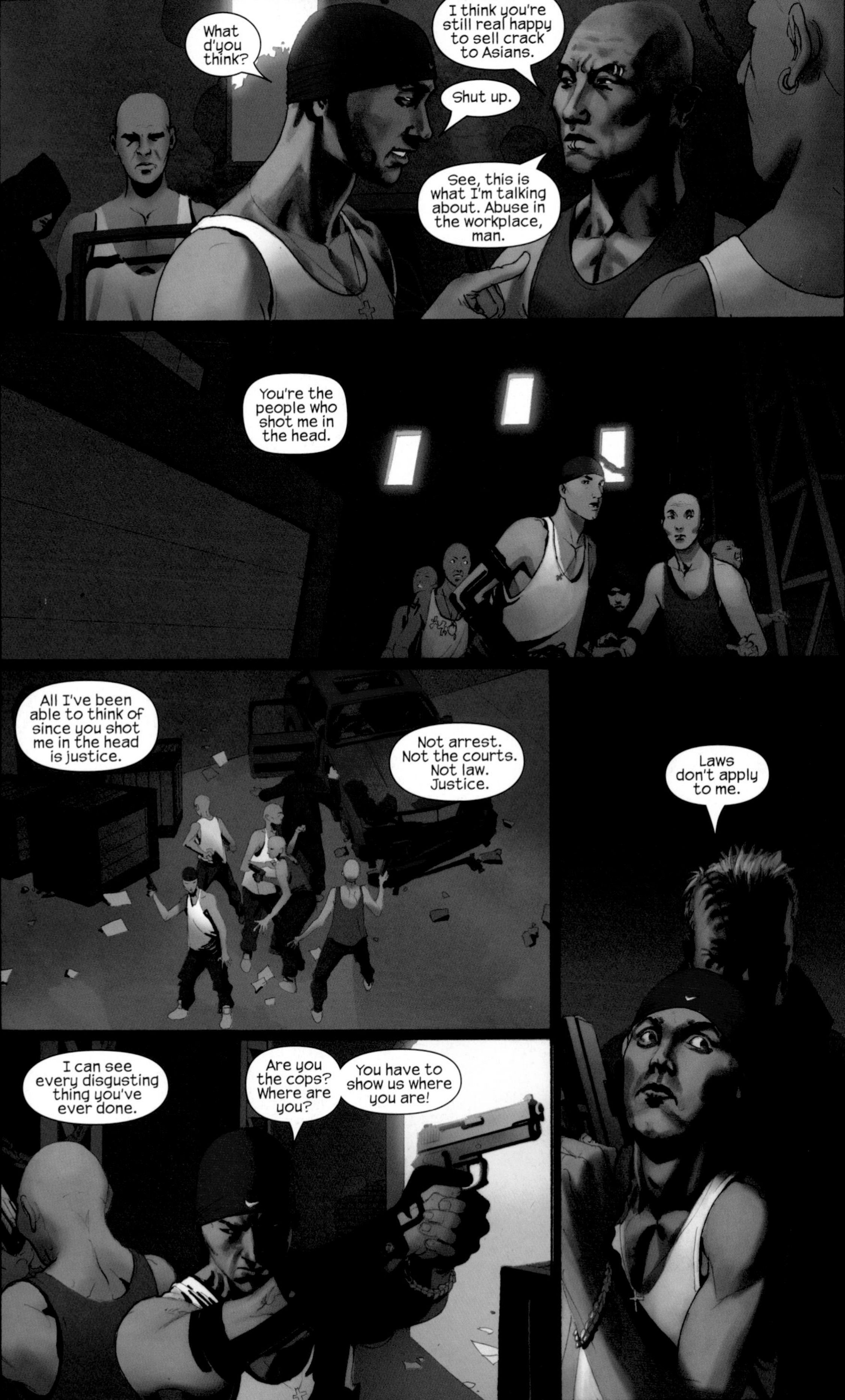
What d'you think?
I think you're still real happy to sell crack to Asians.
Shut up.
See, this is what I'm talking about. Abuse in the workplace, man.
You're the people who shot me in the head.
All I've been able to think of since you shot me in the head is justice.
Not arrest. Not the courts. Not law. Justice.
Laws don't apply to me.
I can see every disgusting thing you've ever done.
Are you the cops? Where are you?
You have to show us where you are!

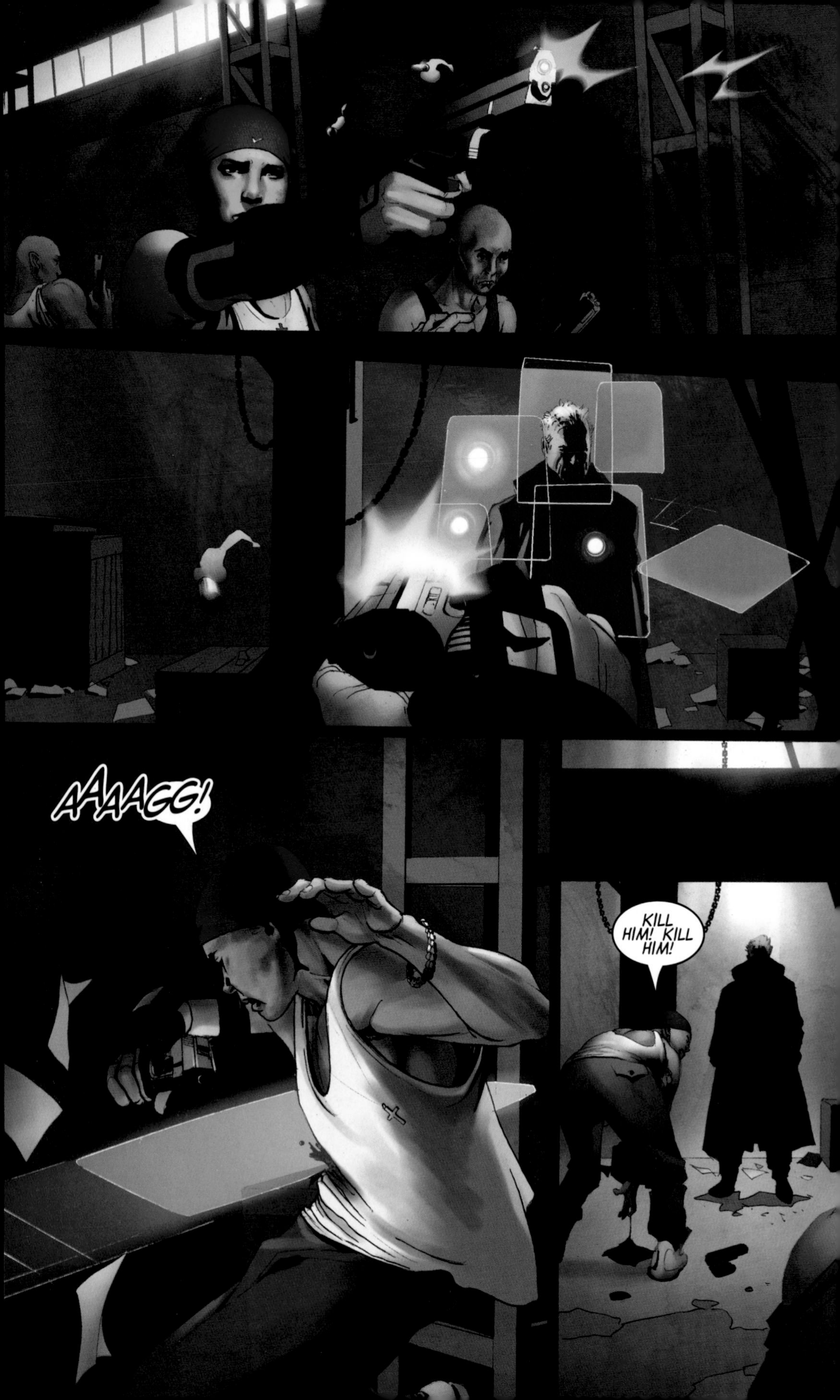
AAAAGG!
KILL HIM! KILL HIM!

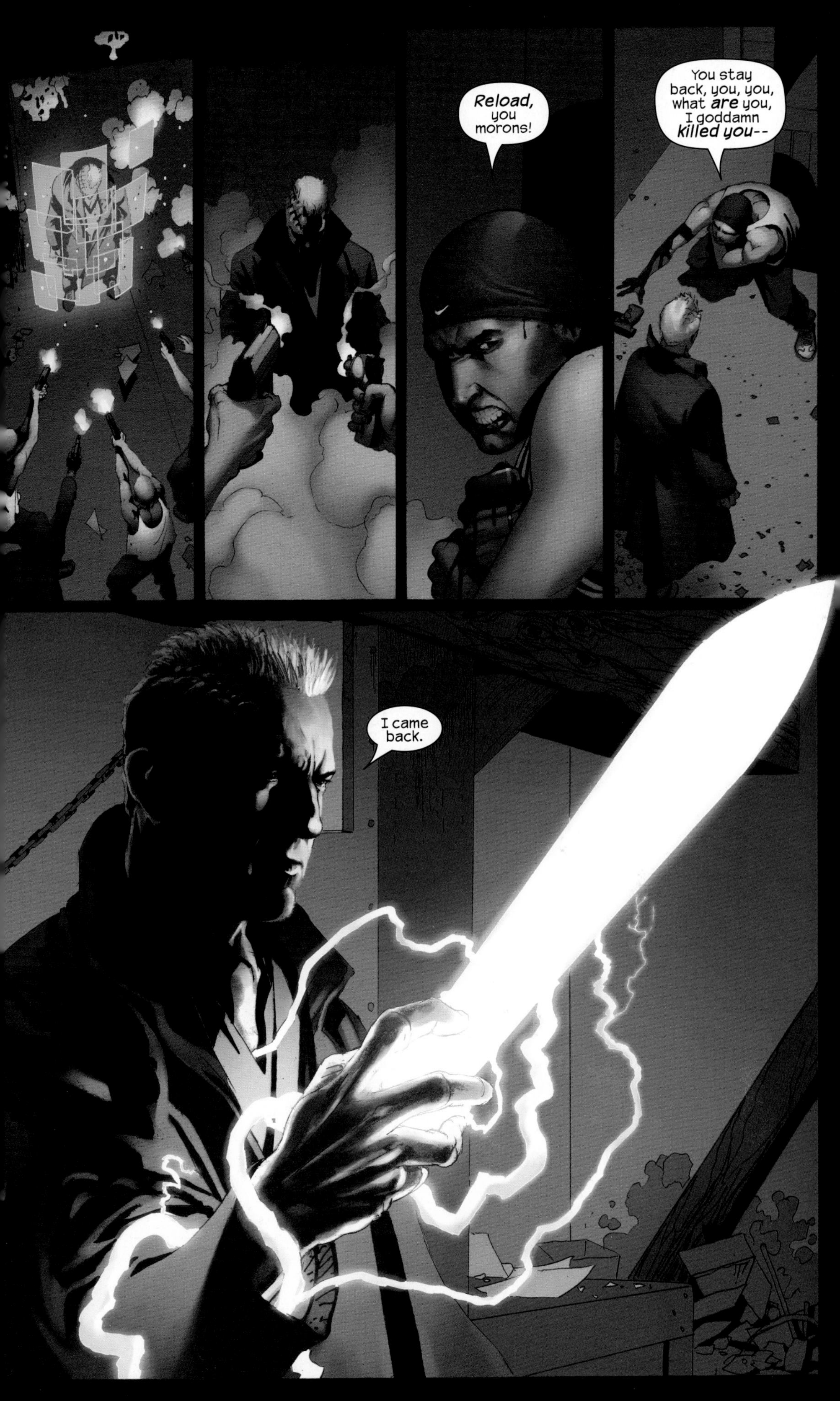
Reload, you morons!
You stay back, you, you, what are you, I goddamn killed you--
I came back.

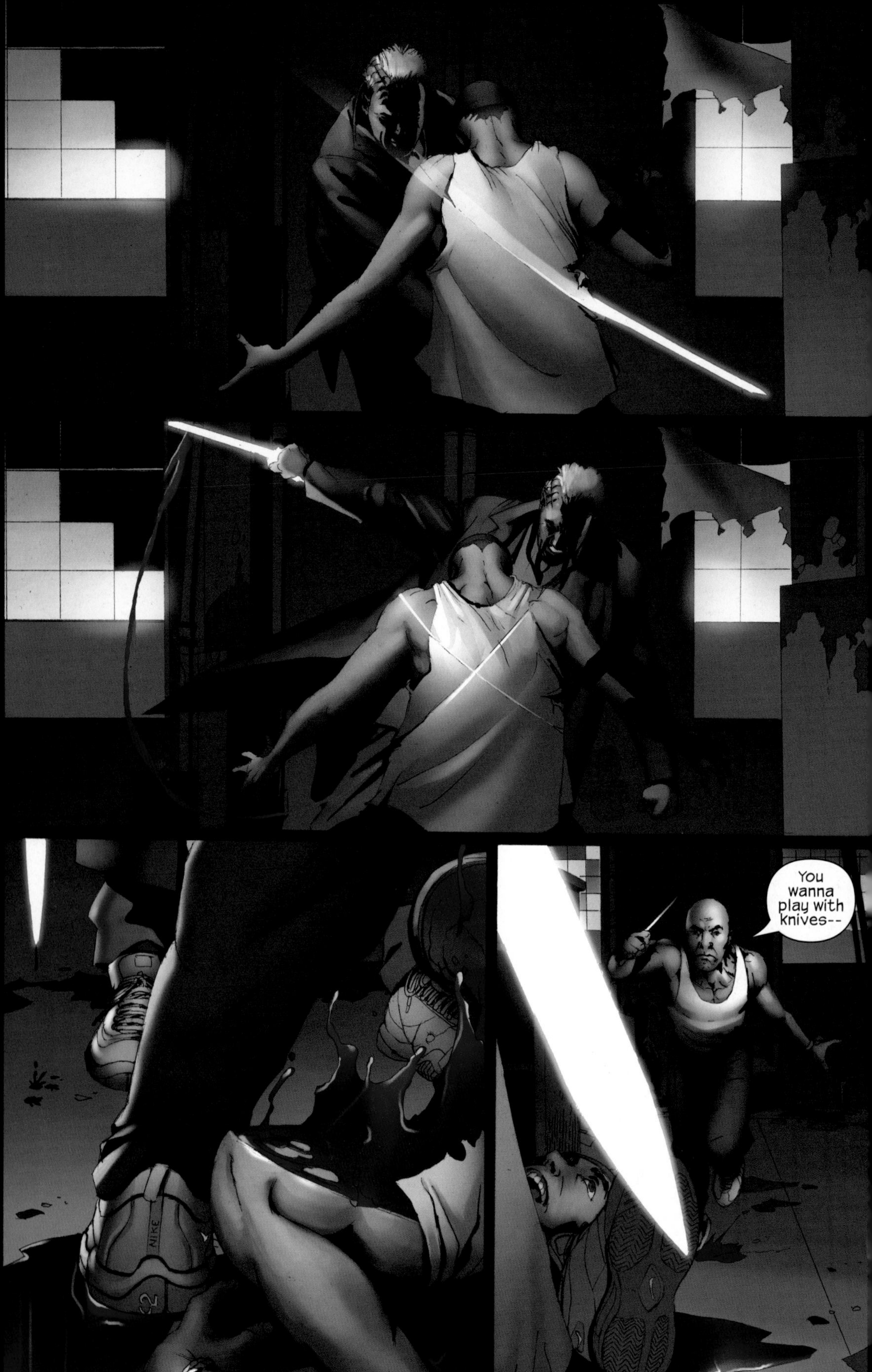
You wanna play with knives--

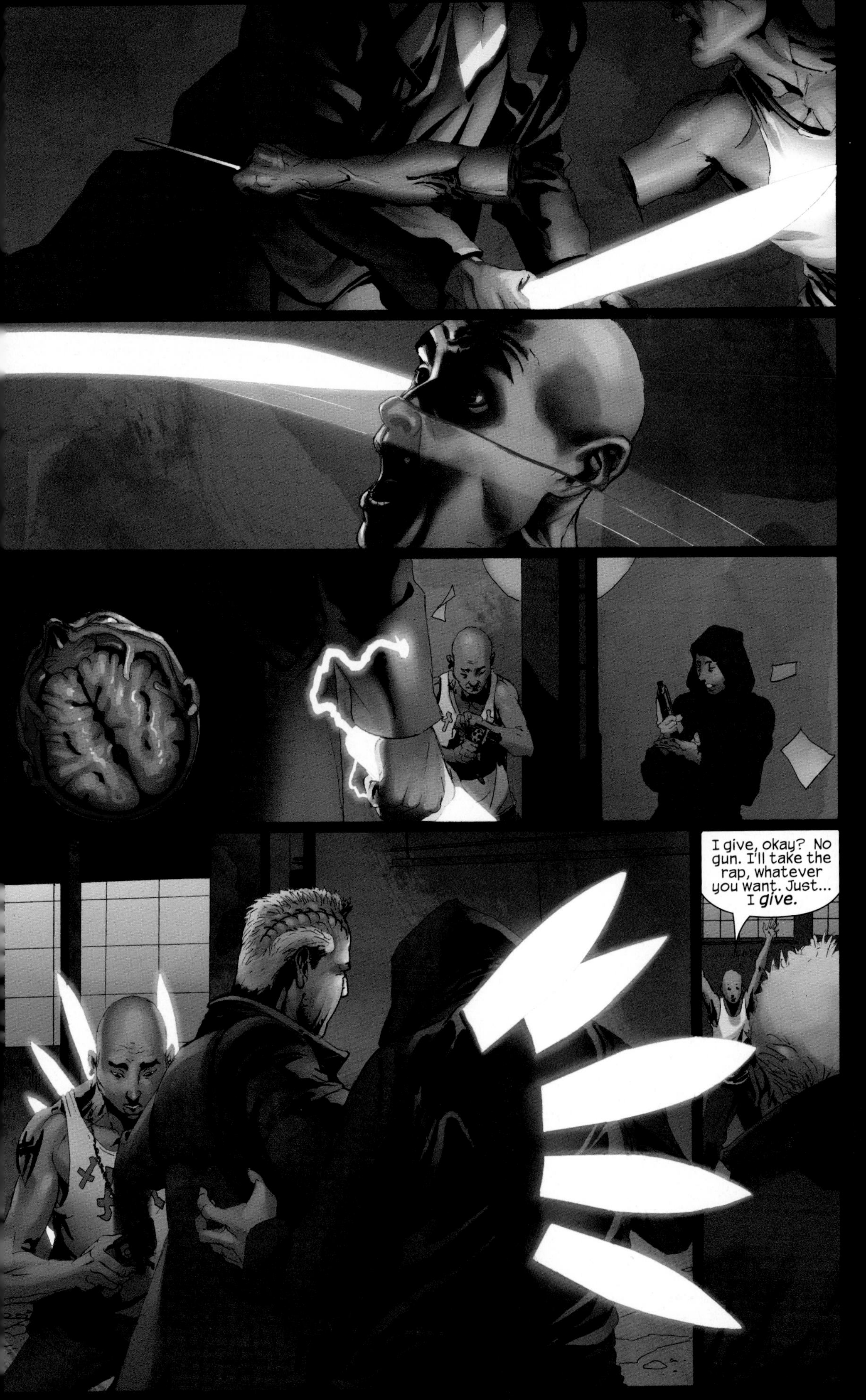
I give, okay? No gun. I'll take the rap, whatever you want. Just... I *give.*

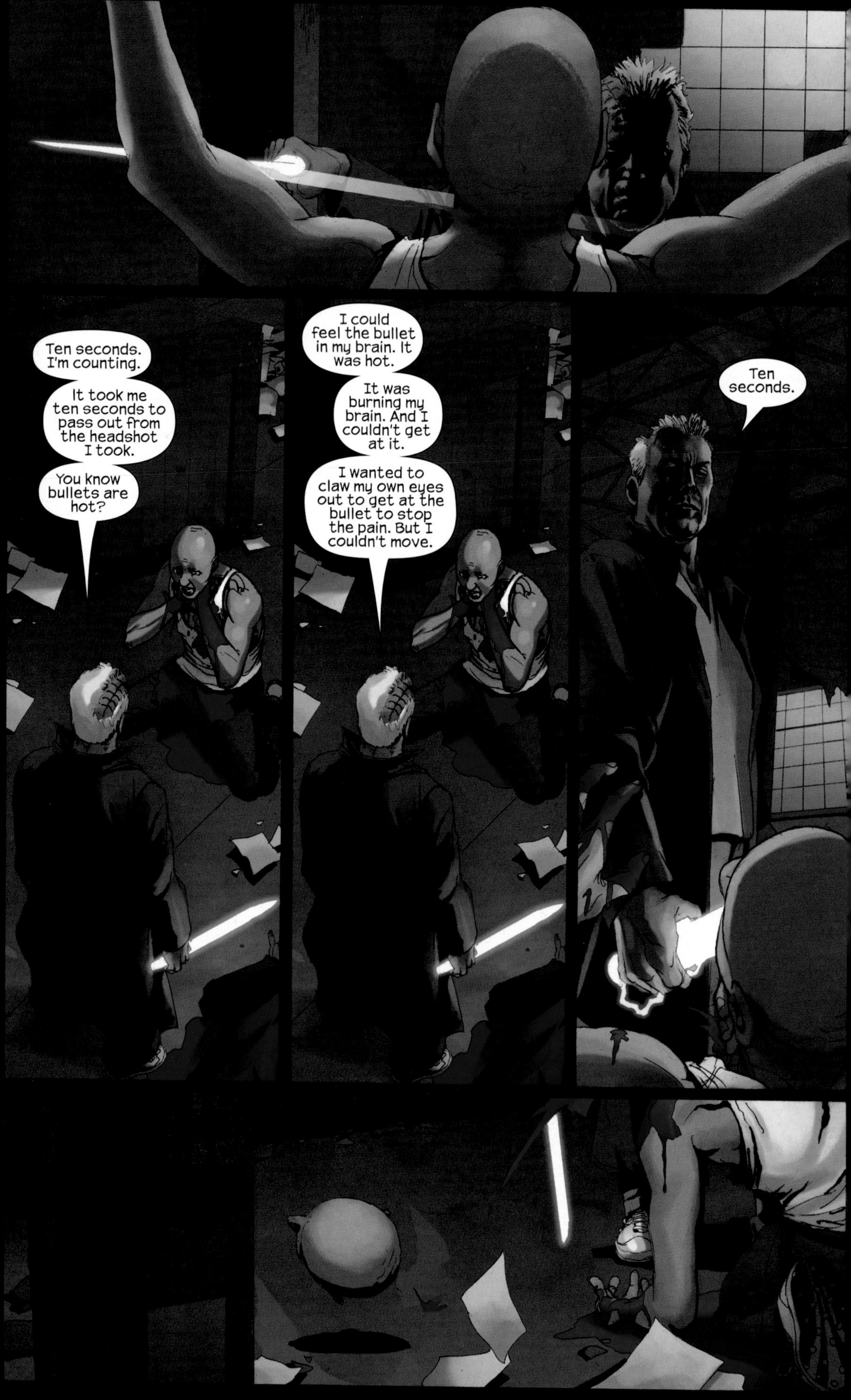
Ten seconds. I'm counting.
It took me ten seconds to pass out from the headshot I took.
You know bullets are hot?
I could feel the bullet in my brain. It was hot.
It was burning my brain. And I couldn't get at it.
I wanted to claw my own eyes out to get at the bullet to stop the pain. But I couldn't move.
Ten seconds.

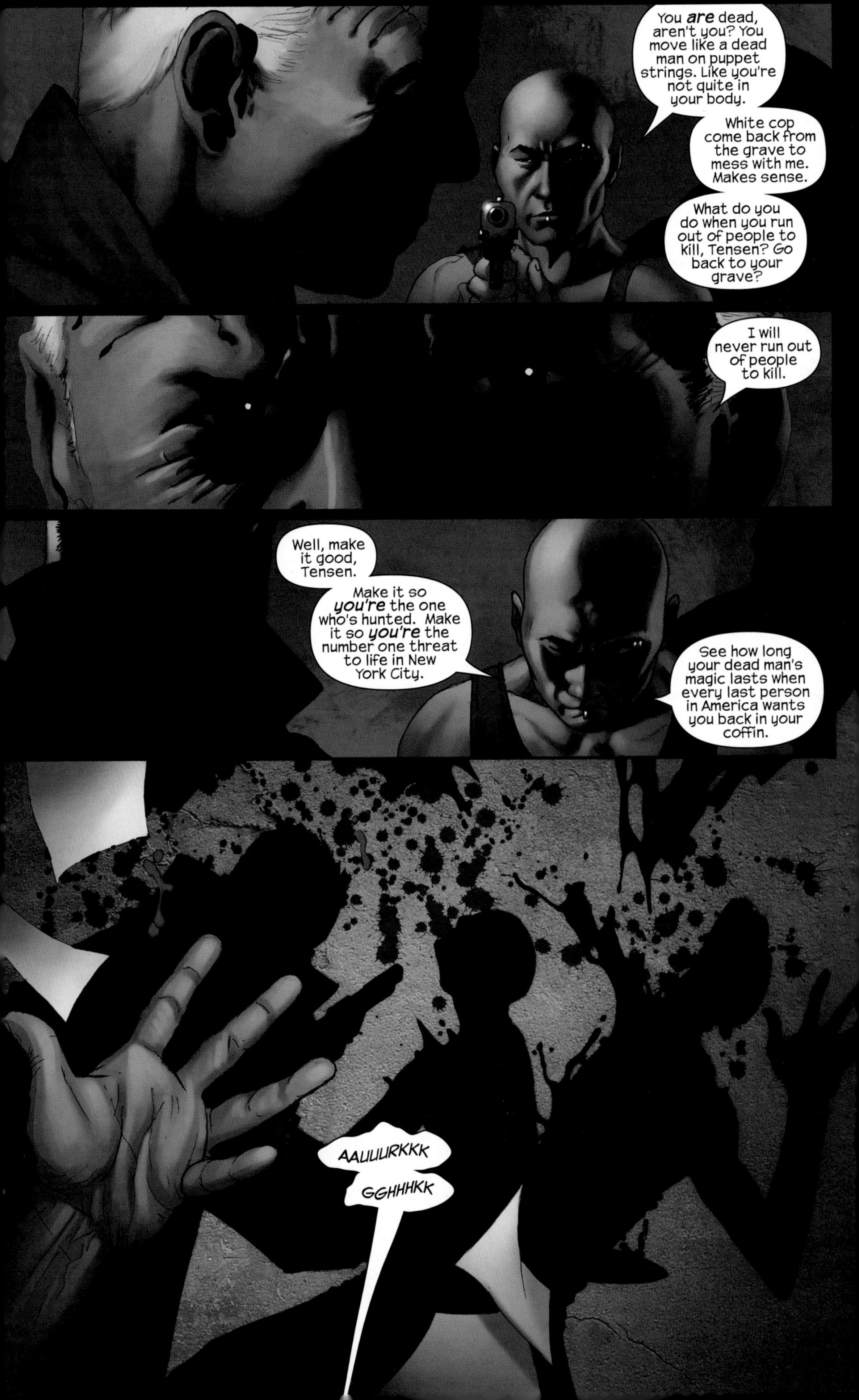
You *are* dead, aren't you? You move like a dead man on puppet strings. Like you're not quite in your body.
White cop come back from the grave to mess with me. Makes sense.
What do you do when you run out of people to kill, Tensen? Go back to your grave?
I will never run out of people to kill.
Well, make it good, Tensen.
Make it so *you're* the one who's hunted. Make it so *you're* the number one threat to life in New York City.
See how long your dead man's magic lasts when every last person in America wants you back in your coffin.
AAUUURKKK
GGHHHKK

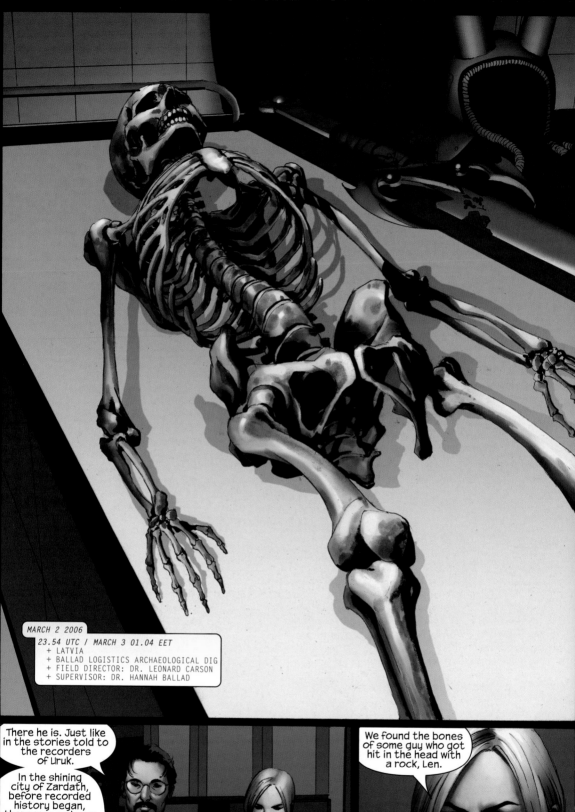

MARCH 2 2006
23.54 UTC / MARCH 3 01.04 EET
+ LATVIA
+ BALLAD LOGISTICS ARCHAEOLOGICAL DIG
+ FIELD DIRECTOR: DR. LEONARD CARSON
+ SUPERVISOR: DR. HANNAH BALLAD

There he is. Just like in the stories told to the recorders of Uruk.

In the shining city of Zardath, before recorded history began, there was a slayer of men touched by the night sky, who became the champion of the city and then its greatest king.

There's an extra character in the name they gave for him. So it transliterates not as "Star", but "Starr."

We found the grave of Starr the Slayer, hero of lost Zardath.

We found the bones of some guy who got hit in the head with a rock, Len.

Oh, for... look at the *size* of him. Were there *any* Indo-Europeans of that height five thousand years ago?

The Uruk texts even described the mark on his head, Hannah. This is Starr. We're in Zardath.

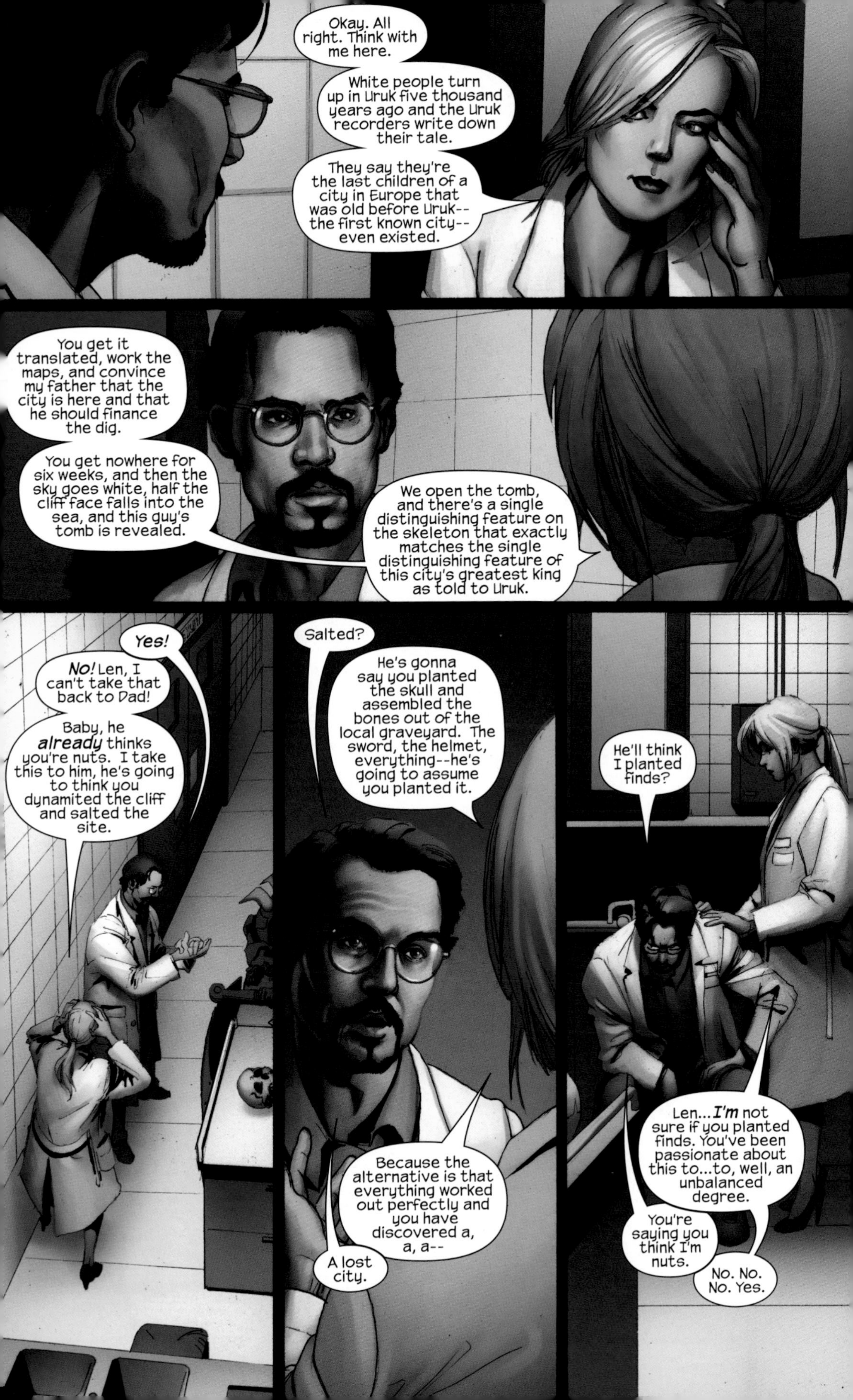

Okay. All right. Think with me here.
White people turn up in Uruk five thousand years ago and the Uruk recorders write down their tale.
They say they're the last children of a city in Europe that was old before Uruk-- the first known city-- even existed.
You get it translated, work the maps, and convince my father that the city is here and that he should finance the dig.
You get nowhere for six weeks, and then the sky goes white, half the cliff face falls into the sea, and this guy's tomb is revealed.
We open the tomb, and there's a single distinguishing feature on the skeleton that exactly matches the single distinguishing feature of this city's greatest king as told to Uruk.
Yes!
No! Len, I can't take that back to Dad!
Baby, he already thinks you're nuts. I take this to him, he's going to think you dynamited the cliff and salted the site.
Salted?
He's gonna say you planted the skull and assembled the bones out of the local graveyard. The sword, the helmet, everything--he's going to assume you planted it.
Because the alternative is that everything worked out perfectly and you have discovered a, a, a--
A lost city.
He'll think I planted finds?
Len... I'm not sure if you planted finds. You've been passionate about this to...to, well, an unbalanced degree.
You're saying you think I'm nuts.
No. No. No. Yes.

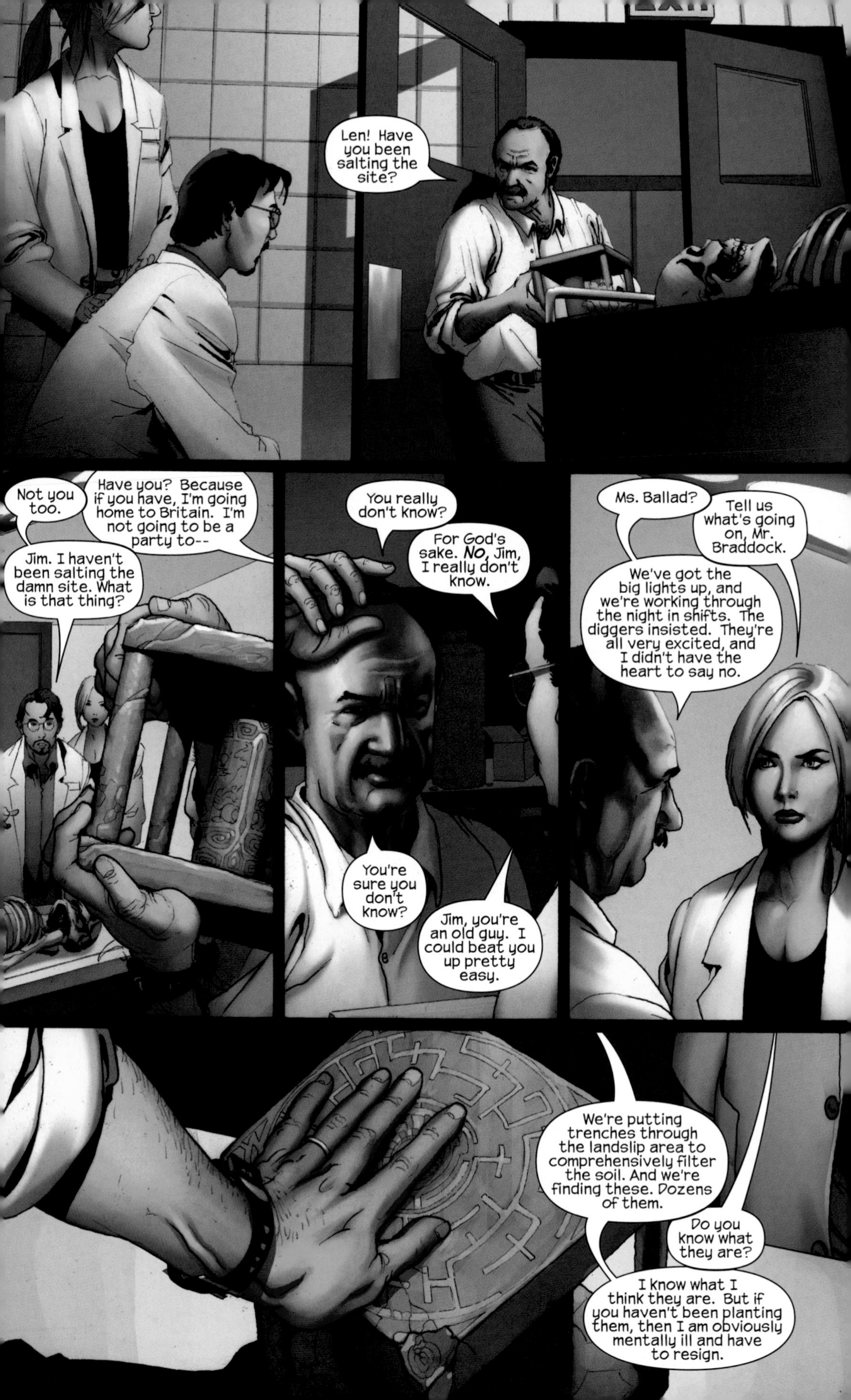

Len! Have you been salting the site?
Not you too.
Have you? Because if you have, I'm going home to Britain. I'm not going to be a party to--
Jim. I haven't been salting the damn site. What is that thing?
You really don't know?
For God's sake. *No*, Jim, I really don't know.
You're sure you don't know?
Jim, you're an old guy. I could beat you up pretty easy.
Ms. Ballad?
Tell us what's going on, Mr. Braddock.
We've got the big lights up, and we're working through the night in shifts. The diggers insisted. They're all very excited, and I didn't have the heart to say no.
We're putting trenches through the landslip area to comprehensively filter the soil. And we're finding these. Dozens of them.
Do you know what they are?
I know what I think they are. But if you haven't been planting them, then I am obviously mentally ill and have to resign.

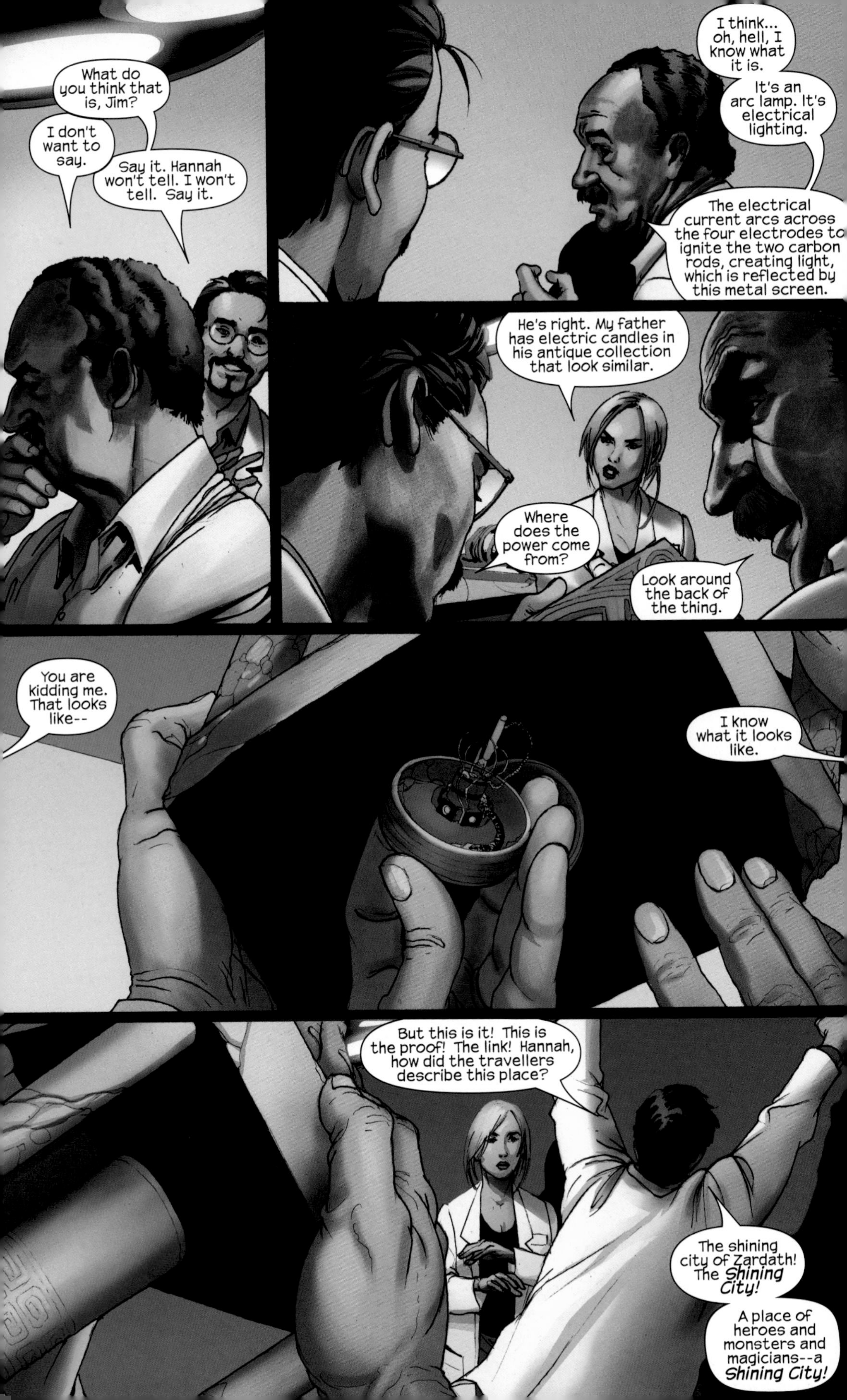
What do you think that is, Jim?
I don't want to say.
Say it. Hannah won't tell. I won't tell. Say it.
I think... oh, hell, I know what it is.
It's an arc lamp. It's electrical lighting.
The electrical current arcs across the four electrodes to ignite the two carbon rods, creating light, which is reflected by this metal screen.
He's right. My father has electric candles in his antique collection that look similar.
Where does the power come from?
Look around the back of the thing.
You are kidding me. That looks like--
I know what it looks like.
But this is it! This is the proof! The link! Hannah, how did the travellers describe this place?
The shining city of Zardath! The Shining City!
A place of heroes and monsters and magicians--a Shining City!

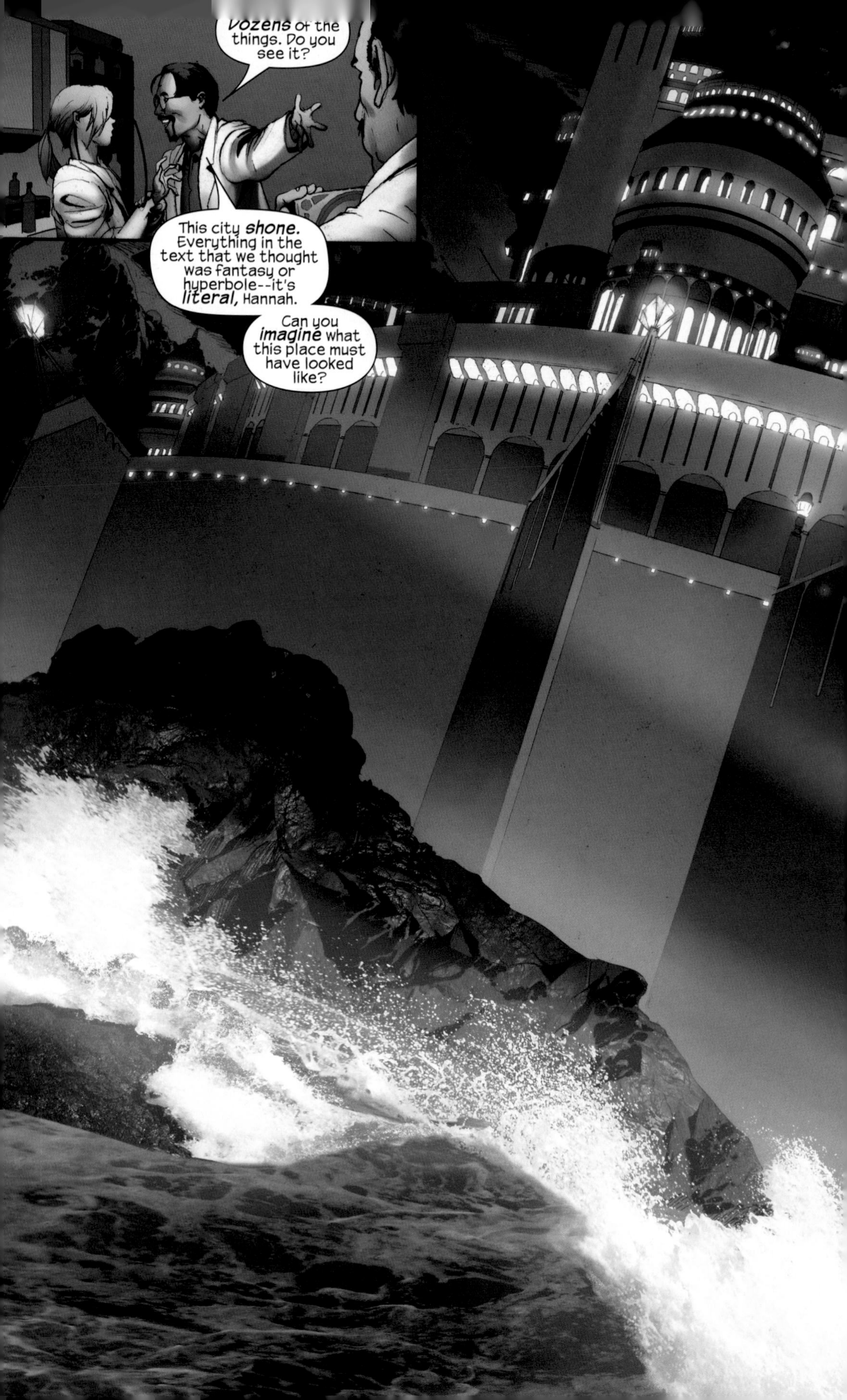
Dozens of the things. Do you see it?
This city shone. Everything in the text that we thought was fantasy or hyperbole--it's literal, Hannah.
Can you imagine what this place must have looked like?

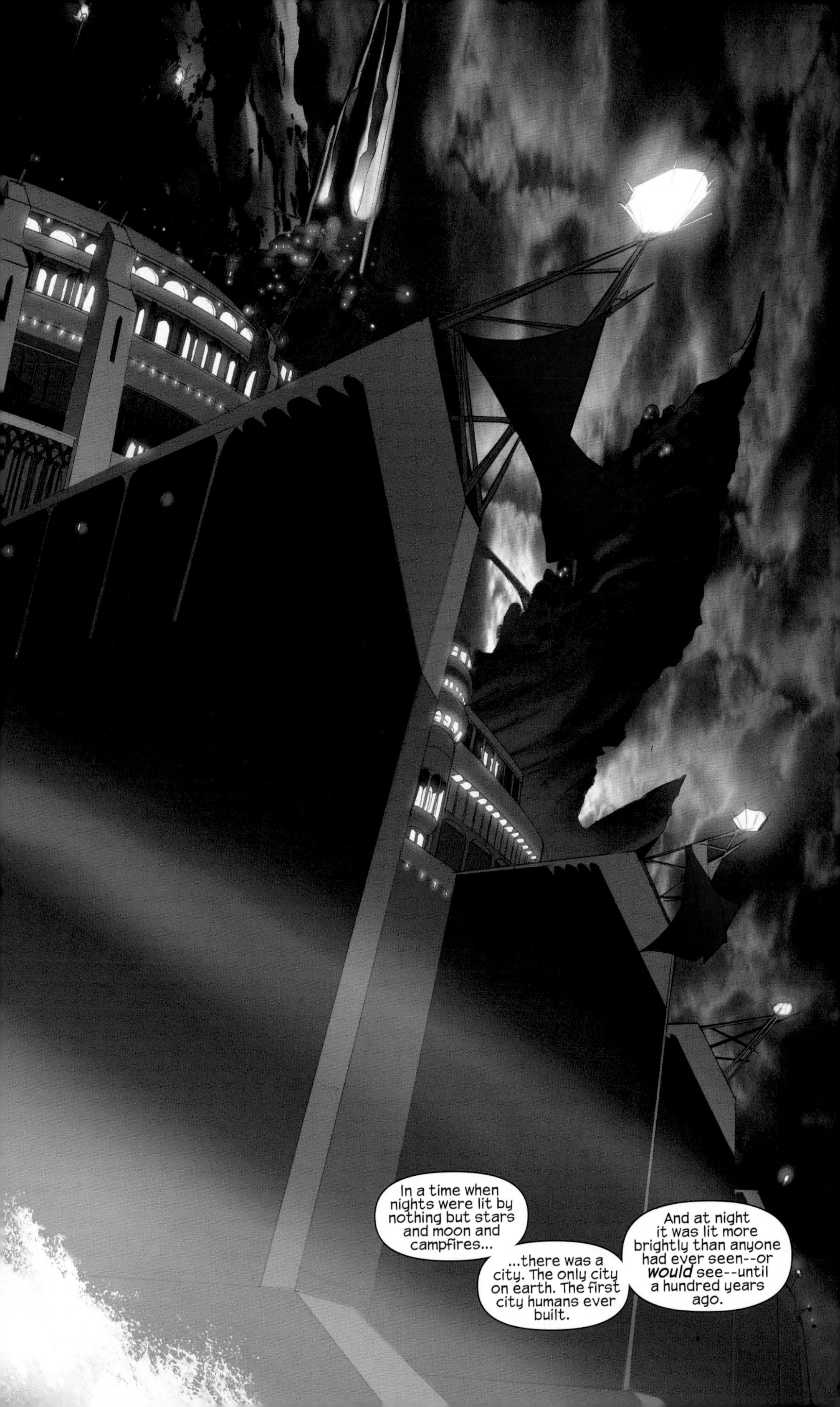
In a time when nights were lit by nothing but stars and moon and campfires...
...there was a city. The only city on earth. The first city humans ever built.
And at night it was lit more brightly than anyone had ever seen--or *would* see--until a hundred years ago.

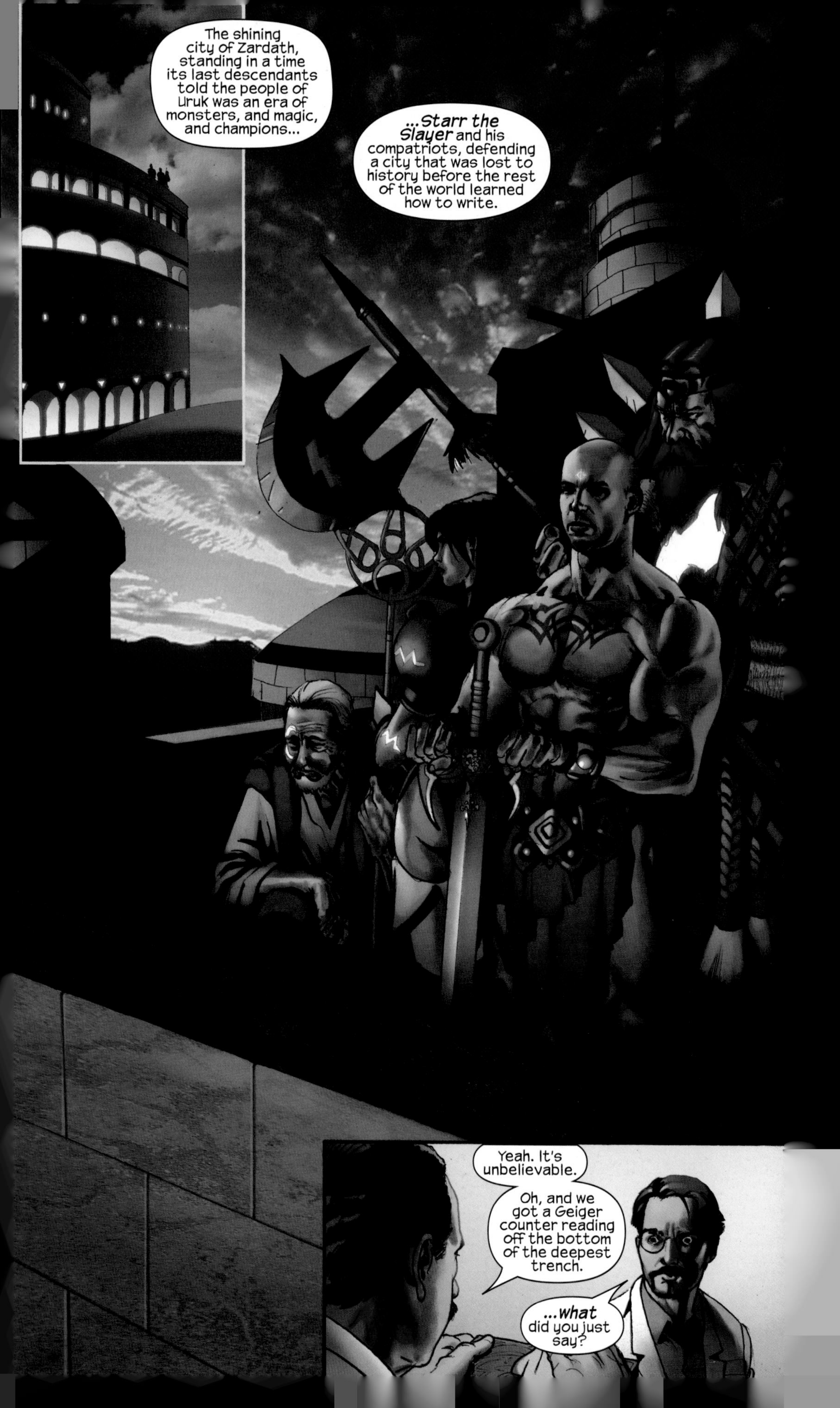

The shining city of Zardath, standing in a time its last descendants told the people of Uruk was an era of monsters, and magic, and champions...
...Starr the Slayer and his compatriots, defending a city that was lost to history before the rest of the world learned how to write.
Yeah. It's unbelievable.
Oh, and we got a Geiger counter reading off the bottom of the deepest trench.
...what did you just say?

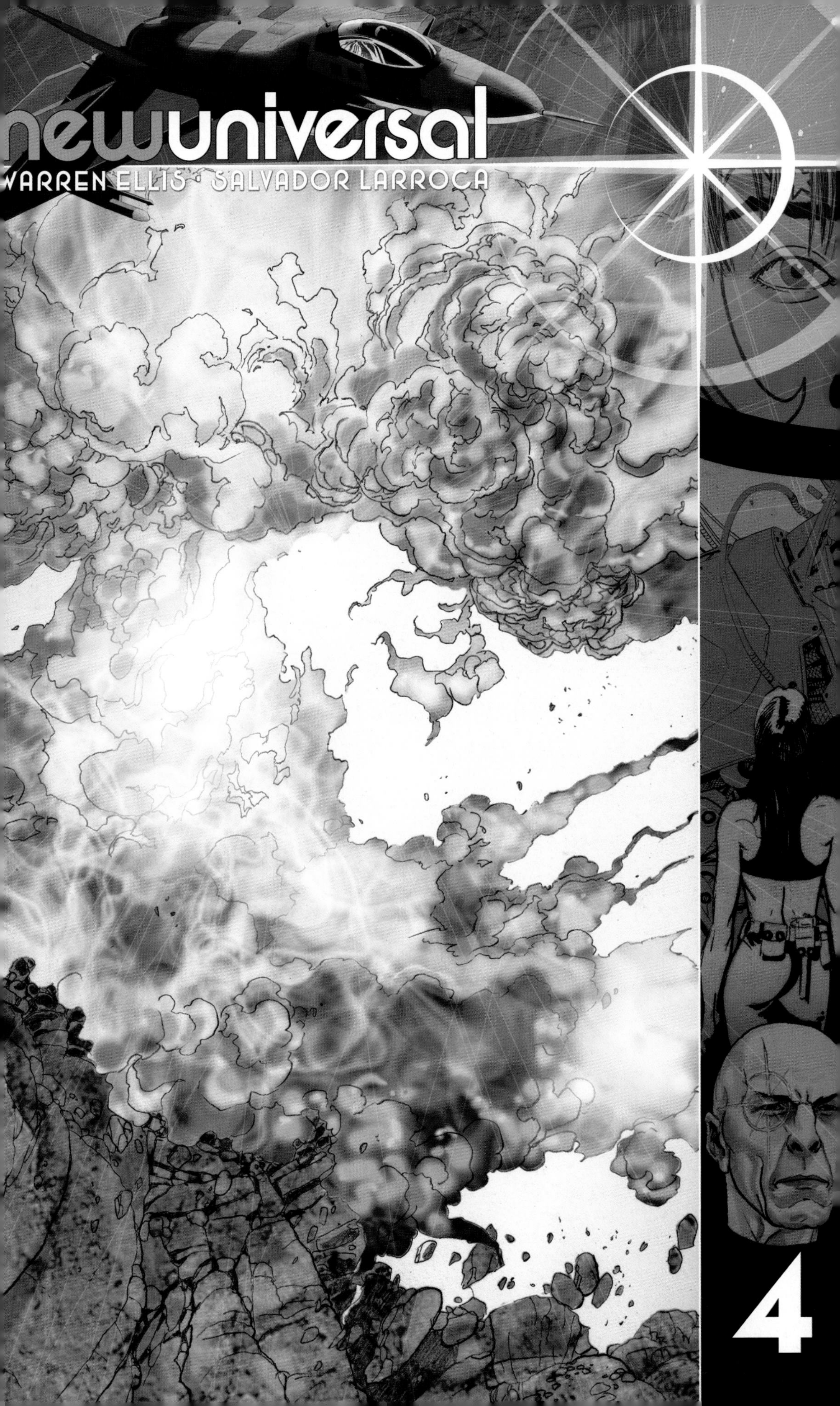

newuniversal
WARREN ELLIS · SALVADOR LARROCA
4

newuniversal
DISTANCE

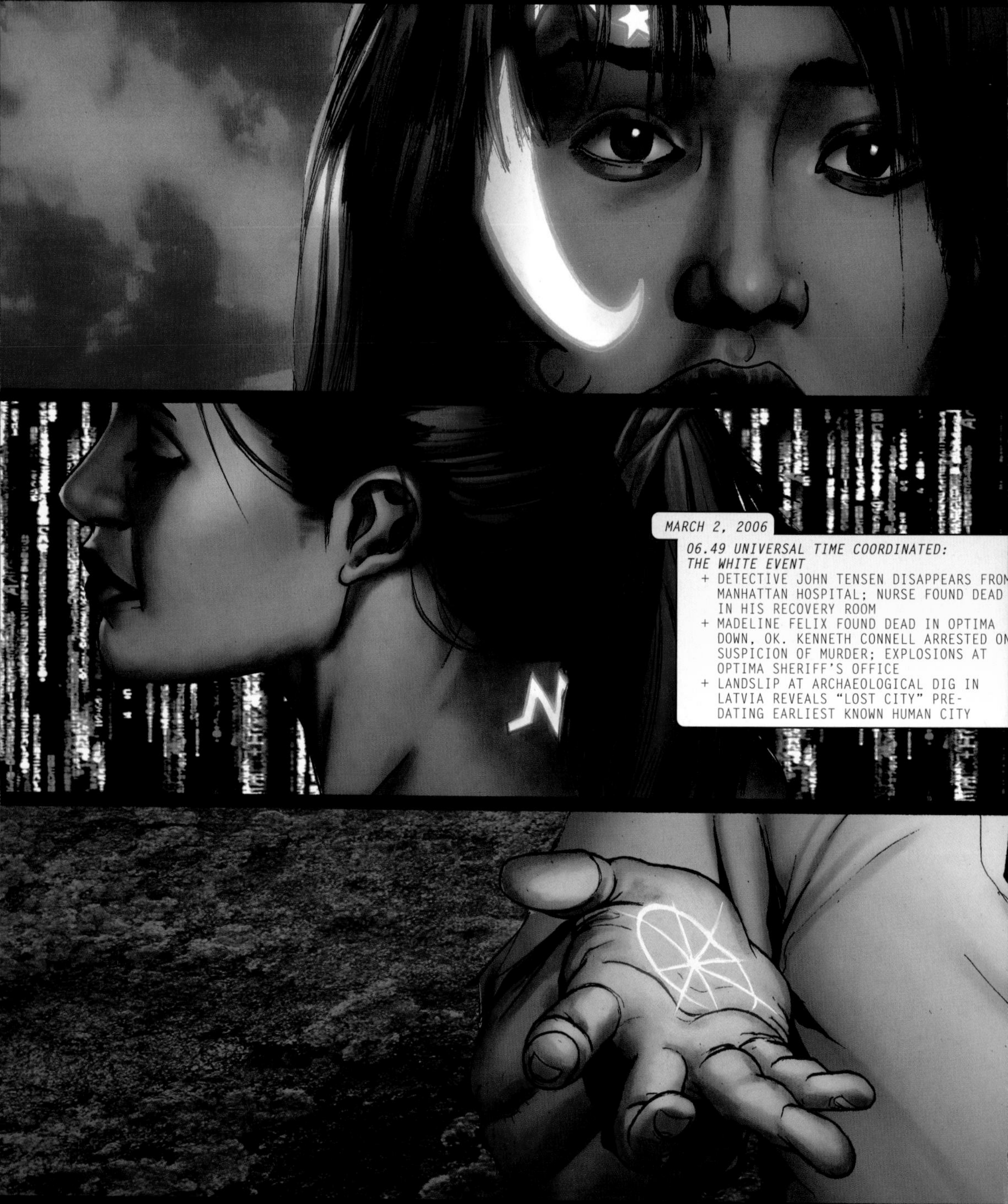

MARCH 2, 2006
06.49 UNIVERSAL TIME COORDINATED: THE WHITE EVENT
+ DETECTIVE JOHN TENSEN DISAPPEARS FROM MANHATTAN HOSPITAL; NURSE FOUND DEAD IN HIS RECOVERY ROOM
+ MADELINE FELIX FOUND DEAD IN OPTIMA DOWN, OK. KENNETH CONNELL ARRESTED ON SUSPICION OF MURDER; EXPLOSIONS AT OPTIMA SHERIFF'S OFFICE
+ LANDSLIP AT ARCHAEOLOGICAL DIG IN LATVIA REVEALS "LOST CITY" PRE-DATING EARLIEST KNOWN HUMAN CITY

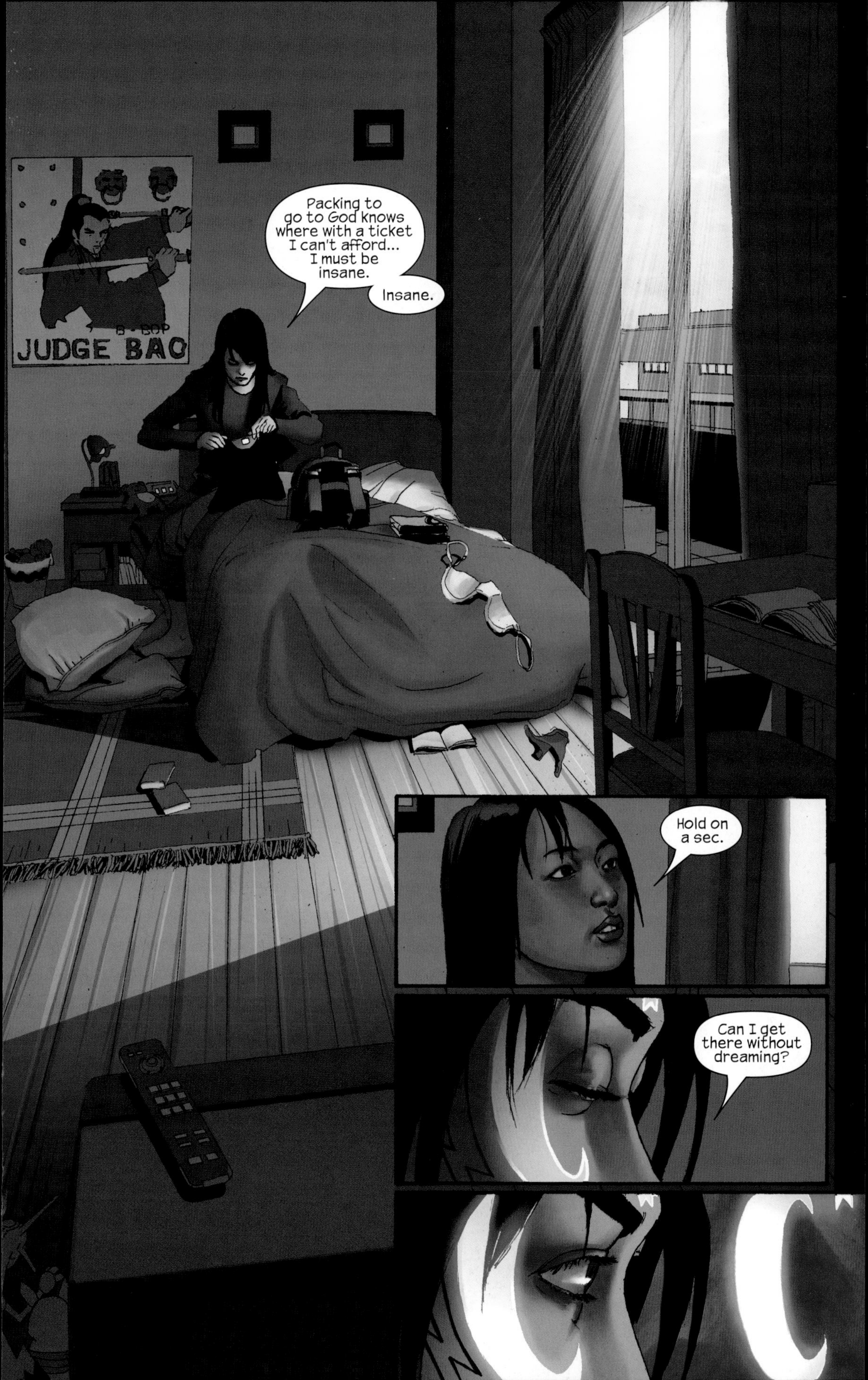

JUDGE BAO
B • BOP
Packing to go to God knows where with a ticket I can't afford... I must be insane.
Insane.
Hold on a sec.
Can I get there without dreaming?

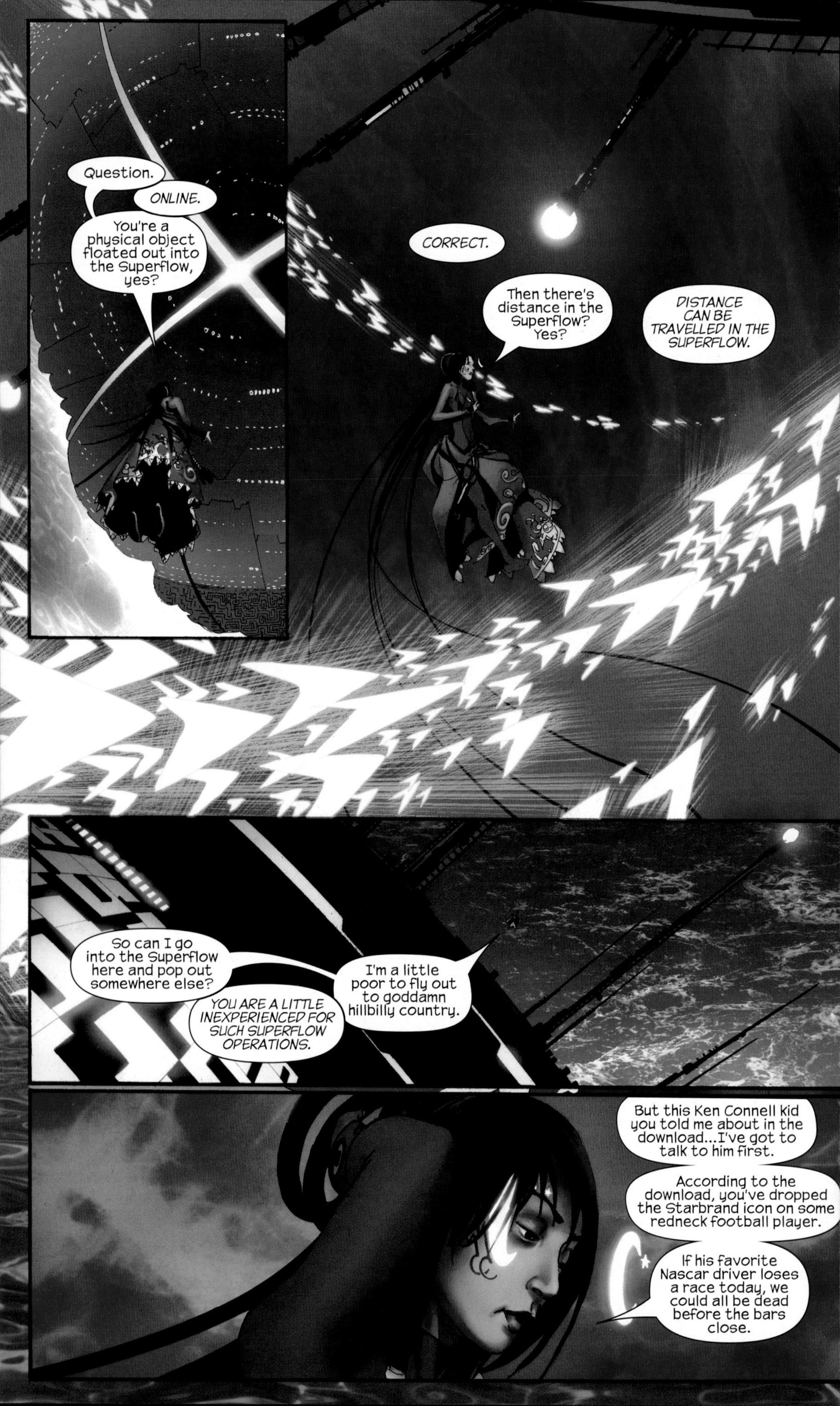
Question.
ONLINE.
You're a physical object floated out into the Superflow, yes?
CORRECT.
Then there's distance in the Superflow? Yes?
DISTANCE CAN BE TRAVELLED IN THE SUPERFLOW.
So can I go into the Superflow here and pop out somewhere else?
YOU ARE A LITTLE INEXPERIENCED FOR SUCH SUPERFLOW OPERATIONS.
I'm a little poor to fly out to goddamn hillbilly country.
But this Ken Connell kid you told me about in the download...I've got to talk to him first.
According to the download, you've dropped the Starbrand icon on some redneck football player.
If his favorite Nascar driver loses a race today, we could all be dead before the bars close.

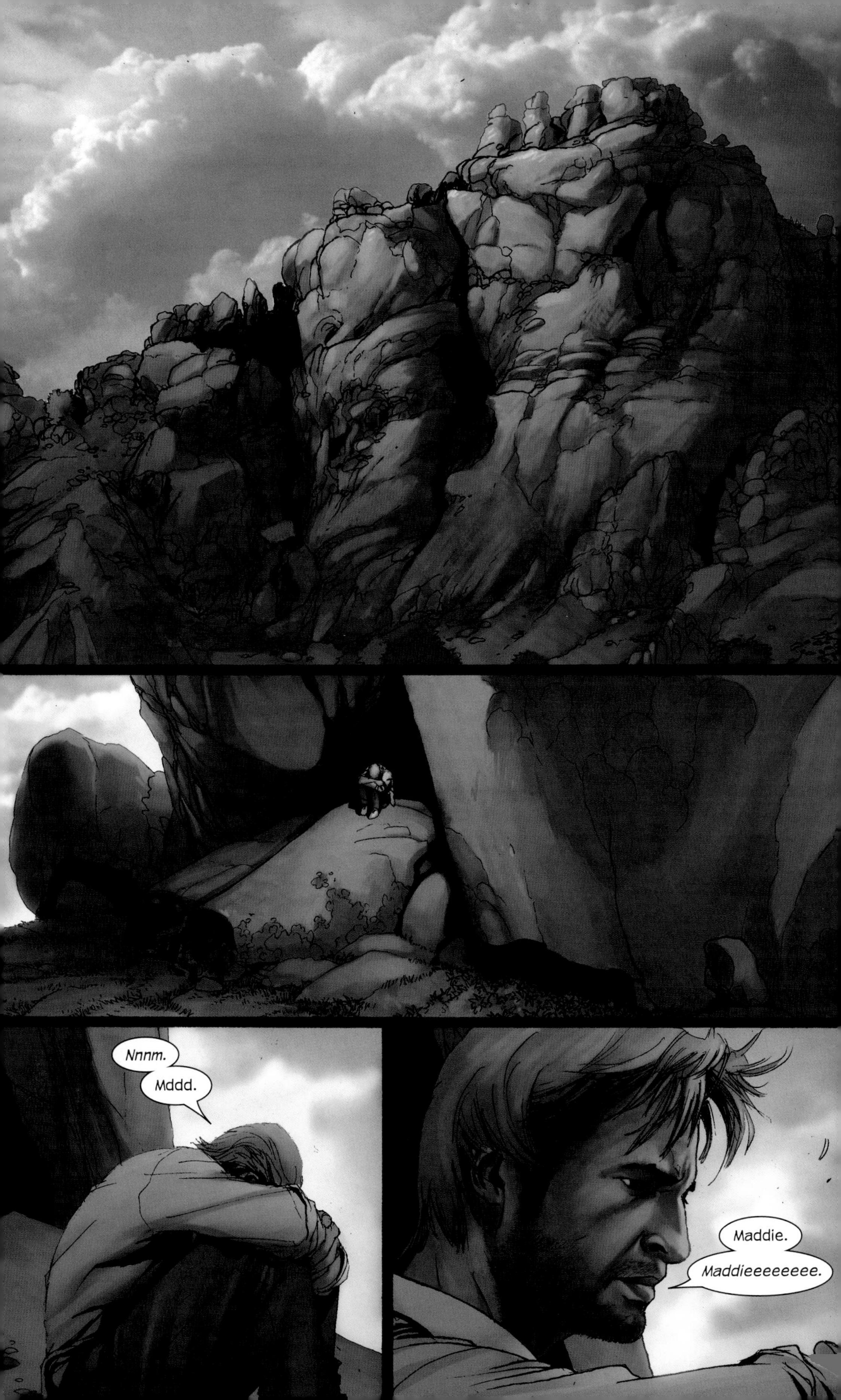
Nnnm.
Mddd.
Maddie.
Maddieeeeeeee.

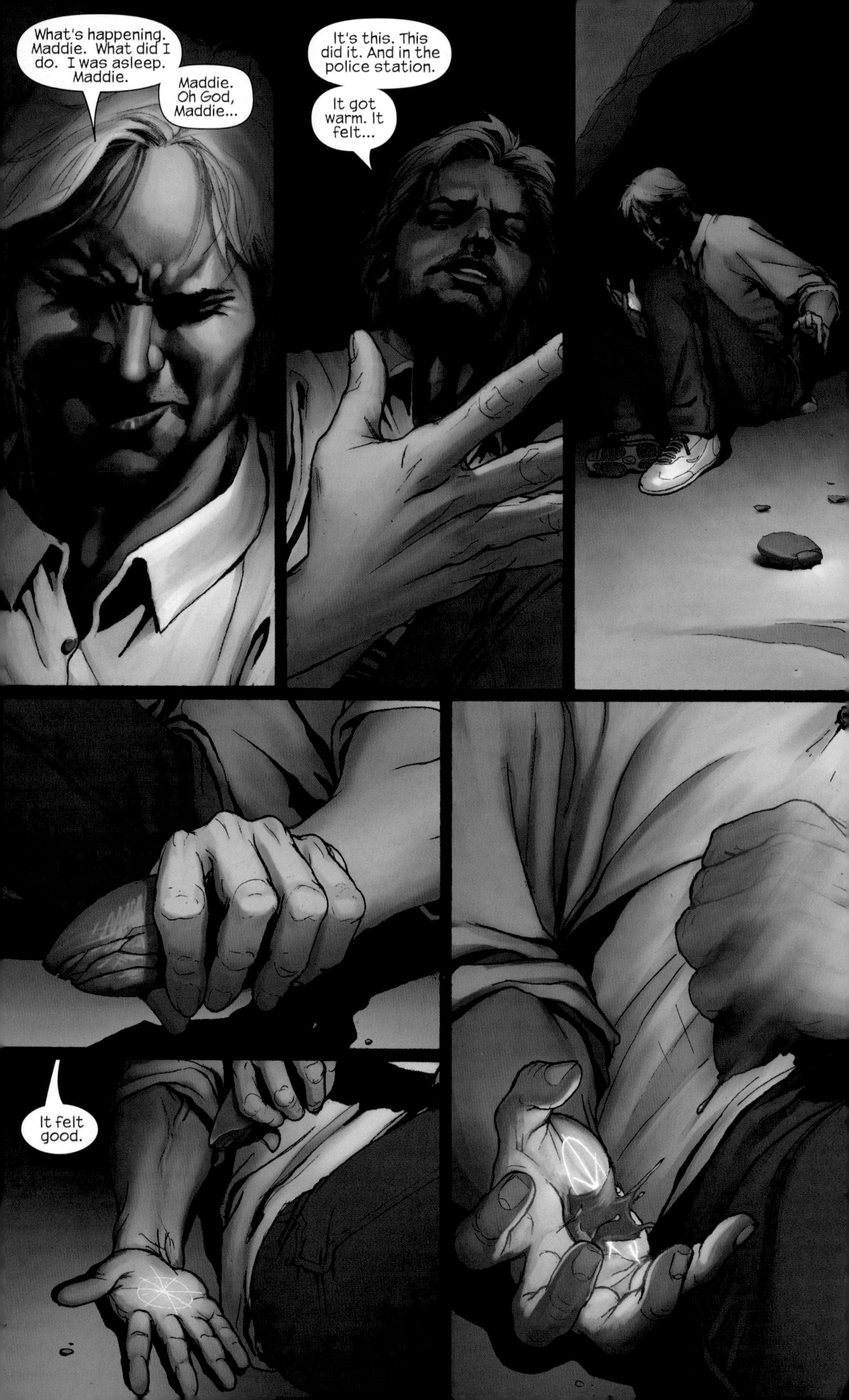
What's happening. Maddie. What did I do. I was asleep. Maddie.
Maddie. Oh God, Maddie...
It's this. This did it. And in the police station.
It got warm. It felt...
It felt good.

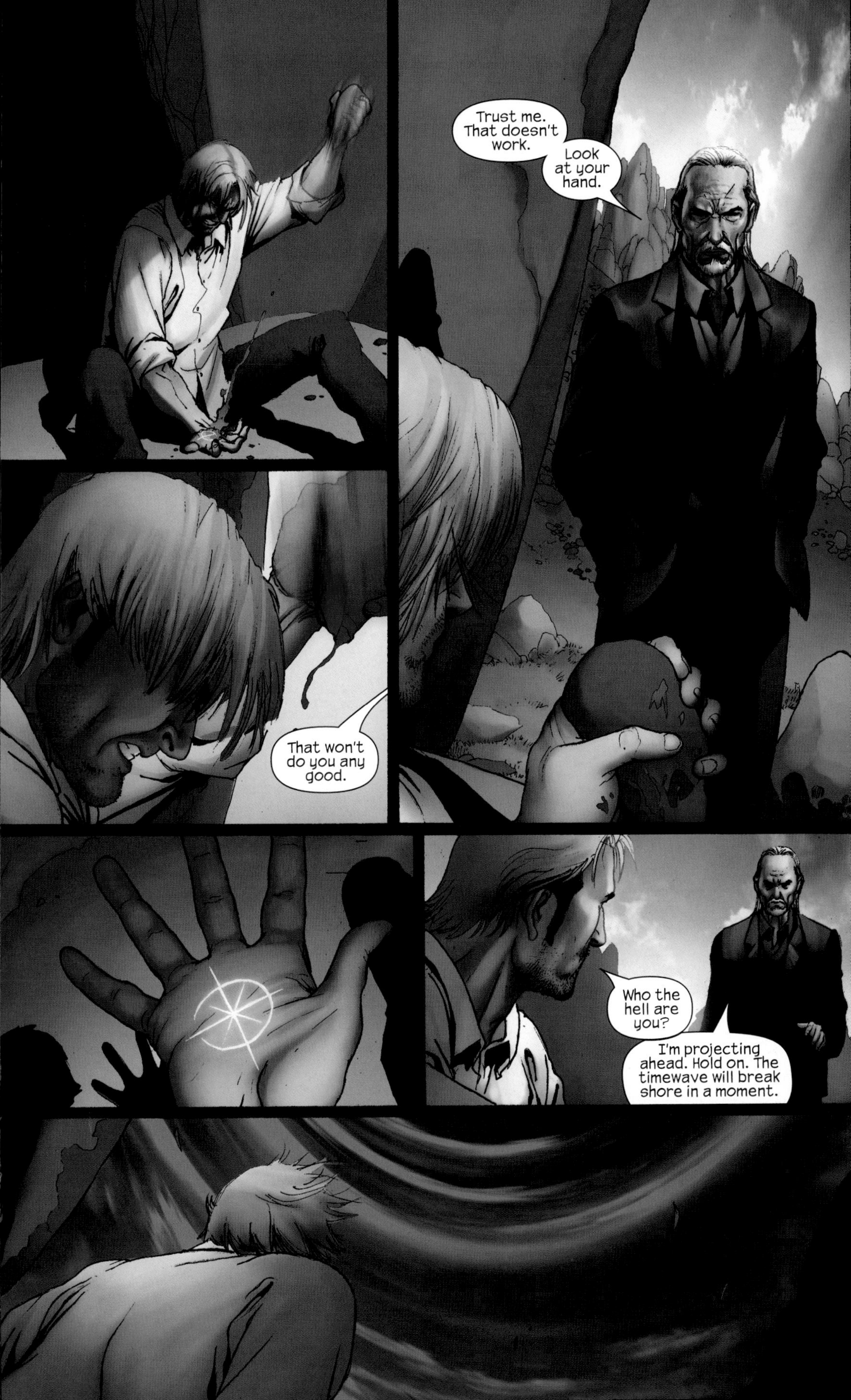
Trust me. That doesn't work.
Look at your hand.
That won't do you any good.
Who the hell are you?
I'm projecting ahead. Hold on. The timewave will break shore in a moment.

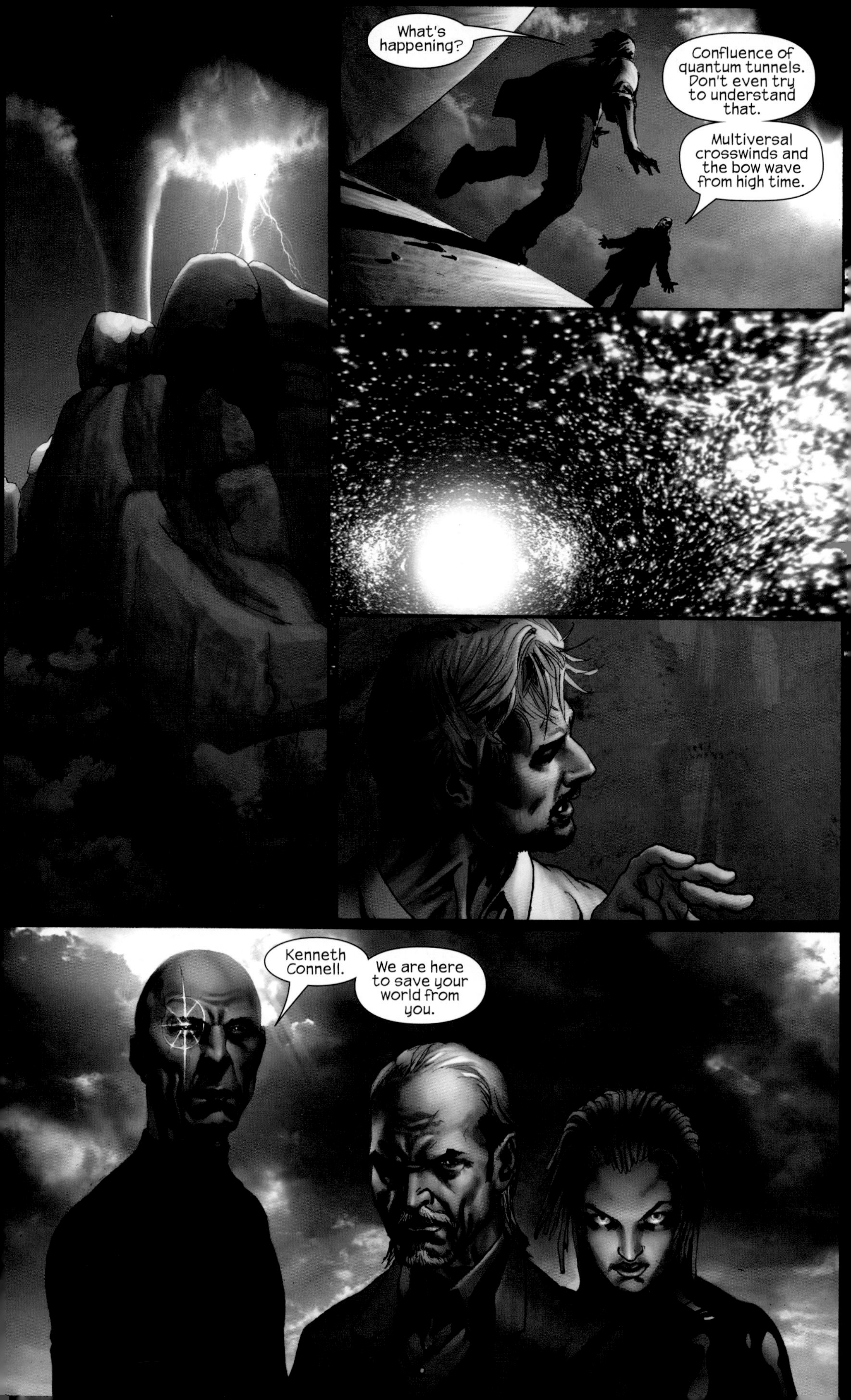
What's happening?
Confluence of quantum tunnels. Don't even try to understand that.
Multiversal crosswinds and the bow wave from high time.
Kenneth Connell.
We are here to save your world from you.

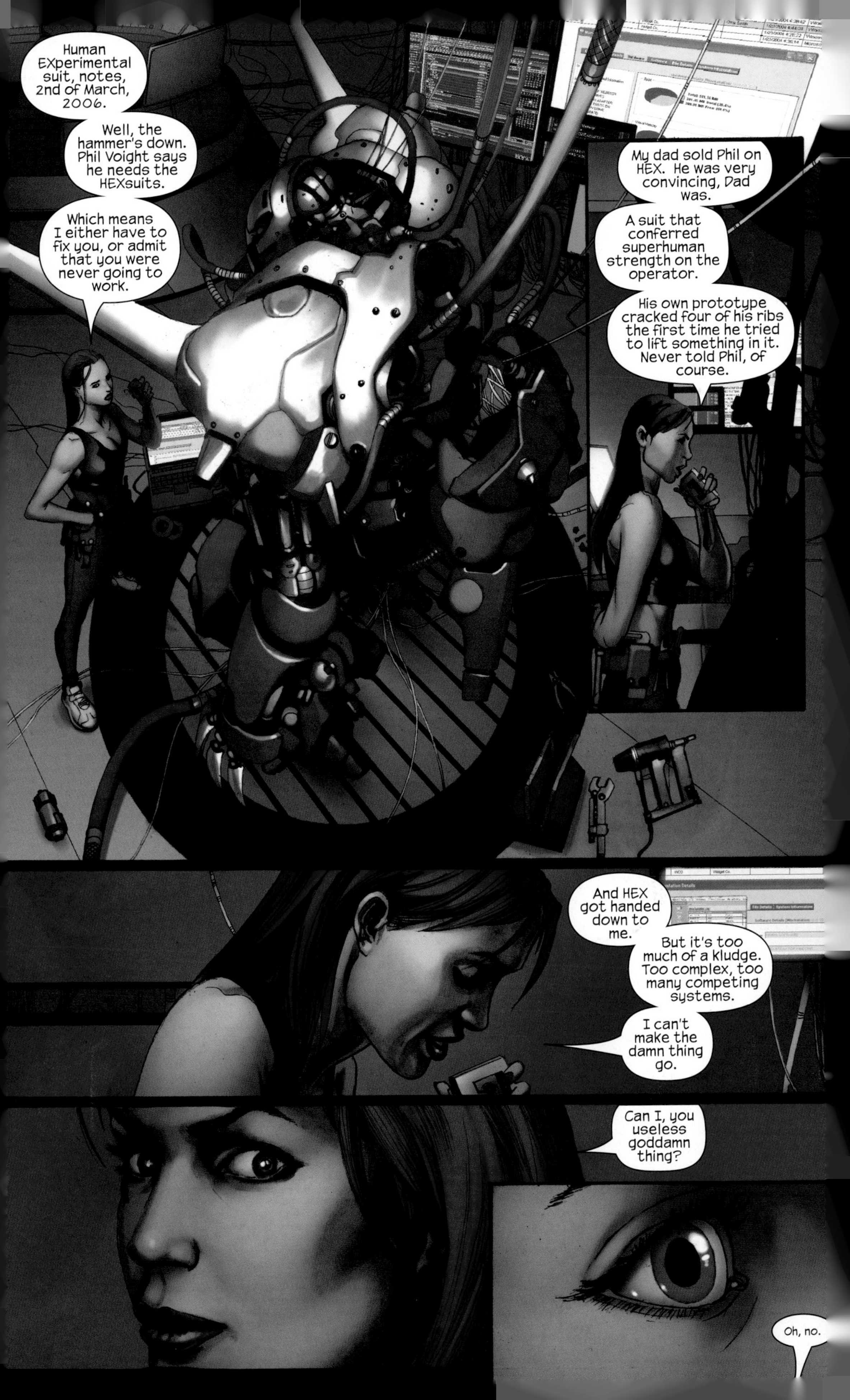

Human EXperimental suit, notes, 2nd of March, 2006.
Well, the hammer's down. Phil Voight says he needs the HEXsuits.
Which means I either have to fix you, or admit that you were never going to work.
My dad sold Phil on HEX. He was very convincing, Dad was.
A suit that conferred superhuman strength on the operator.
His own prototype cracked four of his ribs the first time he tried to lift something in it. Never told Phil, of course.
And HEX got handed down to me.
But it's too much of a kludge. Too complex, too many competing systems.
I can't make the damn thing go.
Can I, you useless goddamn thing?
Oh, no.

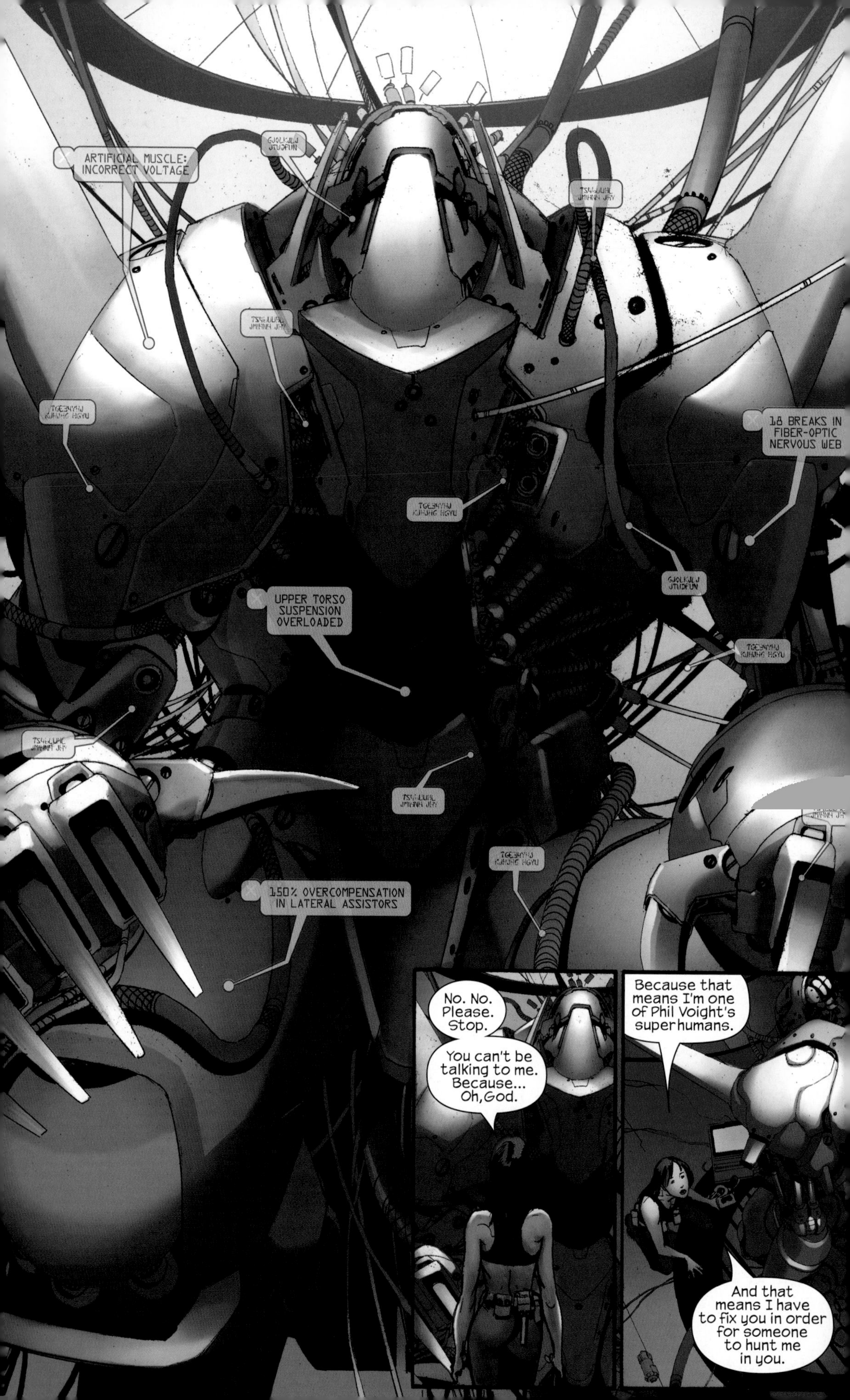
ARTIFICIAL MUSCLE: INCORRECT VOLTAGE
18 BREAKS IN FIBER-OPTIC NERVOUS WEB
UPPER TORSO SUSPENSION OVERLOADED
150% OVERCOMPENSATION IN LATERAL ASSISTORS
No. No. Please. Stop.
You can't be talking to me. Because... Oh, God.
Because that means I'm one of Phil Voight's superhumans.
And that means I have to fix you in order for someone to hunt me in you.

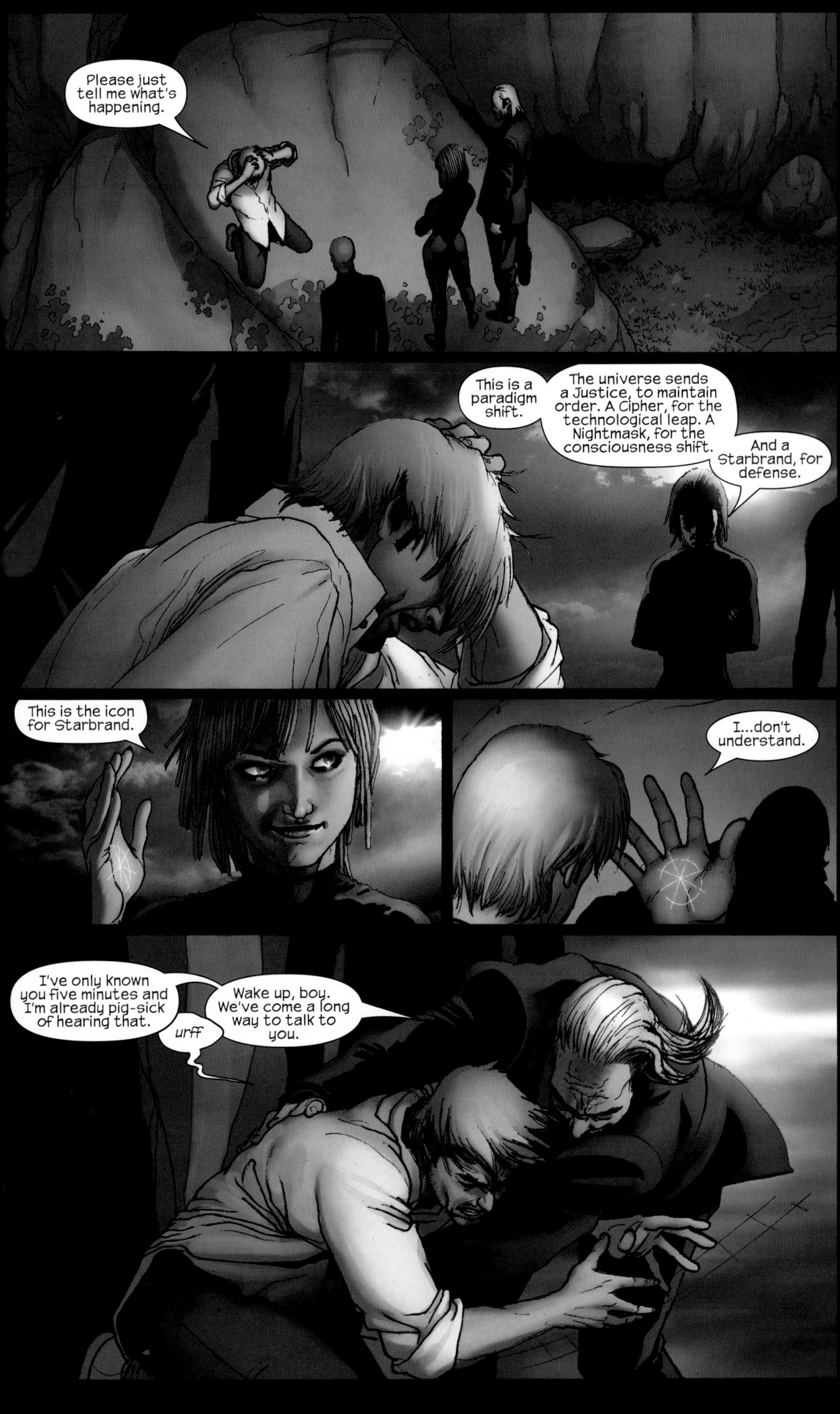
Please just tell me what's happening.
This is a paradigm shift.
The universe sends a Justice, to maintain order. A Cipher, for the technological leap. A Nightmask, for the consciousness shift.
And a Starbrand, for defense.
This is the icon for Starbrand.
I...don't understand.
I've only known you five minutes and I'm already pig-sick of hearing that.
urff
Wake up, boy. We've come a long way to talk to you.

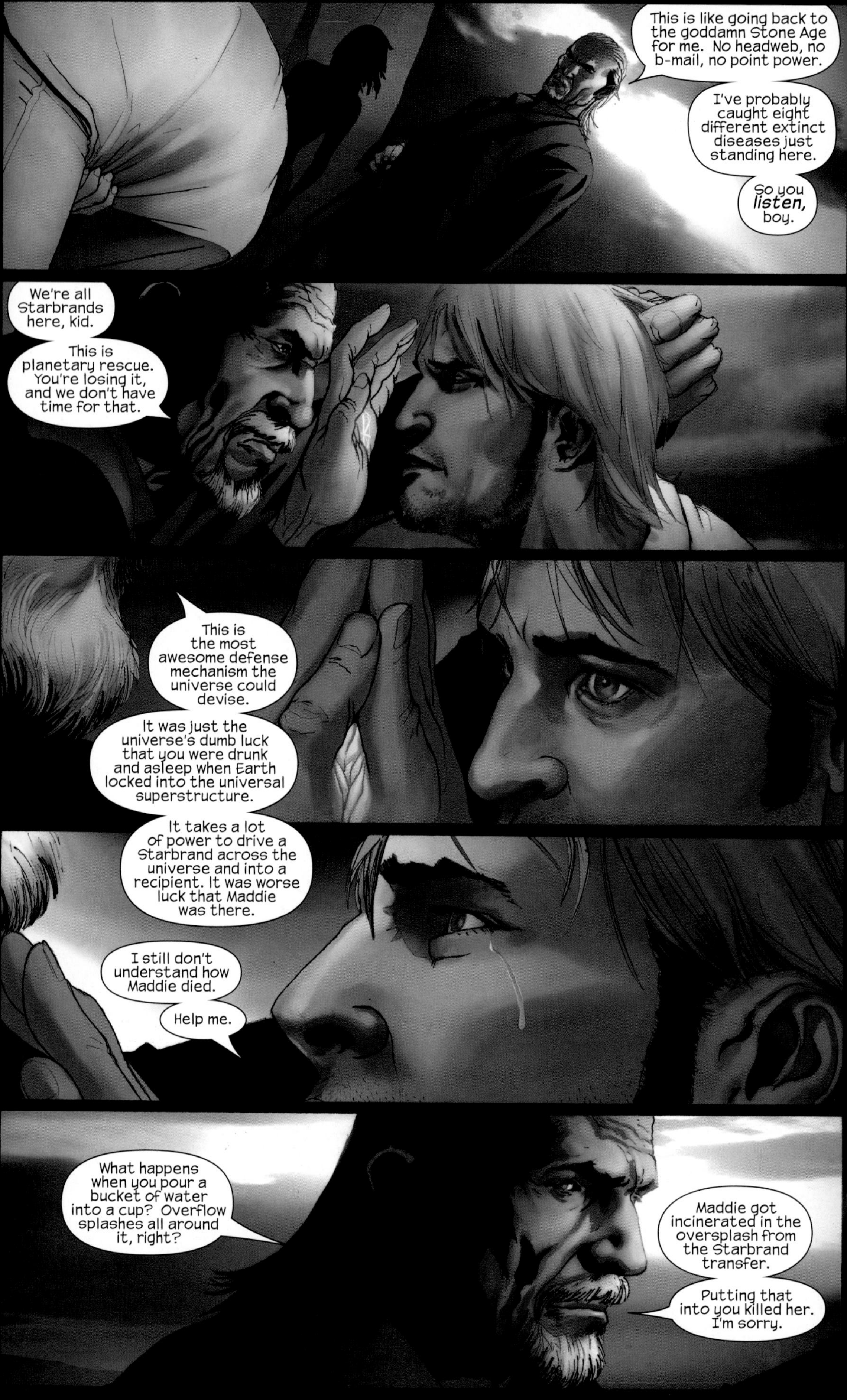
This is like going back to the goddamn Stone Age for me. No headweb, no b-mail, no point power.
I've probably caught eight different extinct diseases just standing here.
So you *listen,* boy.
We're all Starbrands here, kid.
This is planetary rescue. You're losing it, and we don't have time for that.
This is the most awesome defense mechanism the universe could devise.
It was just the universe's dumb luck that you were drunk and asleep when Earth locked into the universal superstructure.
It takes a lot of power to drive a Starbrand across the universe and into a recipient. It was worse luck that Maddie was there.
I still don't understand how Maddie died.
Help me.
What happens when you pour a bucket of water into a cup? Overflow splashes all around it, right?
Maddie got incinerated in the oversplash from the Starbrand transfer.
Putting that into you killed her. I'm sorry.

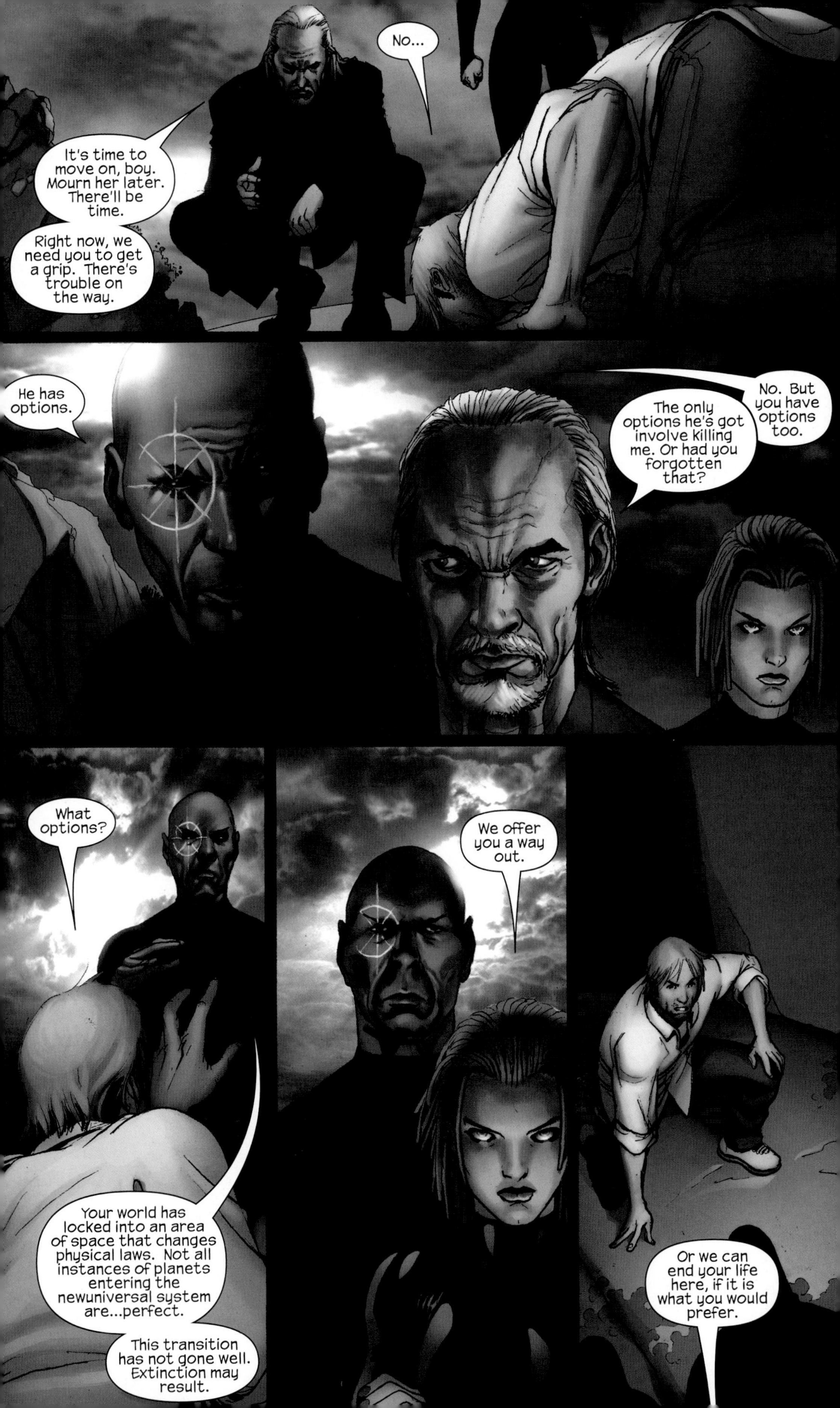

No...
It's time to move on, boy. Mourn her later. There'll be time.
Right now, we need you to get a grip. There's trouble on the way.
He has options.
The only options he's got involve killing me. Or had you forgotten that?
No. But you have options too.
What options?
We offer you a way out.
Your world has locked into an area of space that changes physical laws. Not all instances of planets entering the newuniversal system are...perfect.
This transition has not gone well. Extinction may result.
Or we can end your life here, if it is what you would prefer.

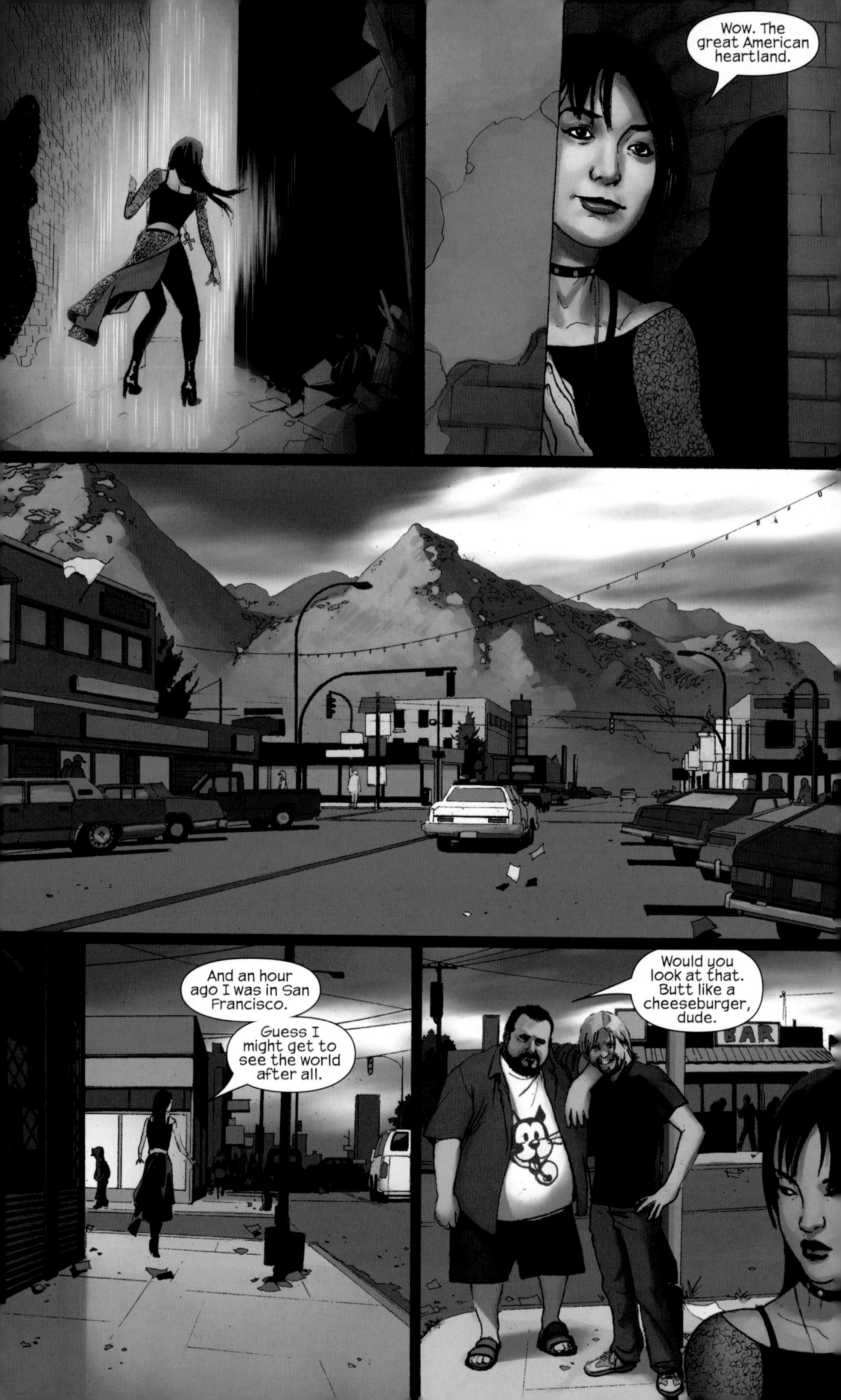
Wow. The great American heartland.
And an hour ago I was in San Francisco.
Guess I might get to see the world after all.
Would you look at that. Butt like a cheeseburger, dude.
BAR

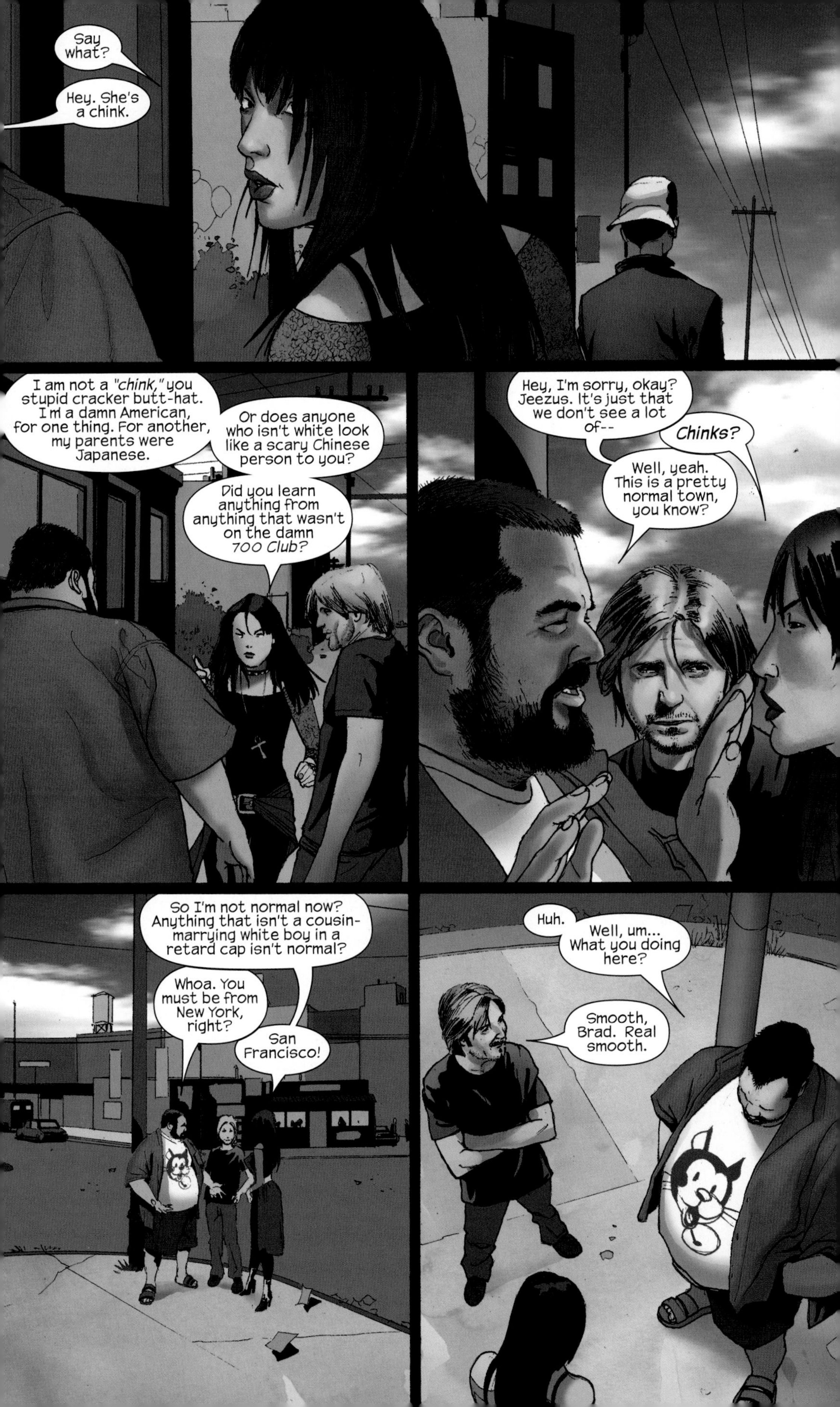
Say what?
Hey. She's a chink.
I am not a "chink," you stupid cracker butt-hat. I'm a damn American, for one thing. For another, my parents were Japanese.
Or does anyone who isn't white look like a scary Chinese person to you?
Did you learn anything from anything that wasn't on the damn 700 Club?
Hey, I'm sorry, okay? Jeezus. It's just that we don't see a lot of--
Chinks?
Well, yeah. This is a pretty normal town, you know?
So I'm not normal now? Anything that isn't a cousin-marrying white boy in a retard cap isn't normal?
Whoa. You must be from New York, right?
San Francisco!
Huh.
Well, um... What you doing here?
Smooth, Brad. Real smooth.

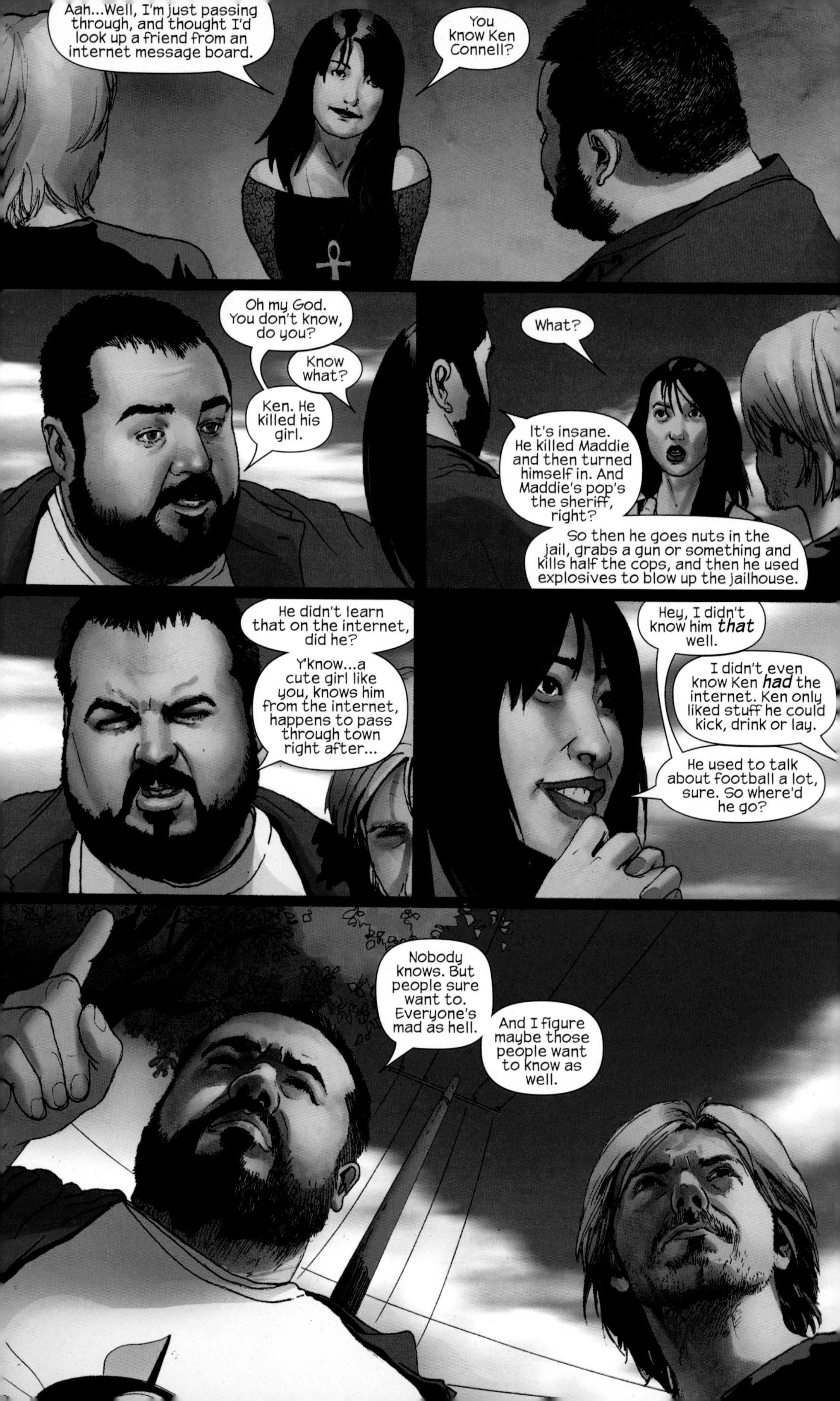
Aah...Well, I'm just passing through, and thought I'd look up a friend from an internet message board.
You know Ken Connell?
Oh my God. You don't know, do you?
Know what?
Ken. He killed his girl.
What?
It's insane. He killed Maddie and then turned himself in. And Maddie's pop's the sheriff, right?
So then he goes nuts in the jail, grabs a gun or something and kills half the cops, and then he used explosives to blow up the jailhouse.
He didn't learn that on the internet, did he?
Y'know...a cute girl like you, knows him from the internet, happens to pass through town right after...
Hey, I didn't know him *that* well.
I didn't even know Ken *had* the internet. Ken only liked stuff he could kick, drink or lay.
He used to talk about football a lot, sure. So where'd he go?
Nobody knows. But people sure want to. Everyone's mad as hell.
And I figure maybe those people want to know as well.

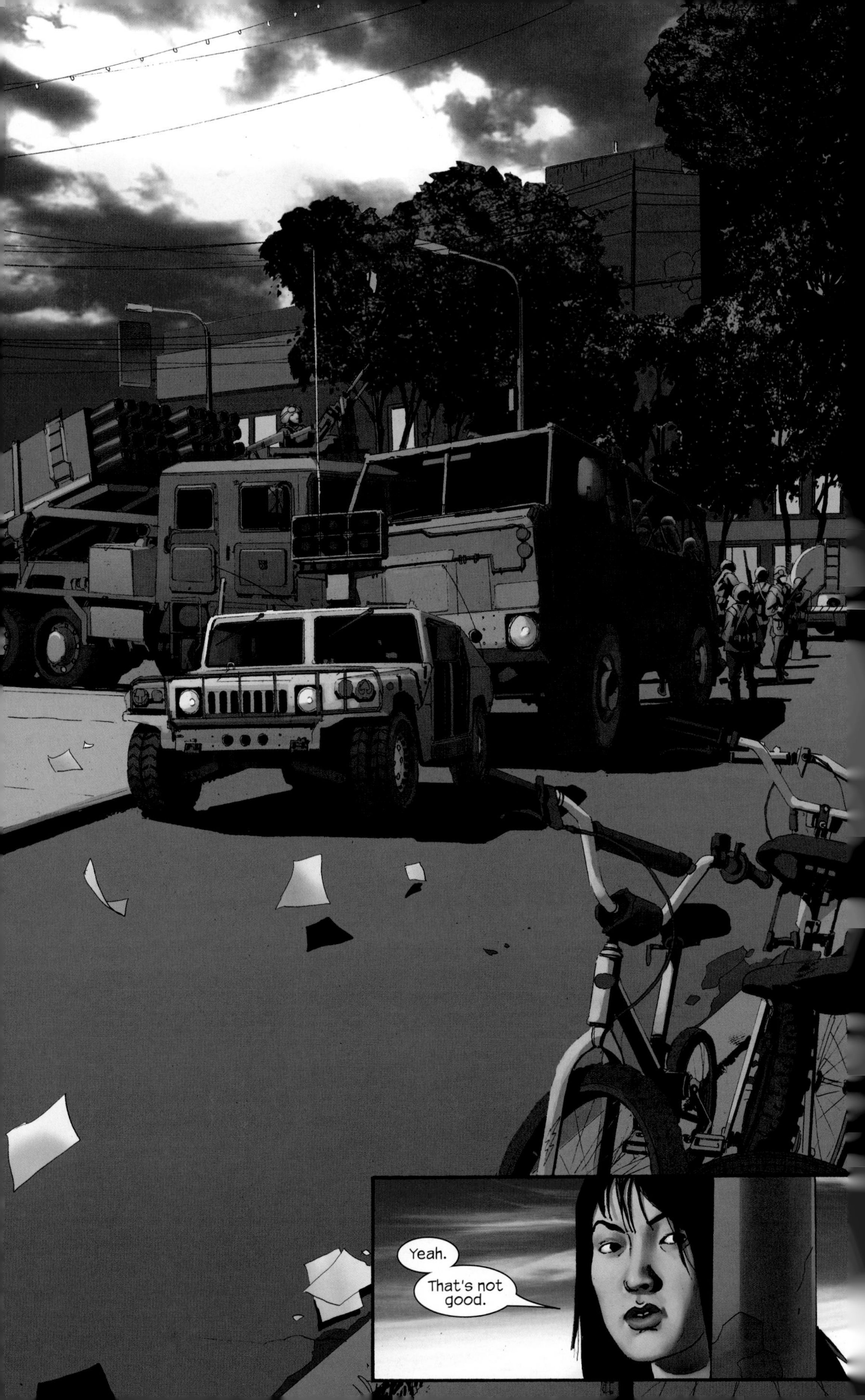
Yeah.
That's not good.

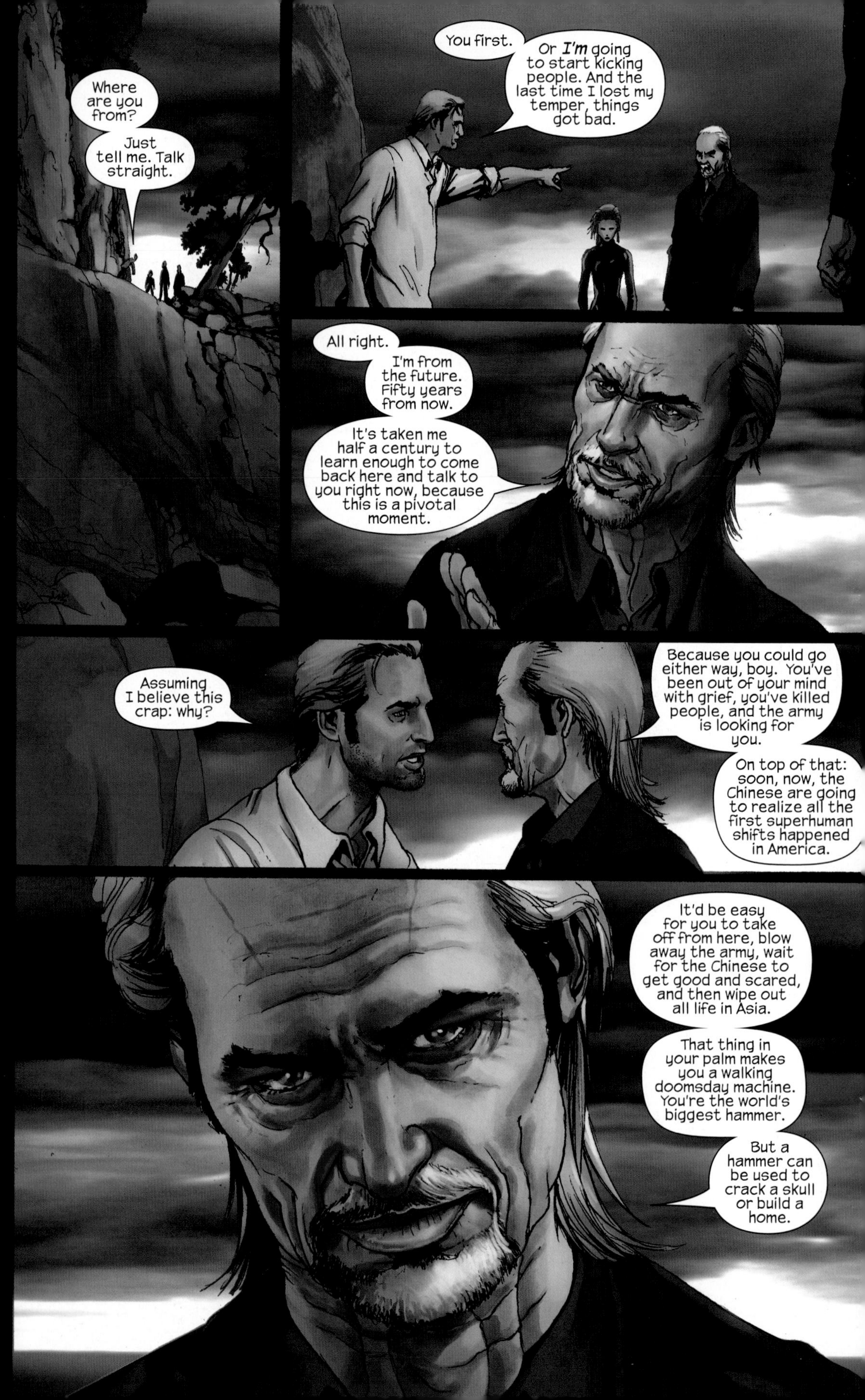

Where are you from?
Just tell me. Talk straight.
You first.
Or *I'm* going to start kicking people. And the last time I lost my temper, things got bad.
All right.
I'm from the future. Fifty years from now.
It's taken me half a century to learn enough to come back here and talk to you right now, because this is a pivotal moment.
Assuming I believe this crap: why?
Because you could go either way, boy. You've been out of your mind with grief, you've killed people, and the army is looking for you.
On top of that: soon, now, the Chinese are going to realize all the first superhuman shifts happened in America.
It'd be easy for you to take off from here, blow away the army, wait for the Chinese to get good and scared, and then wipe out all life in Asia.
That thing in your palm makes you a walking doomsday machine. You're the world's biggest hammer.
But a hammer can be used to crack a skull or build a home.

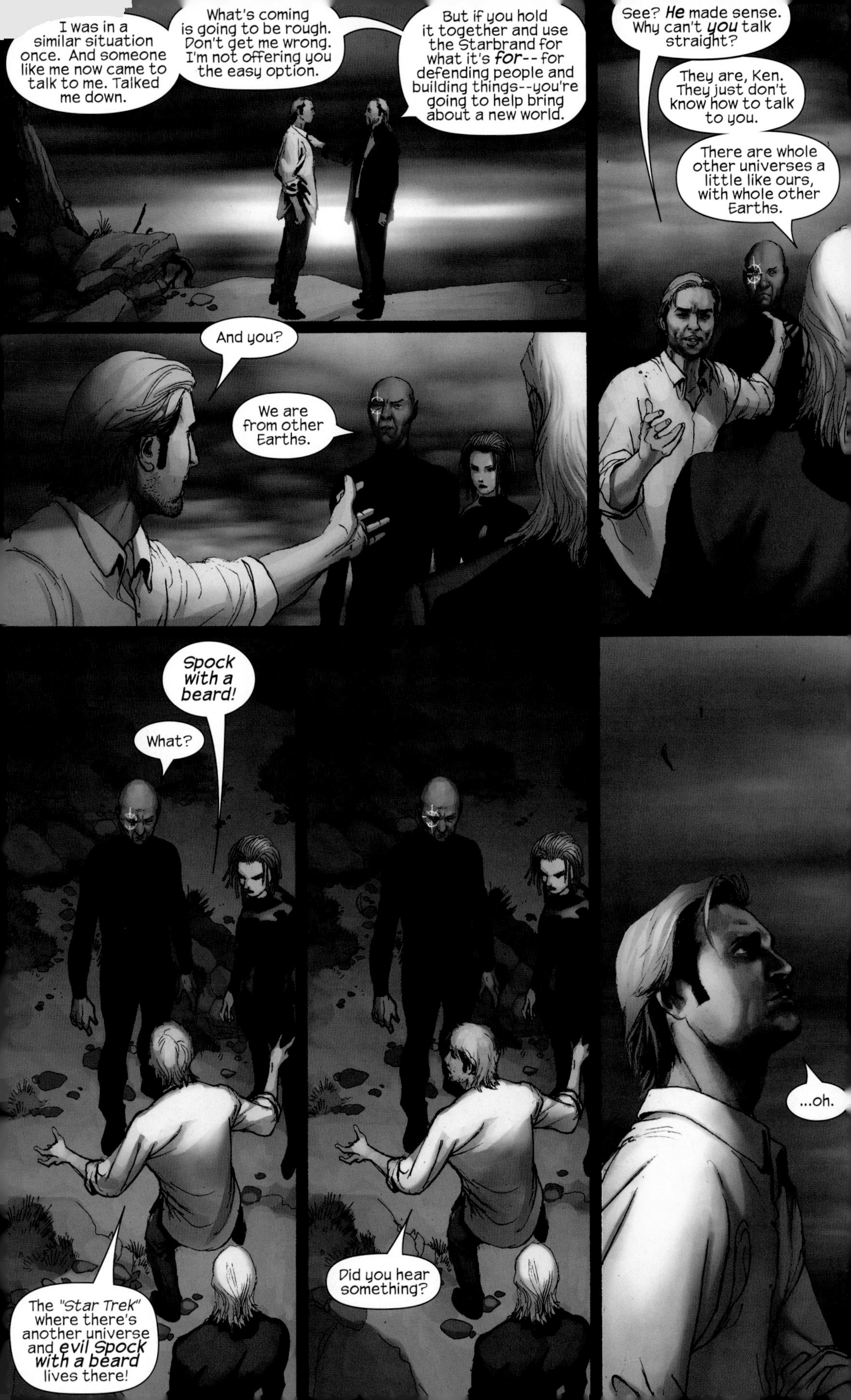

I was in a similar situation once. And someone like me now came to talk to me. Talked me down.
What's coming is going to be rough. Don't get me wrong. I'm not offering you the easy option.
But if you hold it together and use the Starbrand for what it's *for*-- for defending people and building things--you're going to help bring about a new world.
See? *He* made sense. Why can't *you* talk straight?
They are, Ken. They just don't know how to talk to you.
There are whole other universes a little like ours, with whole other Earths.
And you?
We are from other Earths.
Spock with a beard!
What?
The *"Star Trek"* where there's another universe and *evil Spock with a beard* lives there!
Did you hear something?
...oh.

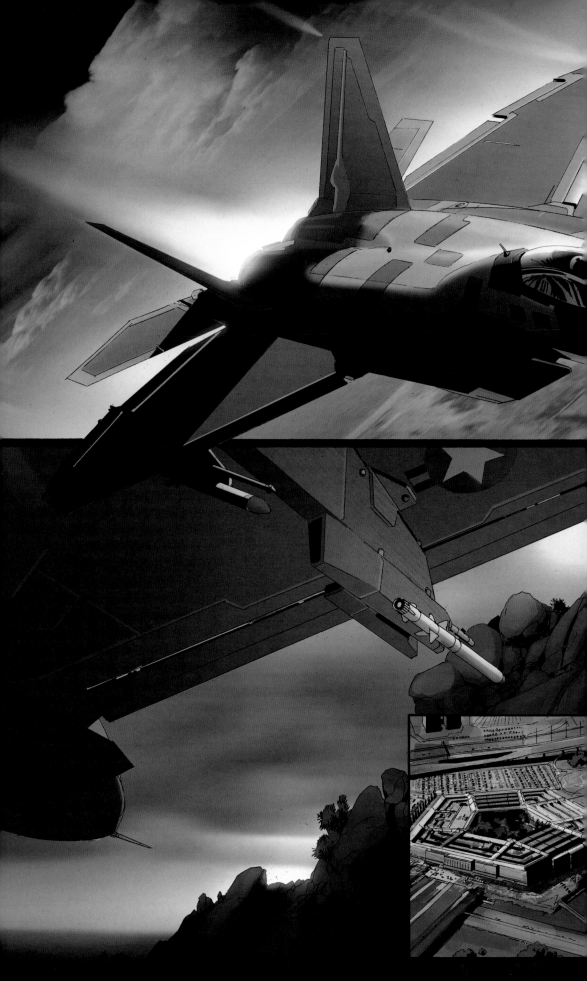

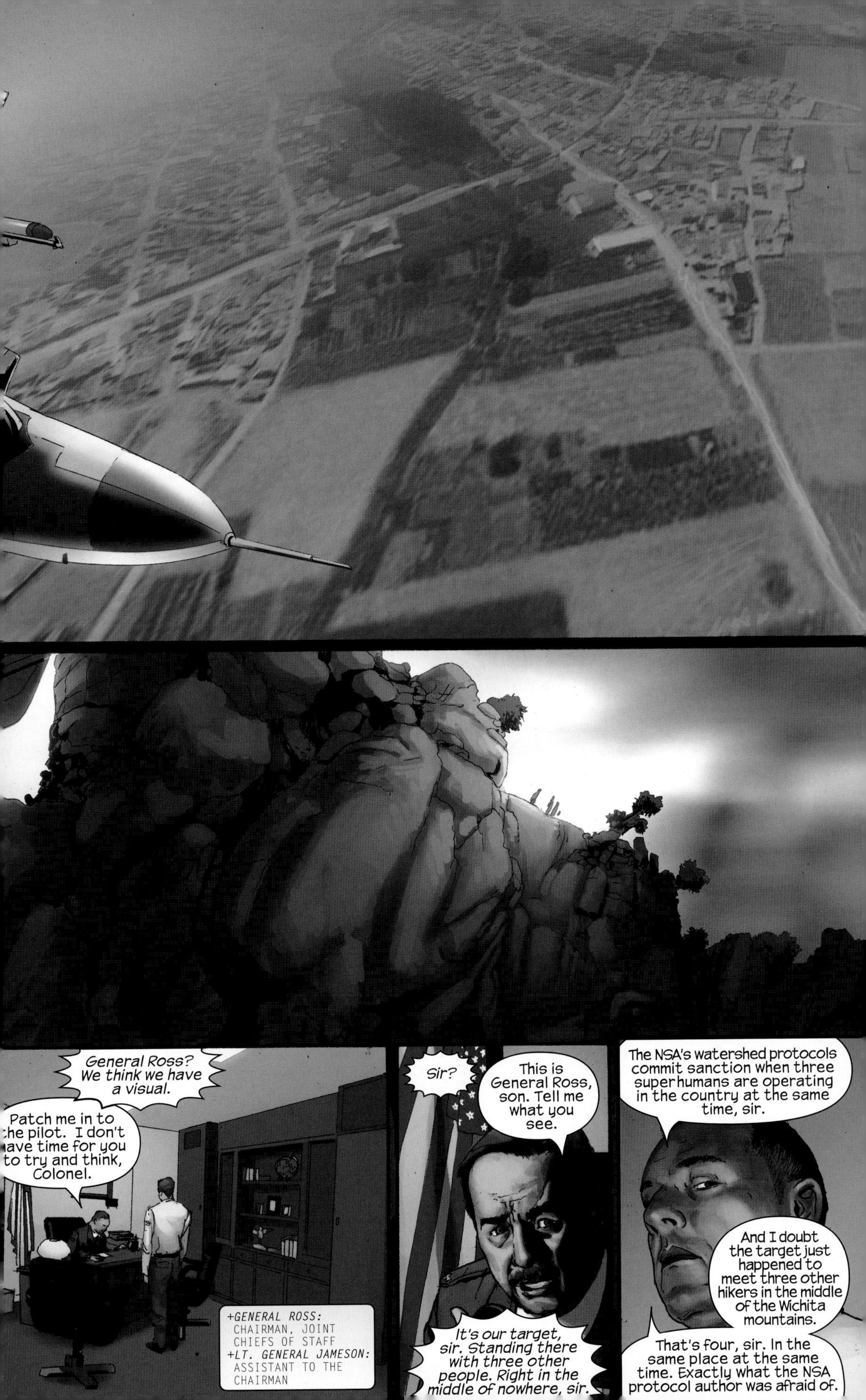
General Ross? We think we have a visual.
Patch me in to the pilot. I don't have time for you to try and think, Colonel.
+GENERAL ROSS: CHAIRMAN, JOINT CHIEFS OF STAFF
+LT. GENERAL JAMESON: ASSISTANT TO THE CHAIRMAN
Sir?
This is General Ross, son. Tell me what you see.
It's our target, sir. Standing there with three other people. Right in the middle of nowhere, sir.
The NSA's watershed protocols commit sanction when three superhumans are operating in the country at the same time, sir.
And I doubt the target just happened to meet three other hikers in the middle of the Wichita mountains.
That's four, sir. In the same place at the same time. Exactly what the NSA protocol author was afraid of.

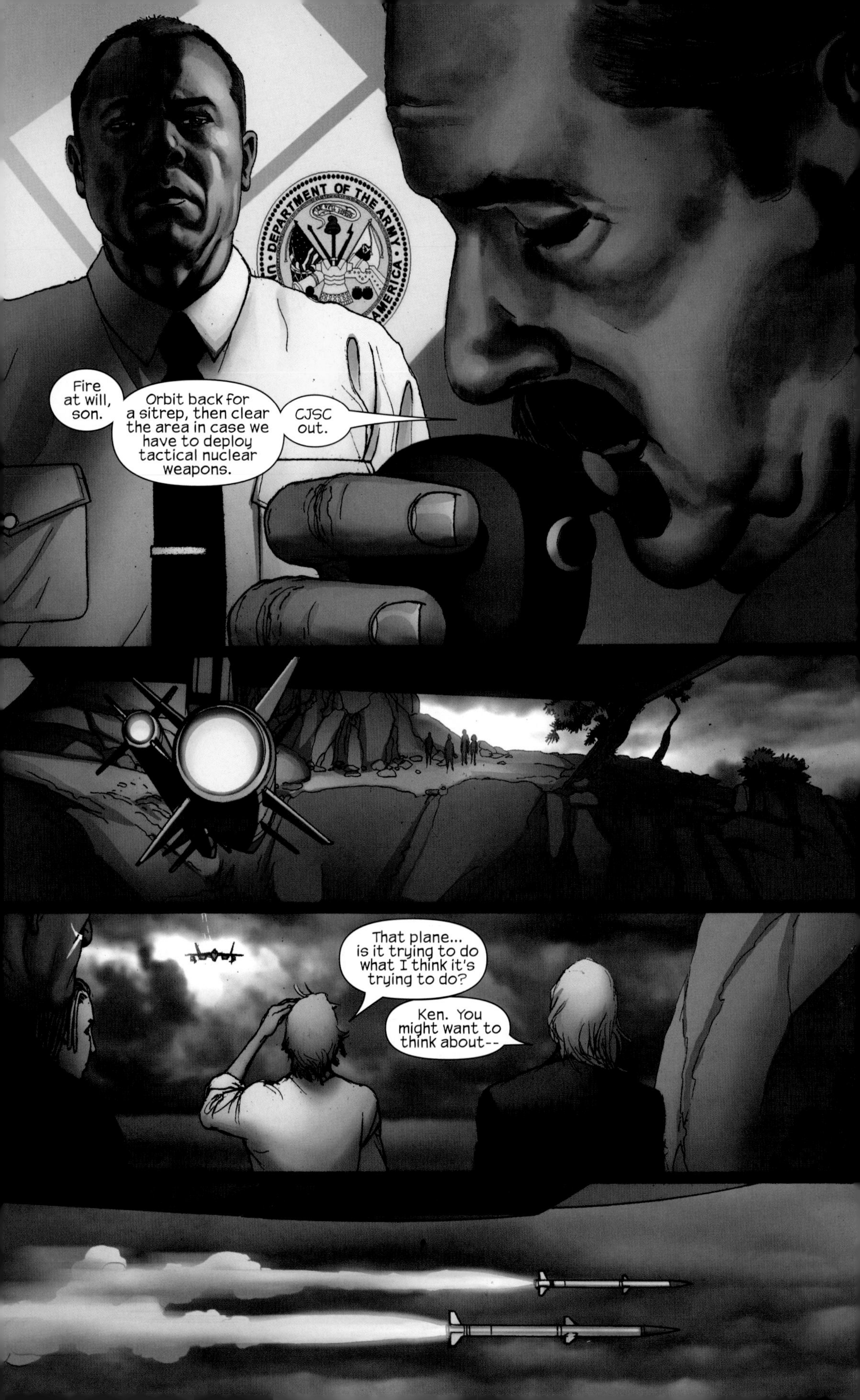
DEPARTMENT OF THE ARMY
Fire at will, son.
Orbit back for a sitrep, then clear the area in case we have to deploy tactical nuclear weapons.
CJSC out.
That plane... is it trying to do what I think it's trying to do?
Ken. You might want to think about--

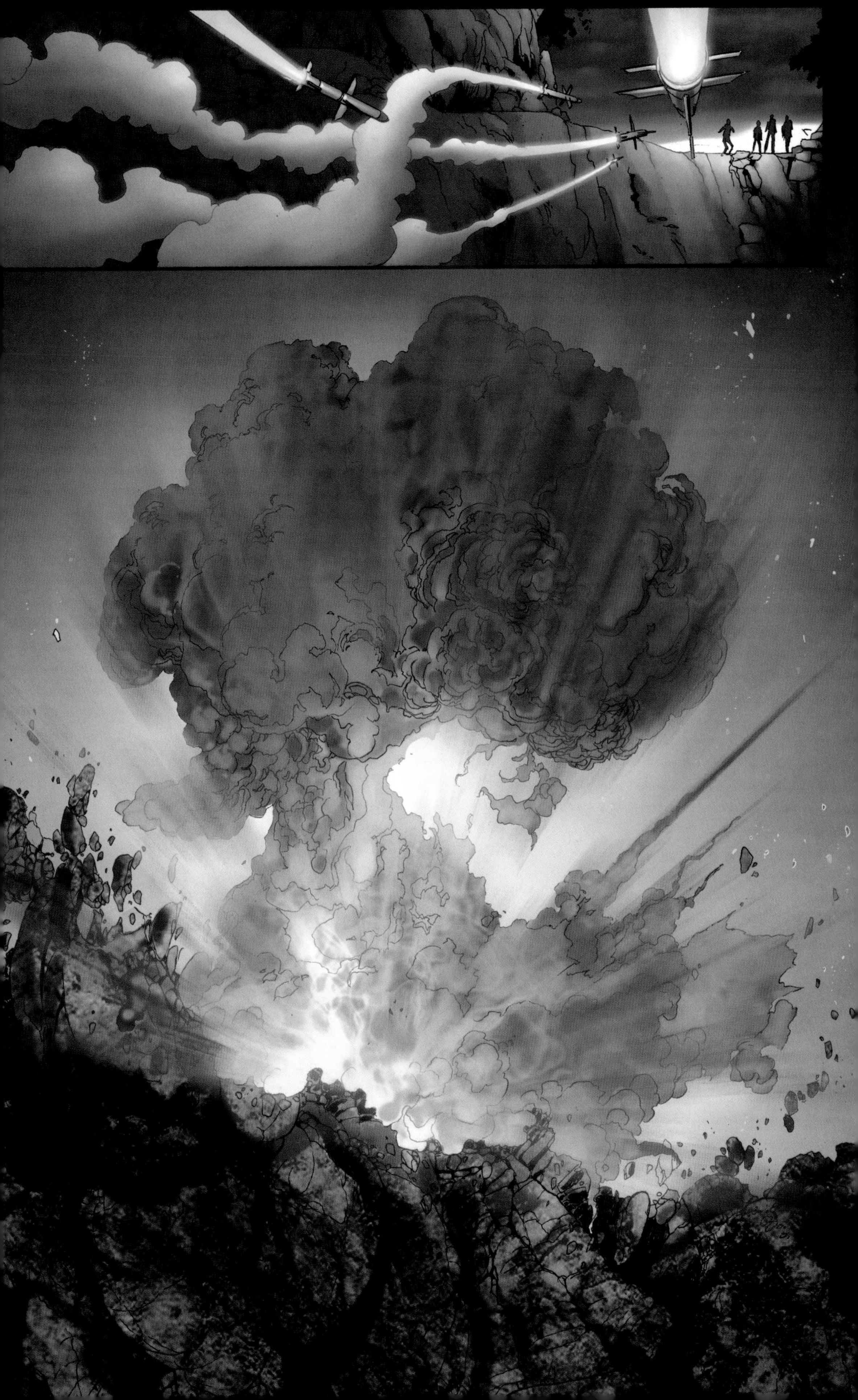

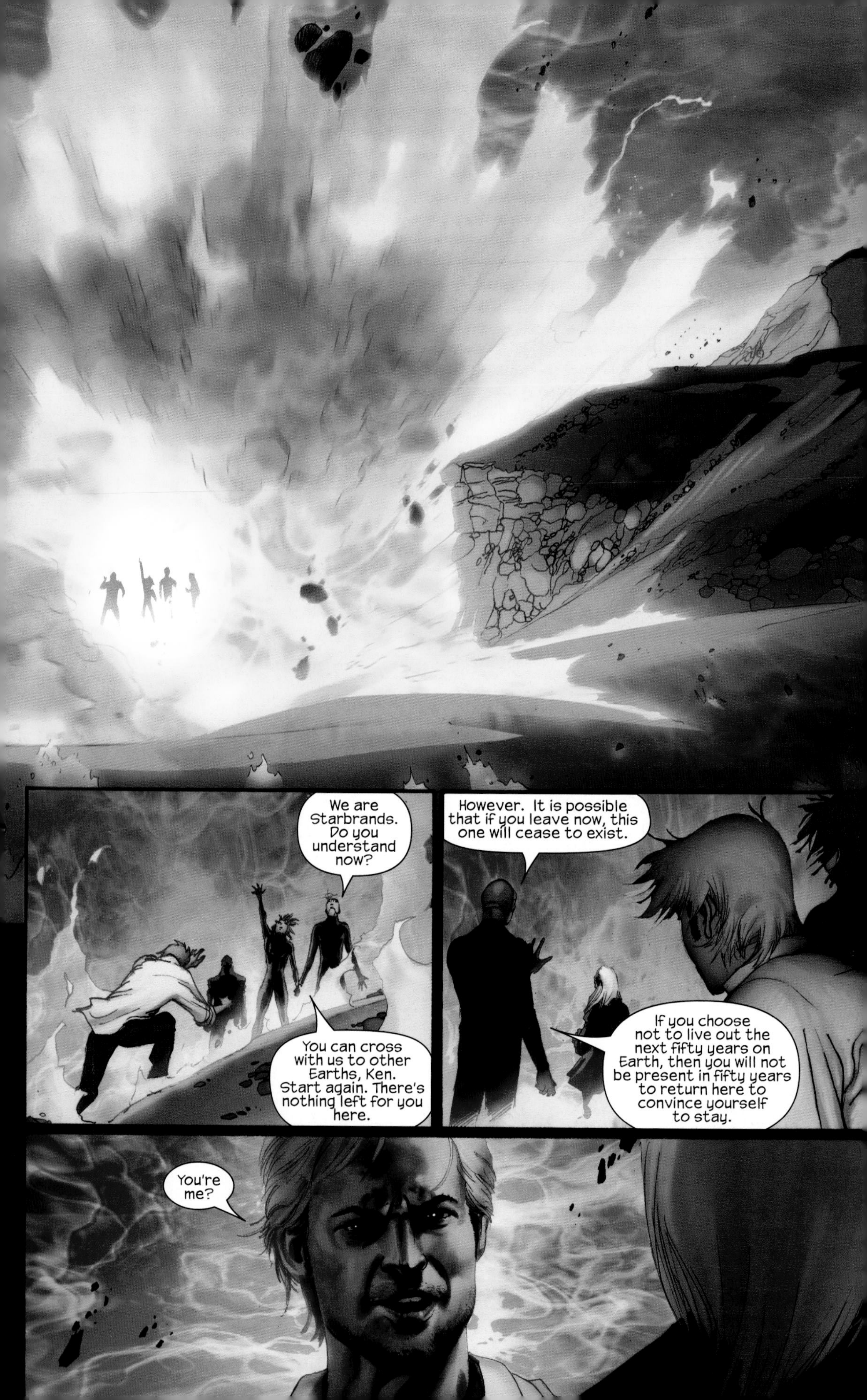
We are Starbrands. Do you understand now?
You can cross with us to other Earths, Ken. Start again. There's nothing left for you here.
However. It is possible that if you leave now, this one will cease to exist.
If you choose not to live out the next fifty years on Earth, then you will not be present in fifty years to return here to convince yourself to stay.
You're me?

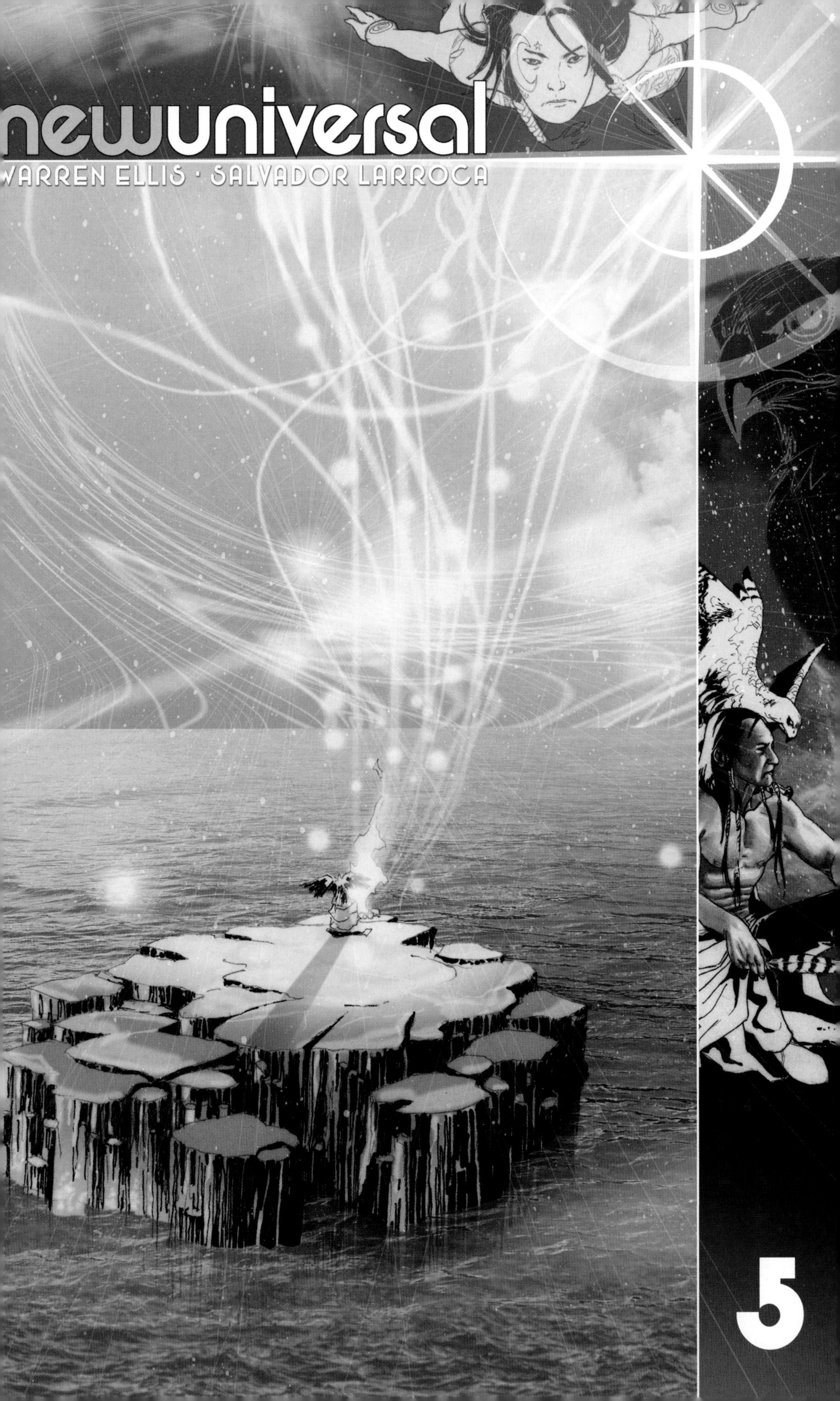

newuniversal
WARREN ELLIS · SALVADOR LARROCA
5

newuniversal MYSTERY

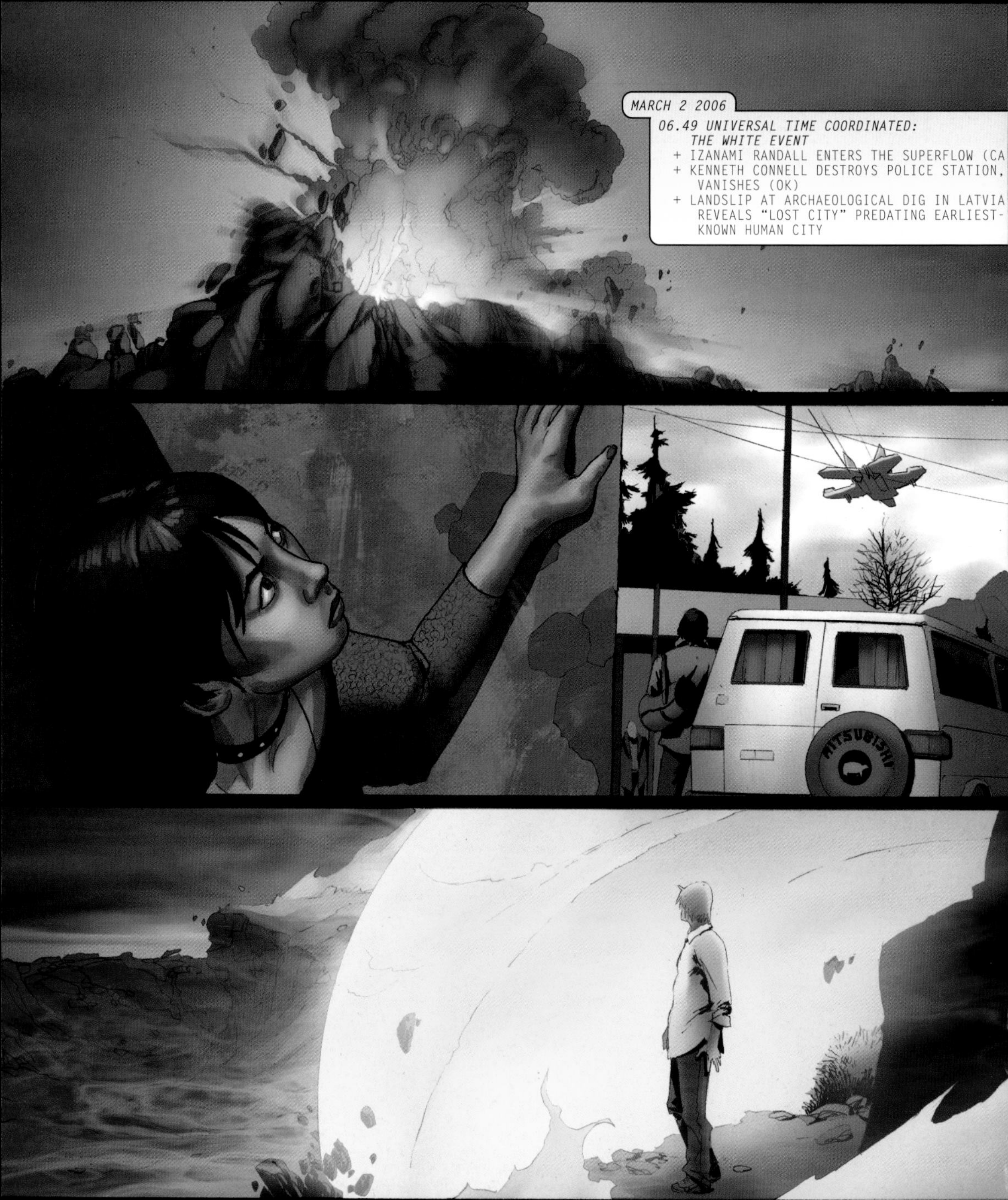

MARCH 2 2006
06.49 UNIVERSAL TIME COORDINATED:
THE WHITE EVENT
+ IZANAMI RANDALL ENTERS THE SUPERFLOW (CA
+ KENNETH CONNELL DESTROYS POLICE STATION, VANISHES (OK)
+ LANDSLIP AT ARCHAEOLOGICAL DIG IN LATVIA REVEALS "LOST CITY" PREDATING EARLIEST-KNOWN HUMAN CITY
MITSUBISHI

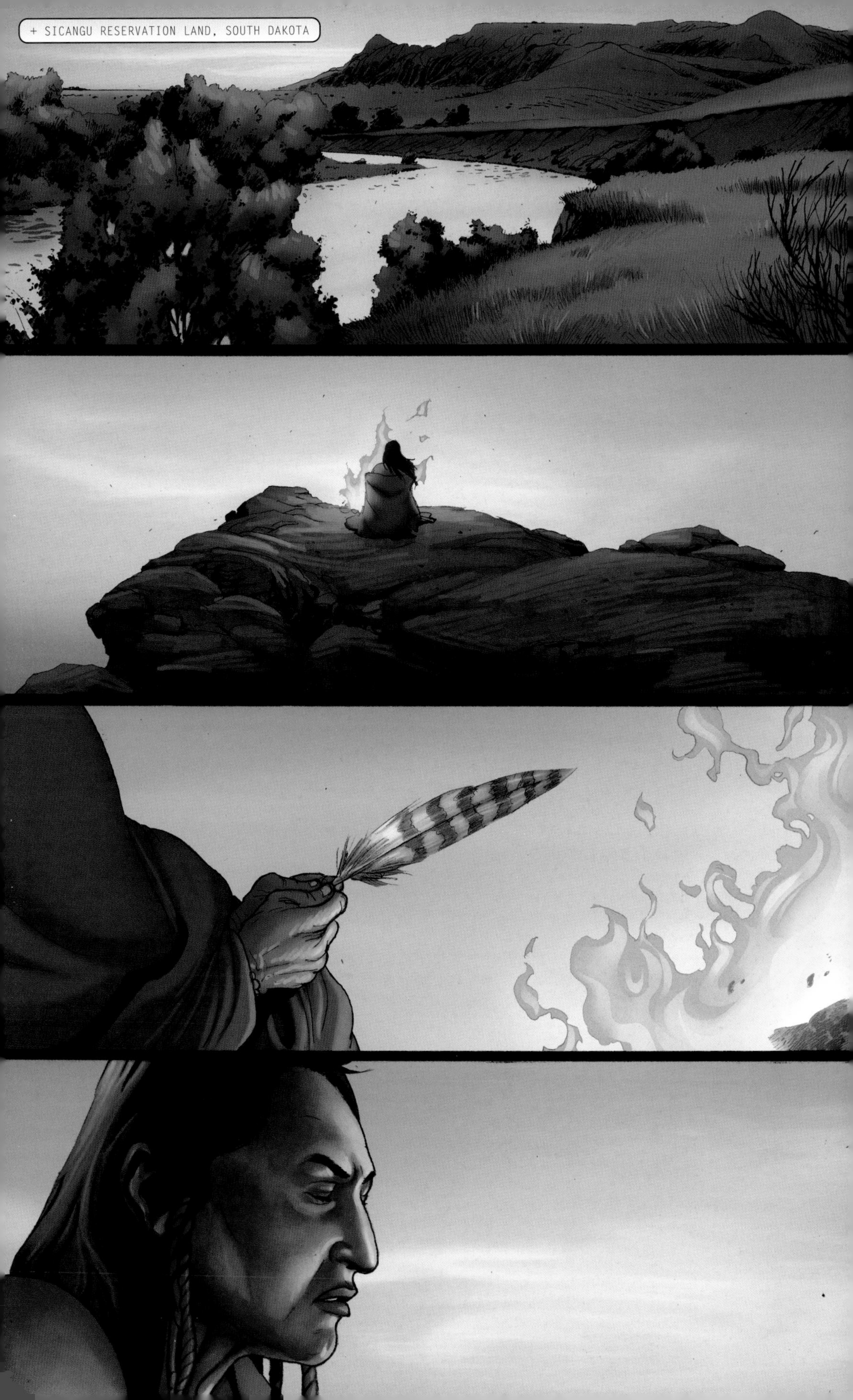
+ SICANGU RESERVATION LAND, SOUTH DAKOTA

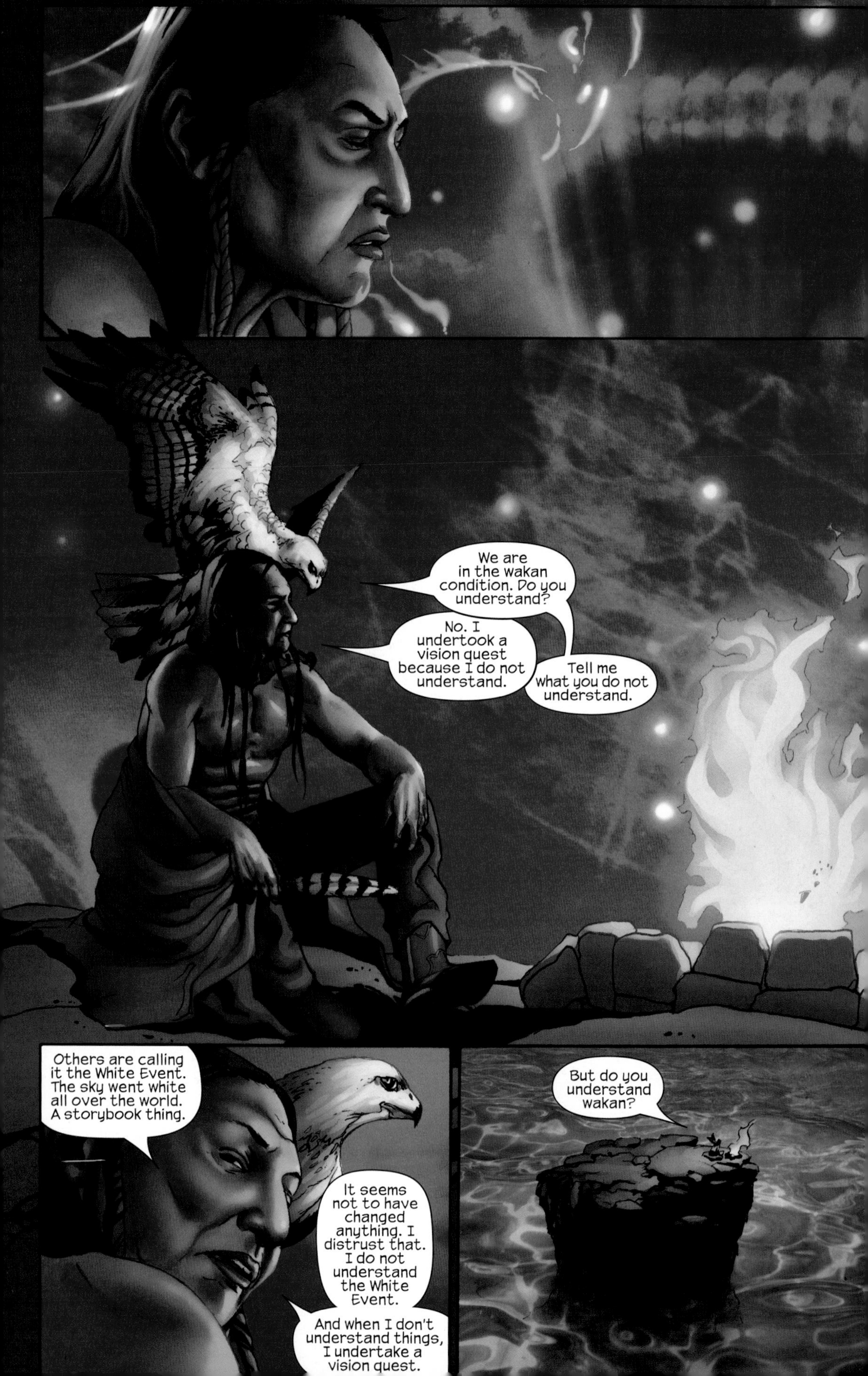
We are in the wakan condition. Do you understand?
No. I undertook a vision quest because I do not understand.
Tell me what you do not understand.
Others are calling it the White Event. The sky went white all over the world. A storybook thing.
It seems not to have changed anything. I distrust that. I do not understand the White Event.
And when I don't understand things, I undertake a vision quest.
But do you understand wakan?

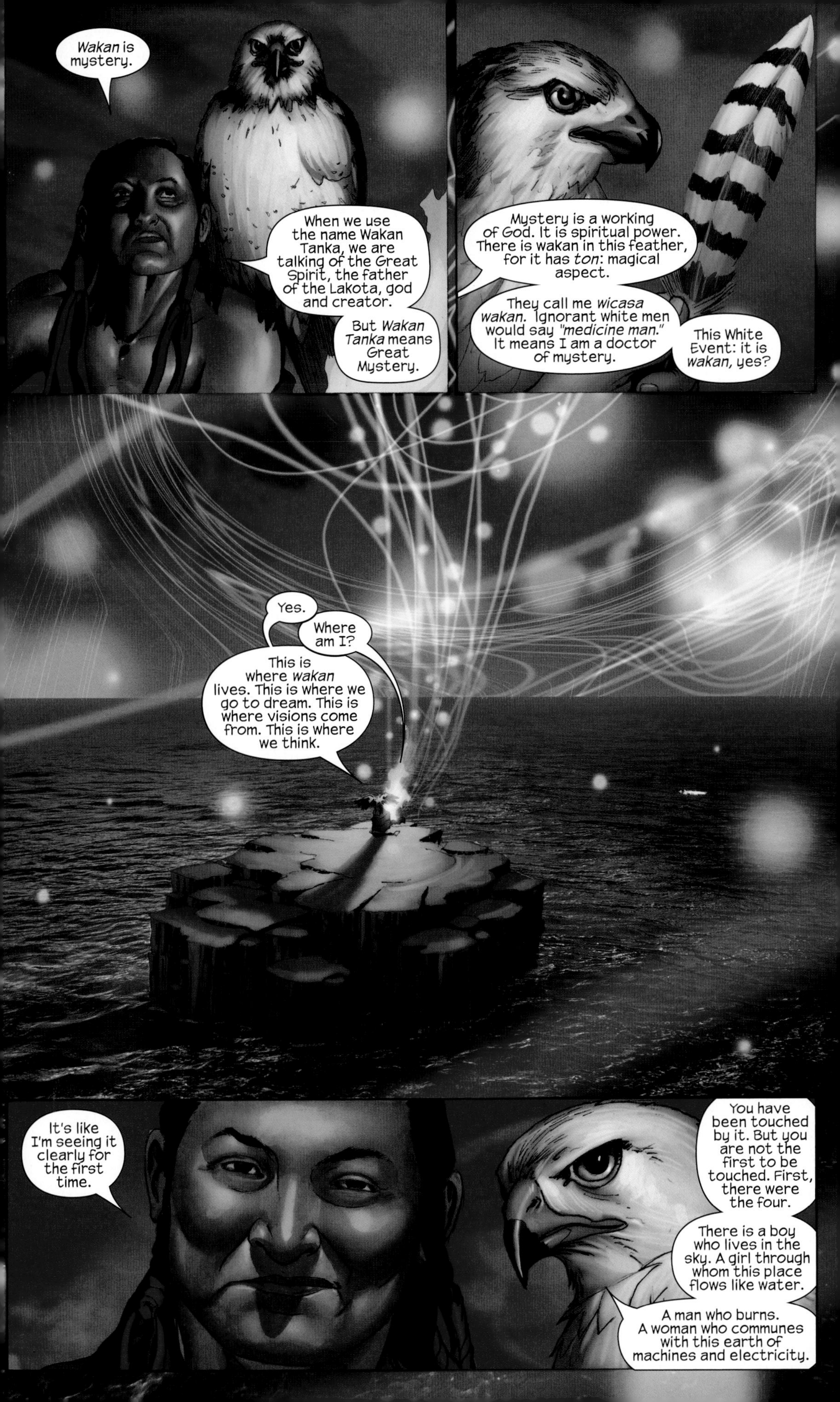
Wakan is mystery.
When we use the name Wakan Tanka, we are talking of the Great Spirit, the father of the Lakota, god and creator.
But *Wakan Tanka* means Great Mystery.
Mystery is a working of God. It is spiritual power. There is wakan in this feather, for it has *ton*: magical aspect.
They call me *wicasa wakan.* Ignorant white men would say *"medicine man."* It means I am a doctor of mystery.
This White Event: it is *wakan*, yes?
Yes.
Where am I?
This is where *wakan* lives. This is where we go to dream. This is where visions come from. This is where we think.
It's like I'm seeing it clearly for the first time.
You have been touched by it. But you are not the first to be touched. First, there were the four.
There is a boy who lives in the sky. A girl through whom this place flows like water.
A man who burns. A woman who communes with this earth of machines and electricity.

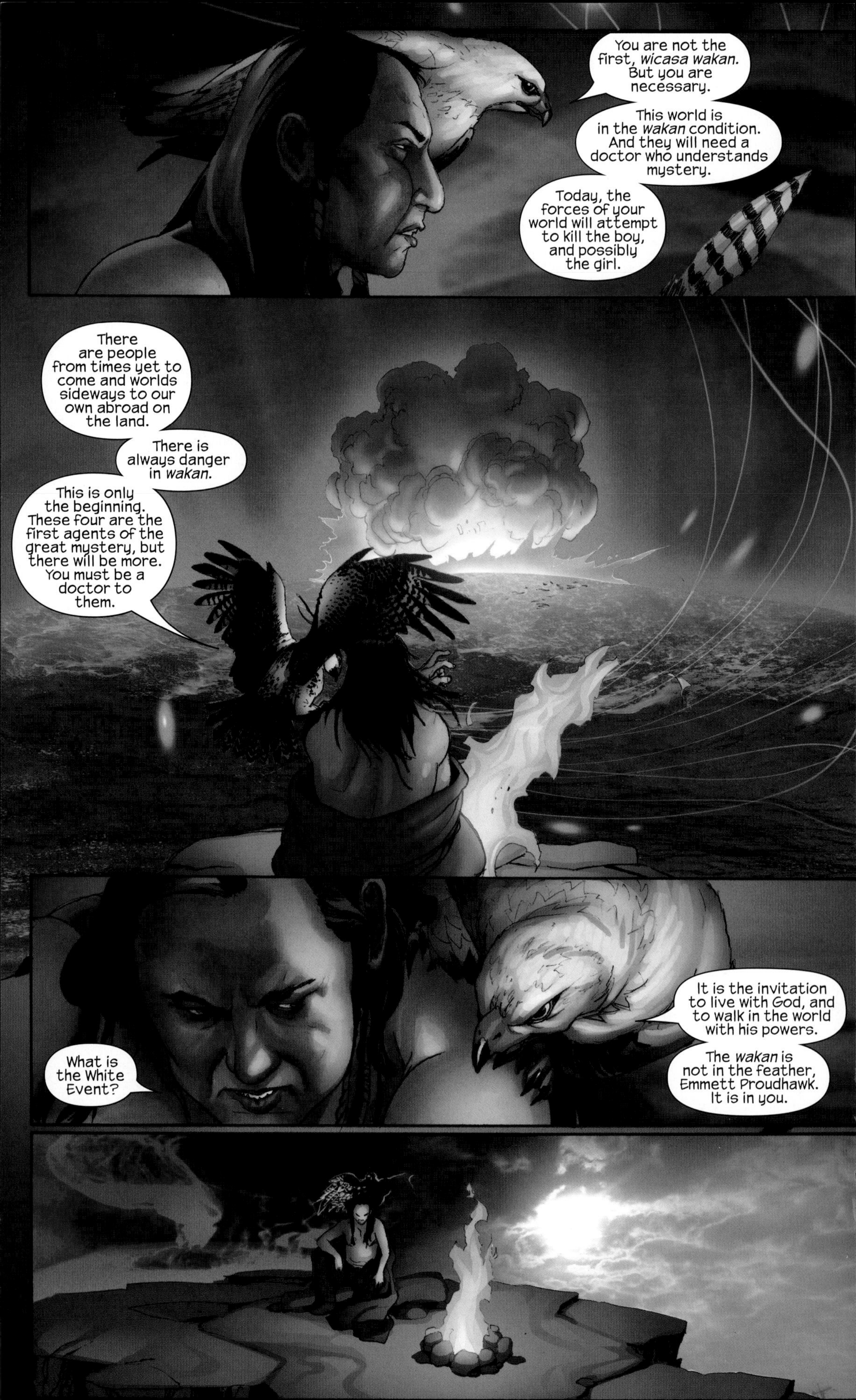
You are not the first, *wicasa wakan.* But you are necessary.
This world is in the *wakan* condition. And they will need a doctor who understands mystery.
Today, the forces of your world will attempt to kill the boy, and possibly the girl.
There are people from times yet to come and worlds sideways to our own abroad on the land.
There is always danger in *wakan.*
This is only the beginning. These four are the first agents of the great mystery, but there will be more. You must be a doctor to them.
What is the White Event?
It is the invitation to live with God, and to walk in the world with his powers.
The *wakan* is not in the feather, Emmett Proudhawk. It is in you.

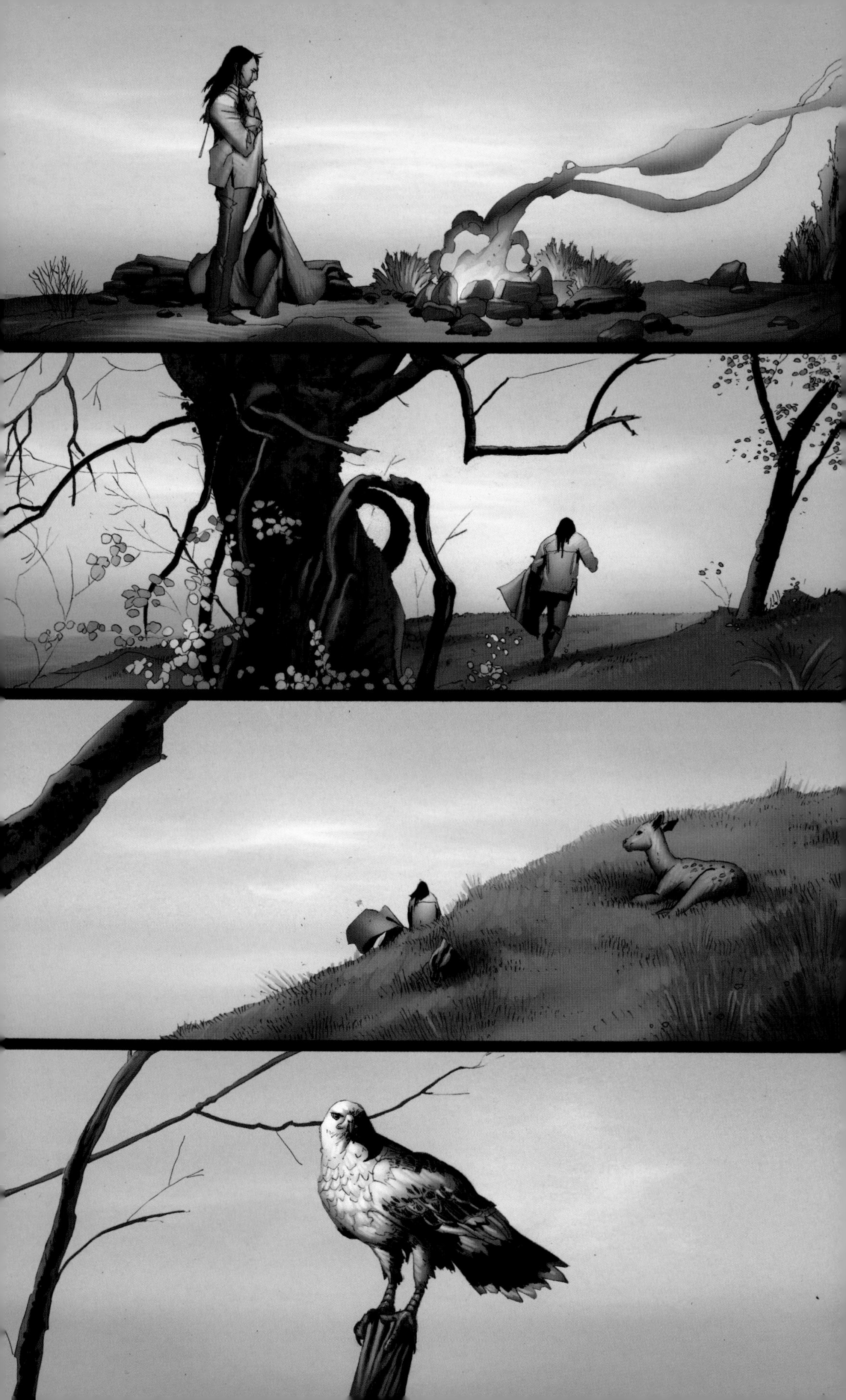

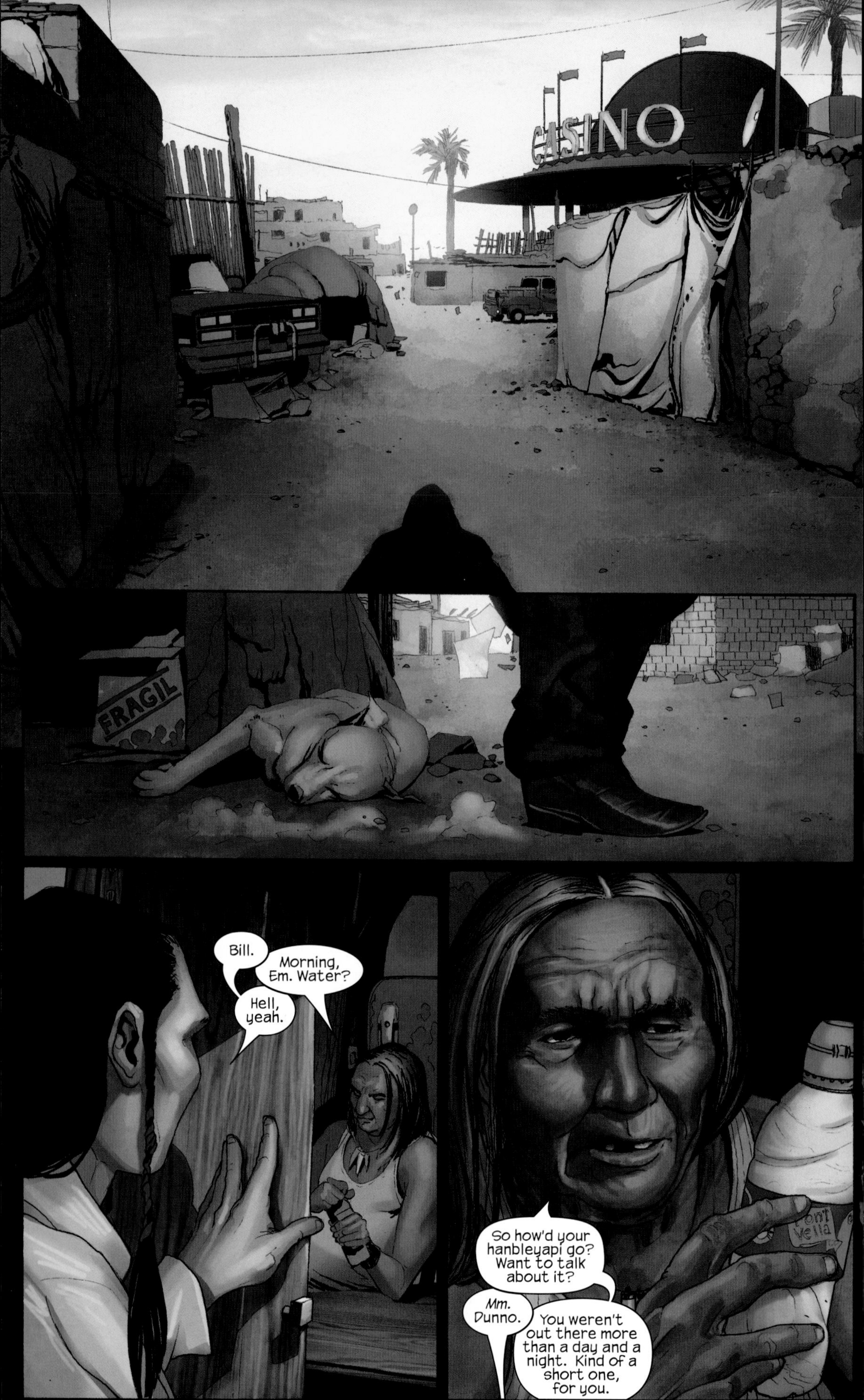
CASINO
FRAGIL
Bill.
Morning, Em. Water?
Hell, yeah.
So how'd your hanbleyapi go? Want to talk about it?
Mm. Dunno.
You weren't out there more than a day and a night. Kind of a short one, for you.

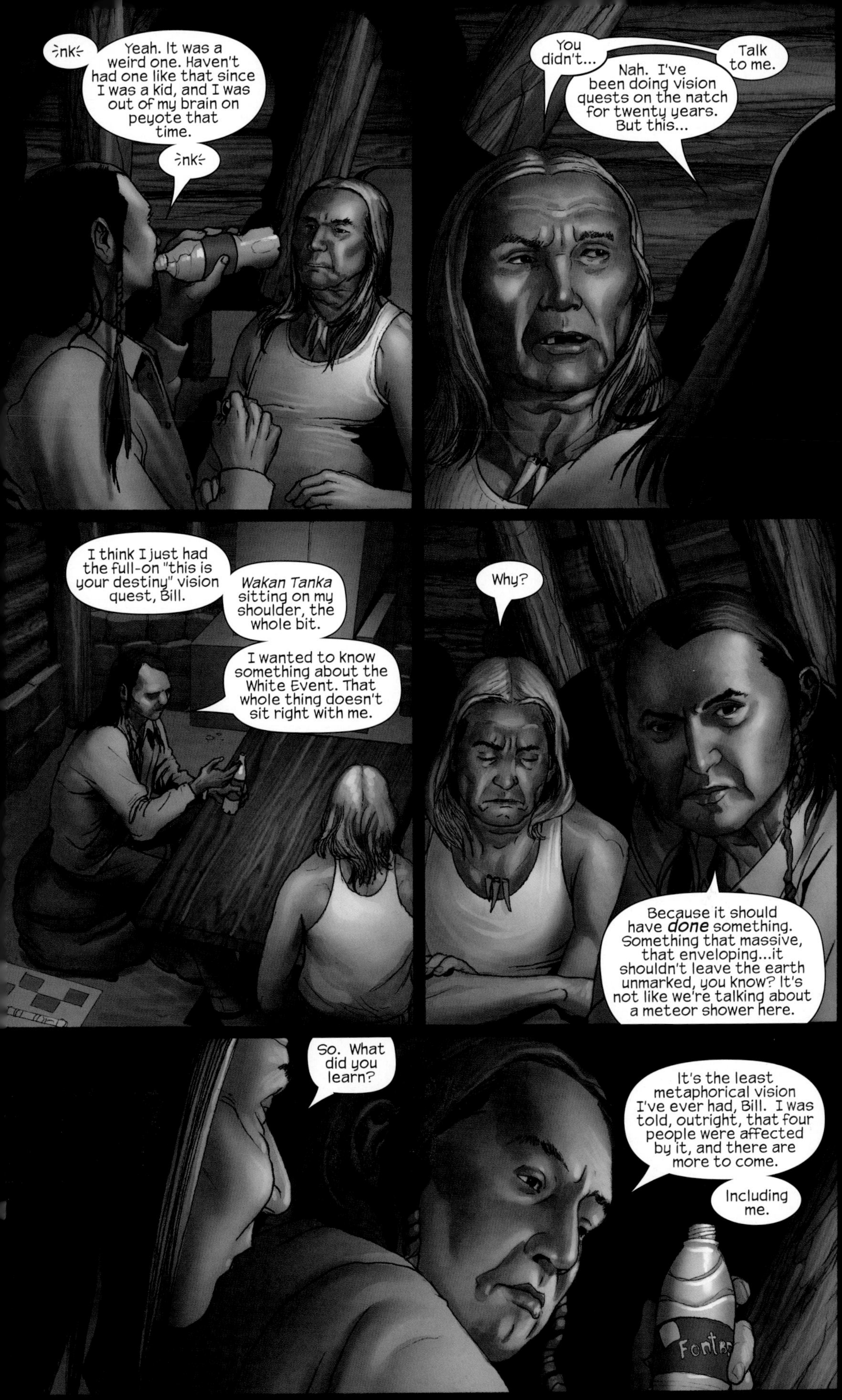

nk
Yeah. It was a weird one. Haven't had one like that since I was a kid, and I was out of my brain on peyote that time.
nk
You didn't...
Talk to me.
Nah. I've been doing vision quests on the natch for twenty years. But this...
I think I just had the full-on "this is your destiny" vision quest, Bill.
Wakan Tanka sitting on my shoulder, the whole bit.
I wanted to know something about the White Event. That whole thing doesn't sit right with me.
Why?
Because it should have ***done*** something. Something that massive, that enveloping...it shouldn't leave the earth unmarked, you know? It's not like we're talking about a meteor shower here.
So. What did you learn?
It's the least metaphorical vision I've ever had, Bill. I was told, outright, that four people were affected by it, and there are more to come.
Including me.

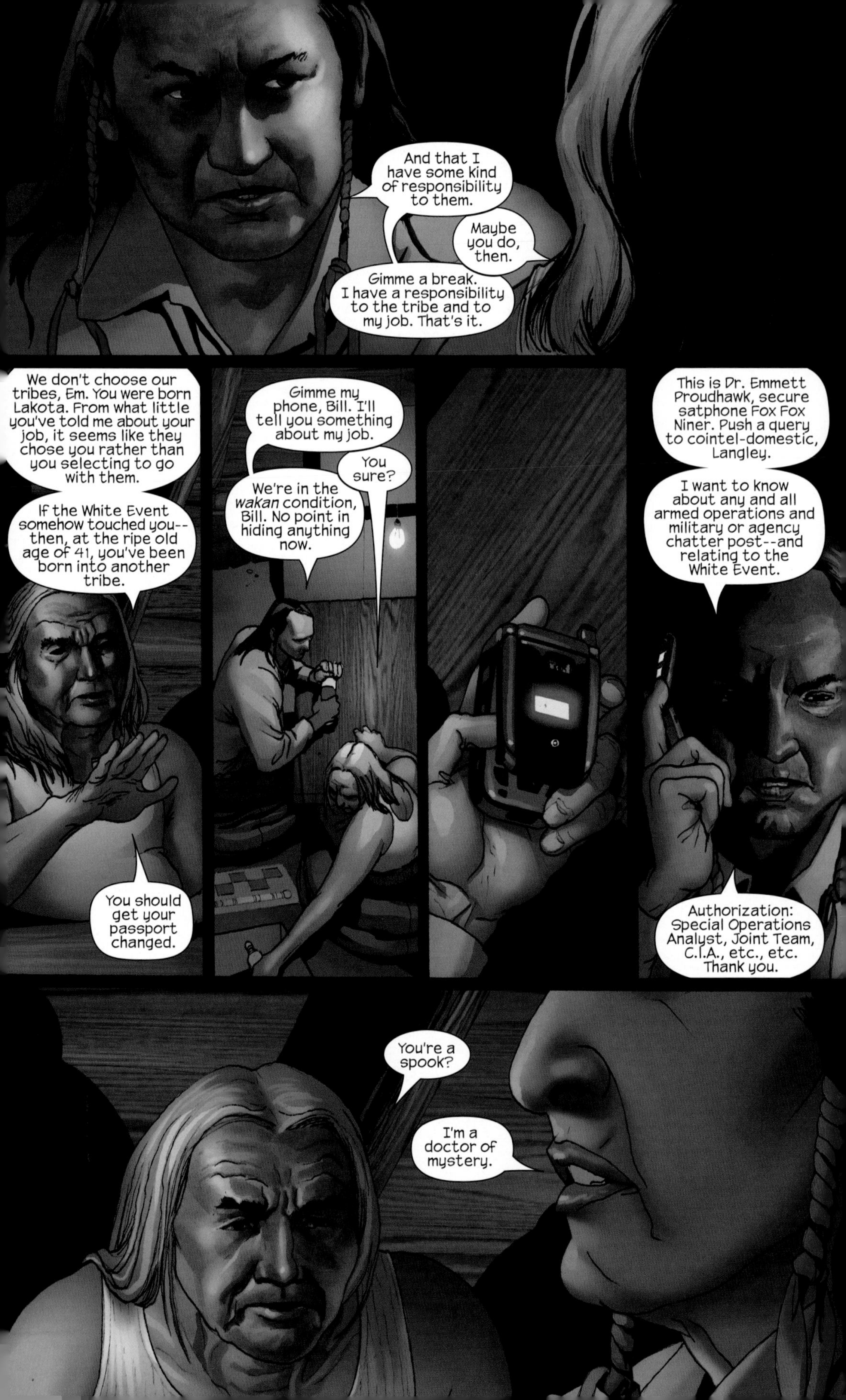
And that I have some kind of responsibility to them.
Maybe you do, then.
Gimme a break. I have a responsibility to the tribe and to my job. That's it.
We don't choose our tribes, Em. You were born Lakota. From what little you've told me about your job, it seems like they chose you rather than you selecting to go with them.
If the White Event somehow touched you--then, at the ripe old age of 41, you've been born into another tribe.
You should get your passport changed.
Gimme my phone, Bill. I'll tell you something about my job.
You sure?
We're in the *wakan* condition, Bill. No point in hiding anything now.
This is Dr. Emmett Proudhawk, secure satphone Fox Fox Niner. Push a query to cointel-domestic, Langley.
I want to know about any and all armed operations and military or agency chatter post--and relating to the White Event.
Authorization: Special Operations Analyst, Joint Team, C.I.A., etc., etc. Thank you.
You're a spook?
I'm a doctor of mystery.

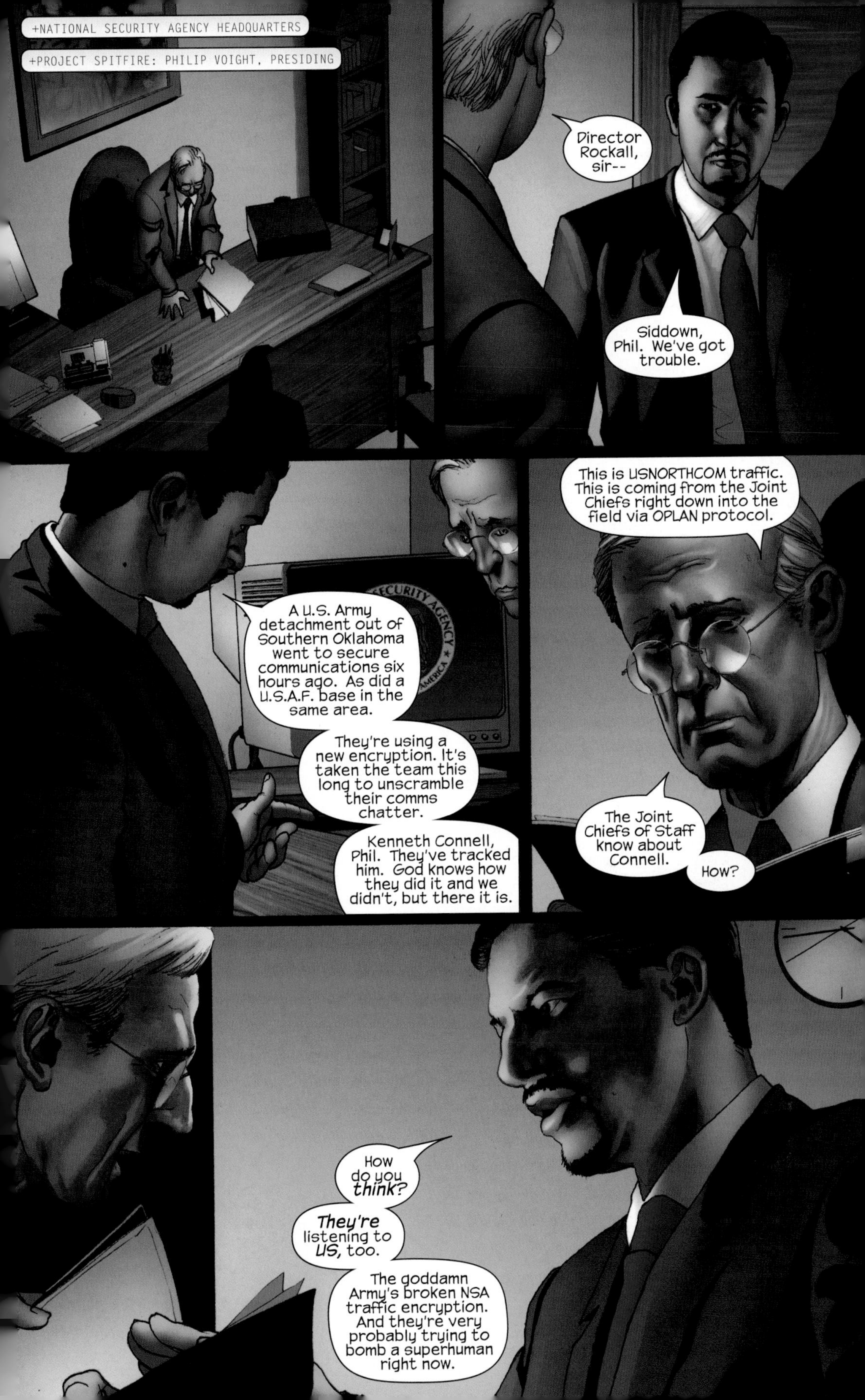
+NATIONAL SECURITY AGENCY HEADQUARTERS
+PROJECT SPITFIRE: PHILIP VOIGHT, PRESIDING
Director Rockall, sir--
Siddown, Phil. We've got trouble.
A U.S. Army detachment out of Southern Oklahoma went to secure communications six hours ago. As did a U.S.A.F. base in the same area.
They're using a new encryption. It's taken the team this long to unscramble their comms chatter.
Kenneth Connell, Phil. They've tracked him. God knows how they did it and we didn't, but there it is.
This is USNORTHCOM traffic. This is coming from the Joint Chiefs right down into the field via OPLAN protocol.
The Joint Chiefs of Staff know about Connell.
How?
How do you *think?*
They're listening to *US,* too.
The goddamn Army's broken NSA traffic encryption. And they're very probably trying to bomb a superhuman right now.

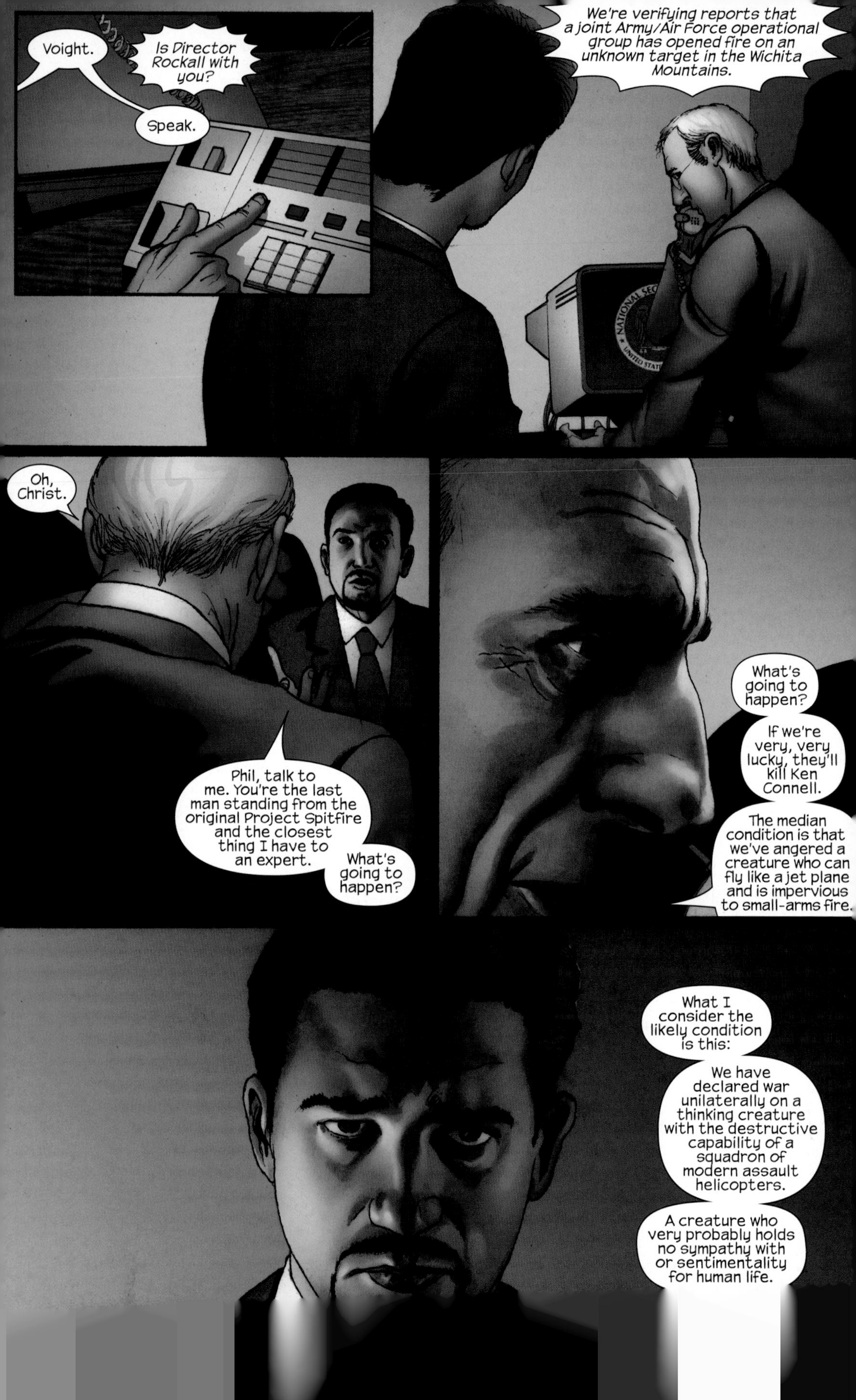
Voight.
Is Director Rockall with you?
Speak.
We're verifying reports that a joint Army/Air Force operational group has opened fire on an unknown target in the Wichita Mountains.
Oh, Christ.
Phil, talk to me. You're the last man standing from the original Project Spitfire and the closest thing I have to an expert.
What's going to happen?
What's going to happen?
If we're very, very lucky, they'll kill Ken Connell.
The median condition is that we've angered a creature who can fly like a jet plane and is impervious to small-arms fire.
What I consider the likely condition is this:
We have declared war unilaterally on a thinking creature with the destructive capability of a squadron of modern assault helicopters.
A creature who very probably holds no sympathy with or sentimentality for human life.

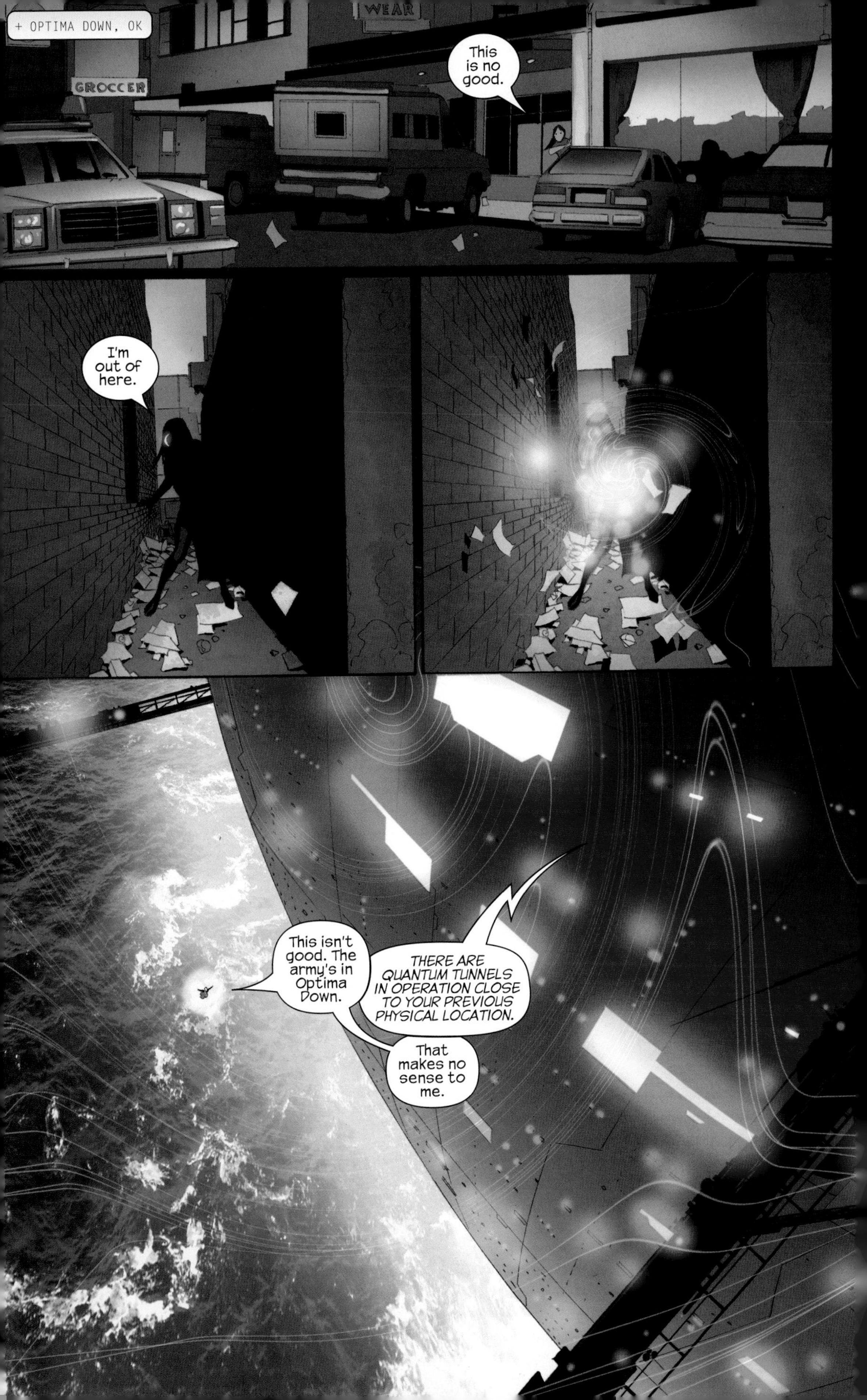
+ OPTIMA DOWN, OK
GROCCER
WEAR
This is no good.
I'm out of here.
This isn't good. The army's in Optima Down.
THERE ARE QUANTUM TUNNELS IN OPERATION CLOSE TO YOUR PREVIOUS PHYSICAL LOCATION.
That makes no sense to me.

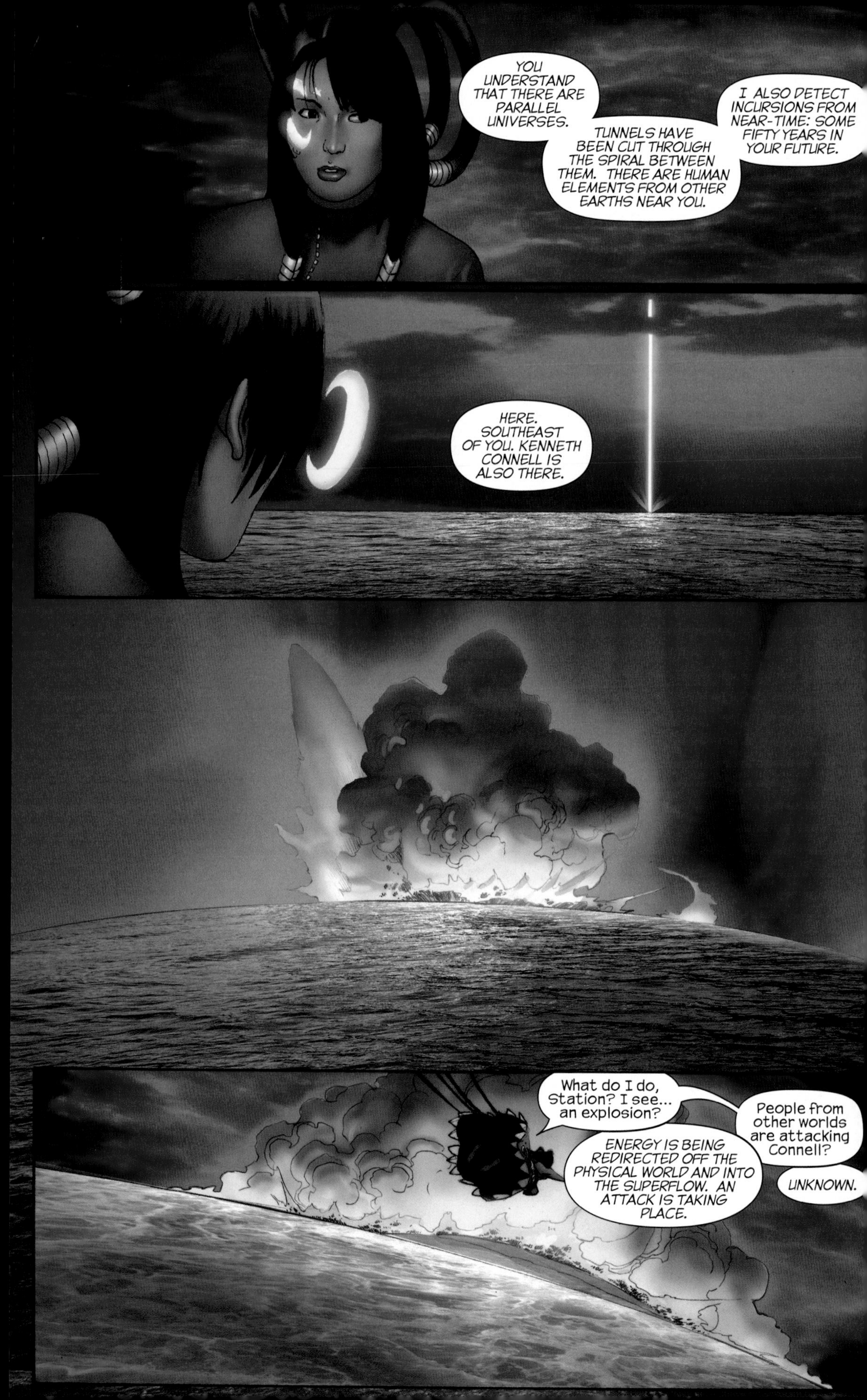
YOU UNDERSTAND THAT THERE ARE PARALLEL UNIVERSES.
TUNNELS HAVE BEEN CUT THROUGH THE SPIRAL BETWEEN THEM. THERE ARE HUMAN ELEMENTS FROM OTHER EARTHS NEAR YOU.
I ALSO DETECT INCURSIONS FROM NEAR-TIME: SOME FIFTY YEARS IN YOUR FUTURE.
HERE. SOUTHEAST OF YOU. KENNETH CONNELL IS ALSO THERE.
What do I do, Station? I see... an explosion?
ENERGY IS BEING REDIRECTED OFF THE PHYSICAL WORLD AND INTO THE SUPERFLOW. AN ATTACK IS TAKING PLACE.
People from other worlds are attacking Connell?
UNKNOWN.

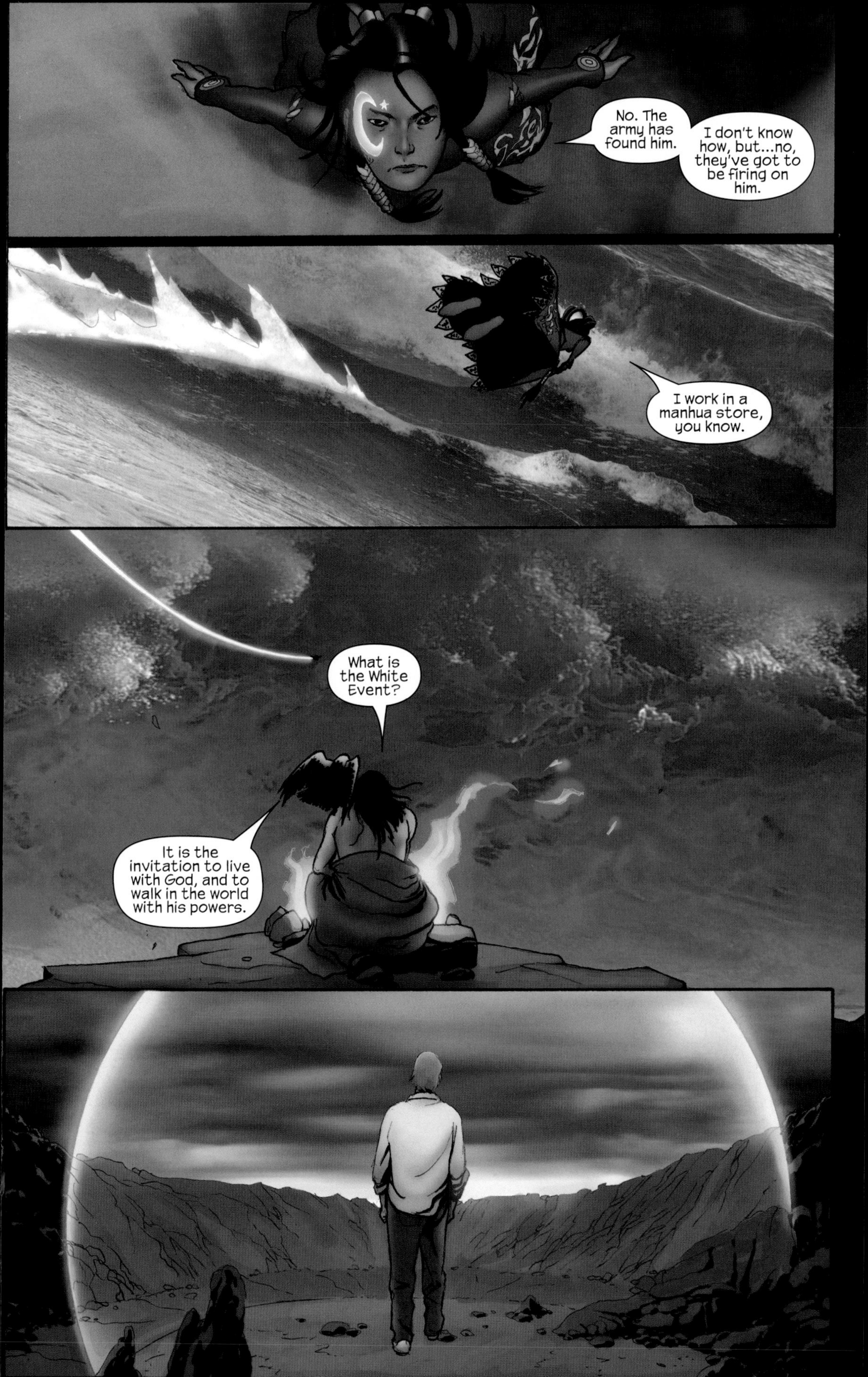
No. The army has found him.
I don't know how, but...no, they've got to be firing on him.
I work in a manhua store, you know.
What is the White Event?
It is the invitation to live with God, and to walk in the world with his powers.

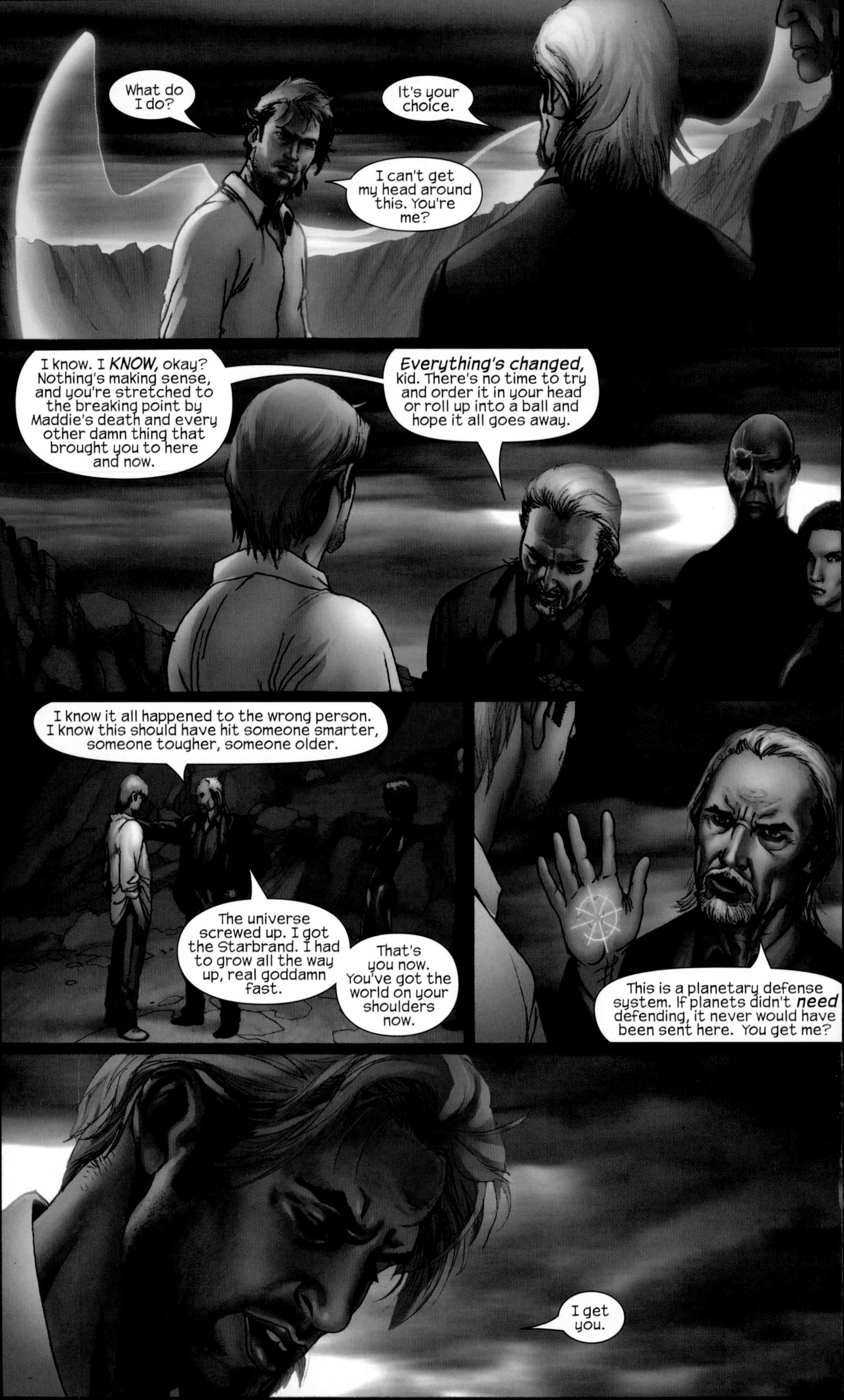
What do I do?
It's your choice.
I can't get my head around this. You're me?
I know. I *KNOW,* okay? Nothing's making sense, and you're stretched to the breaking point by Maddie's death and every other damn thing that brought you to here and now.
Everything's changed, kid. There's no time to try and order it in your head or roll up into a ball and hope it all goes away.
I know it all happened to the wrong person. I know this should have hit someone smarter, someone tougher, someone older.
The universe screwed up. I got the Starbrand. I had to grow all the way up, real goddamn fast.
That's you now. You've got the world on your shoulders now.
This is a planetary defense system. If planets didn't *need* defending, it never would have been sent here. You get me?
I get you.

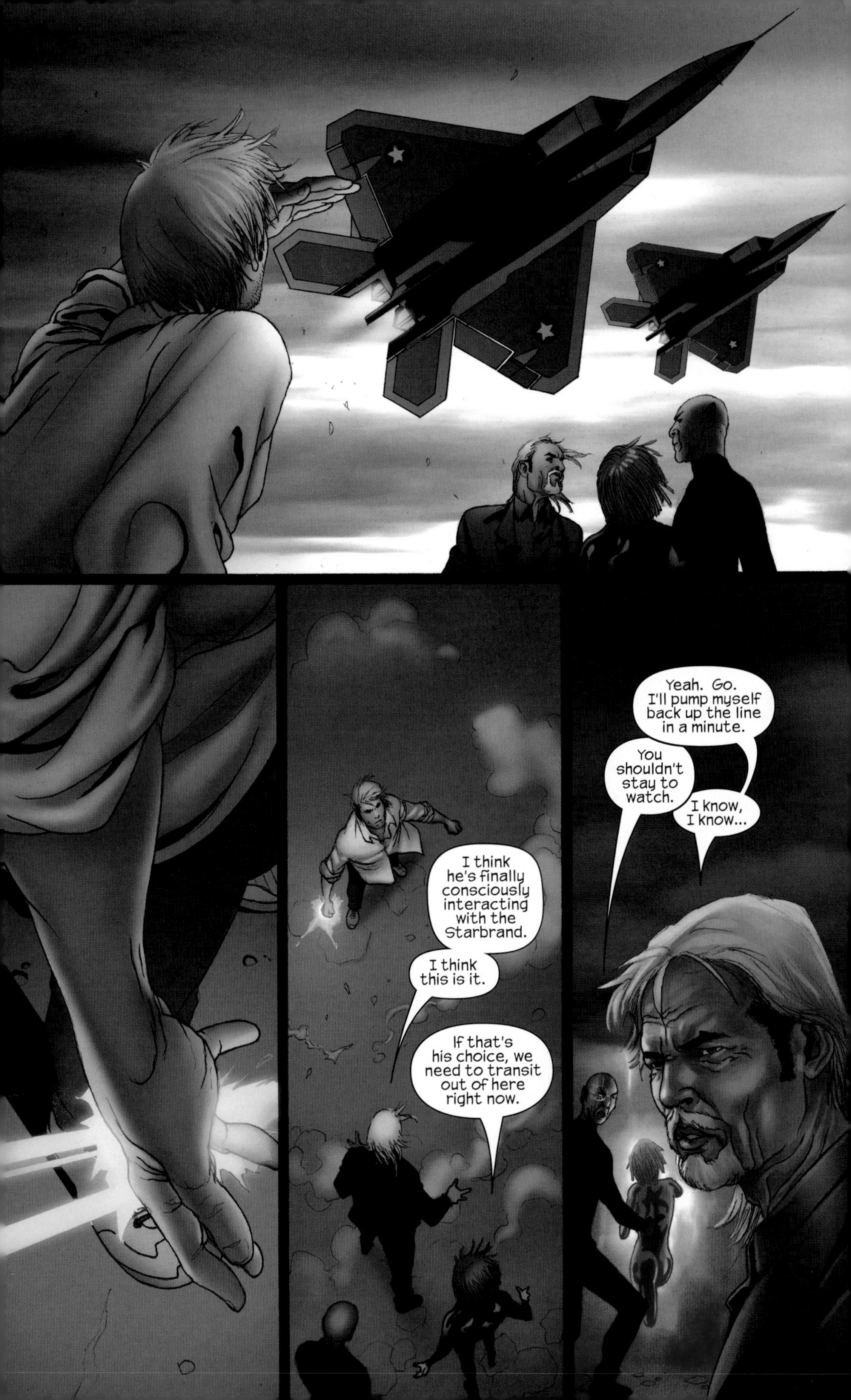
I think he's finally consciously interacting with the Starbrand.
I think this is it.
If that's his choice, we need to transit out of here right now.
Yeah. Go. I'll pump myself back up the line in a minute.
You shouldn't stay to watch.
I know, I know...

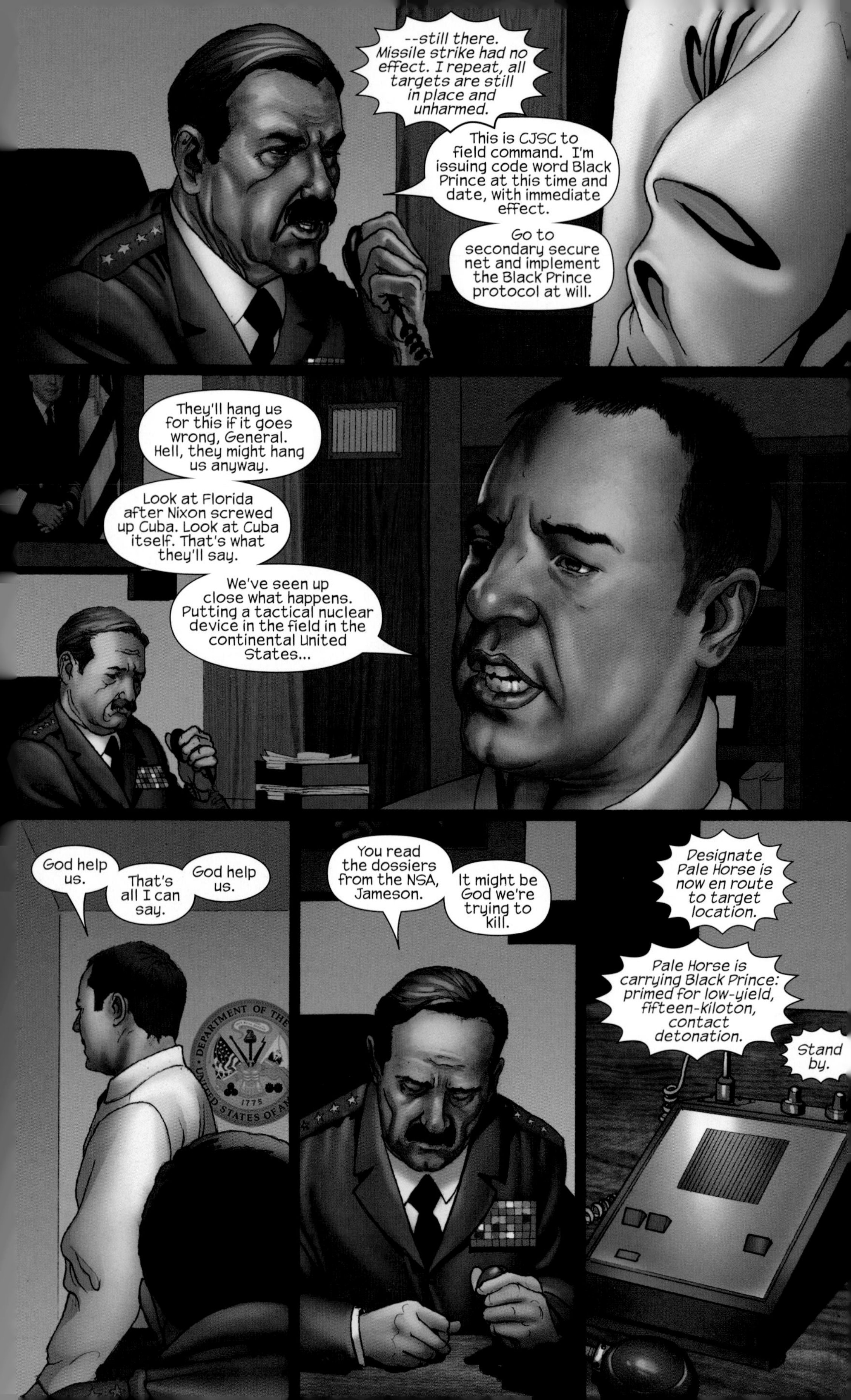
--still there. Missile strike had no effect. I repeat, all targets are still in place and unharmed.
This is CJSC to field command. I'm issuing code word Black Prince at this time and date, with immediate effect.
Go to secondary secure net and implement the Black Prince protocol at will.
They'll hang us for this if it goes wrong, General. Hell, they might hang us anyway.
Look at Florida after Nixon screwed up Cuba. Look at Cuba itself. That's what they'll say.
We've seen up close what happens. Putting a tactical nuclear device in the field in the continental United States...
God help us.
That's all I can say.
God help us.
DEPARTMENT OF THE
UNITED STATES OF A
1775
You read the dossiers from the NSA, Jameson.
It might be God we're trying to kill.
Designate Pale Horse is now en route to target location.
Pale Horse is carrying Black Prince: primed for low-yield, fifteen-kiloton, contact detonation.
Stand by.

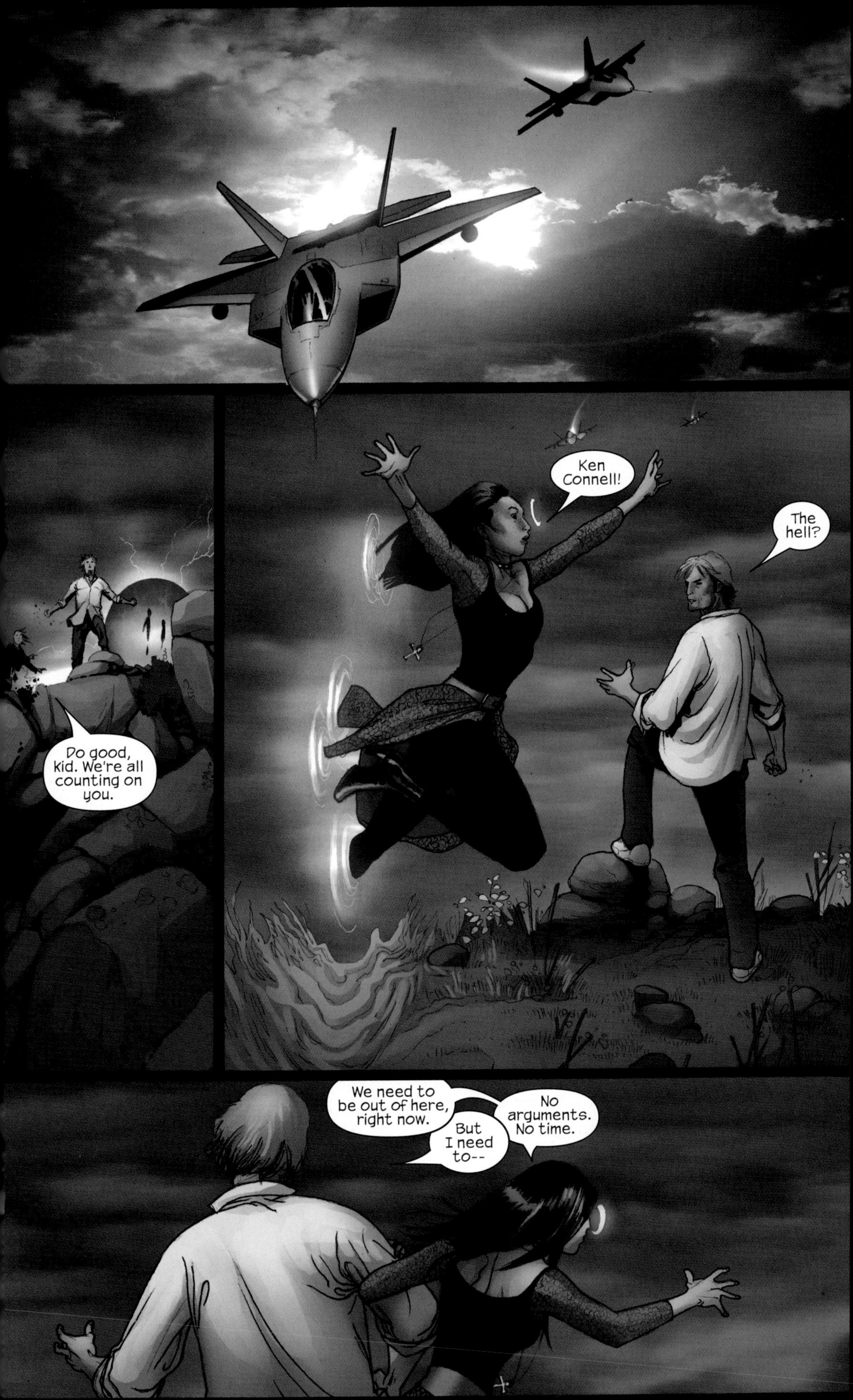

Do good, kid. We're all counting on you.
Ken Connell!
The hell?
We need to be out of here, right now.
But I need to--
No arguments. No time.

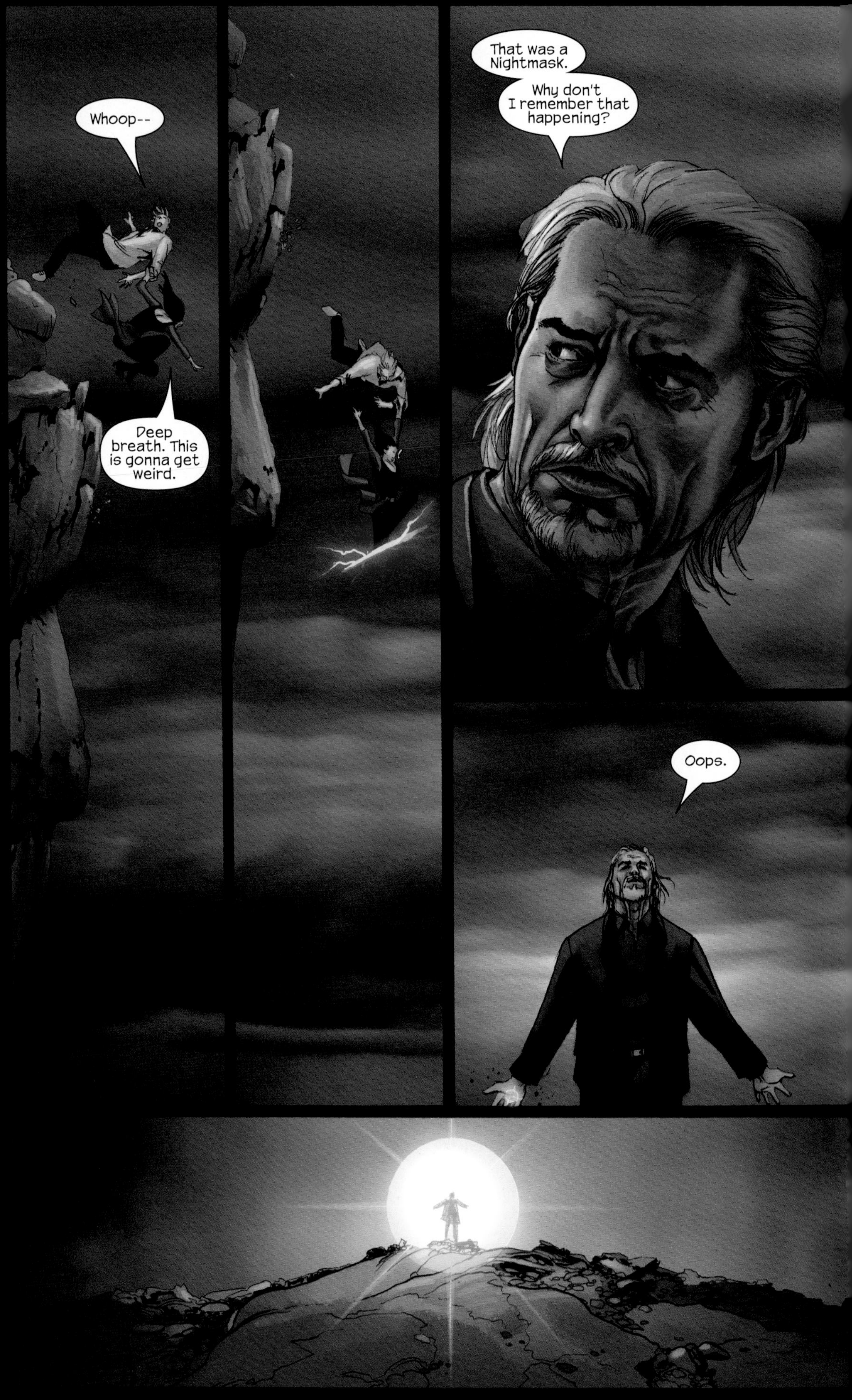
Whoop--
Deep breath. This is gonna get weird.
That was a Nightmask.
Why don't I remember that happening?
Oops.

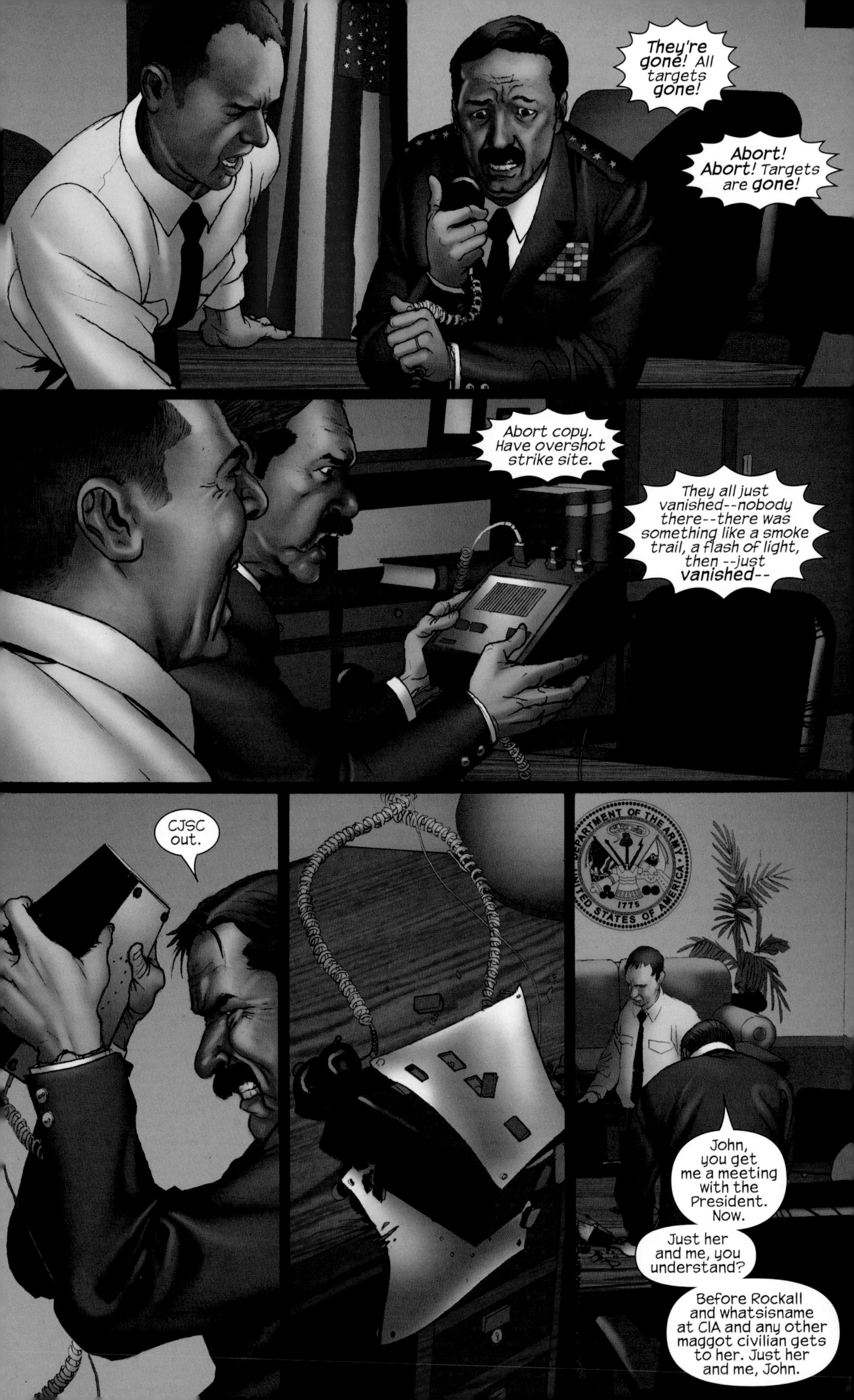
They're gone! All targets gone!
Abort! Abort! Targets are gone!
Abort copy. Have overshot strike site.
They all just vanished--nobody there--there was something like a smoke trail, a flash of light, then --just vanished--
CJSC out.
DEPARTMENT OF THE ARMY
UNITED STATES OF AMERICA
1775
John, you get me a meeting with the President. Now.
Just her and me, you understand?
Before Rockall and whatsisname at CIA and any other maggot civilian gets to her. Just her and me, John.

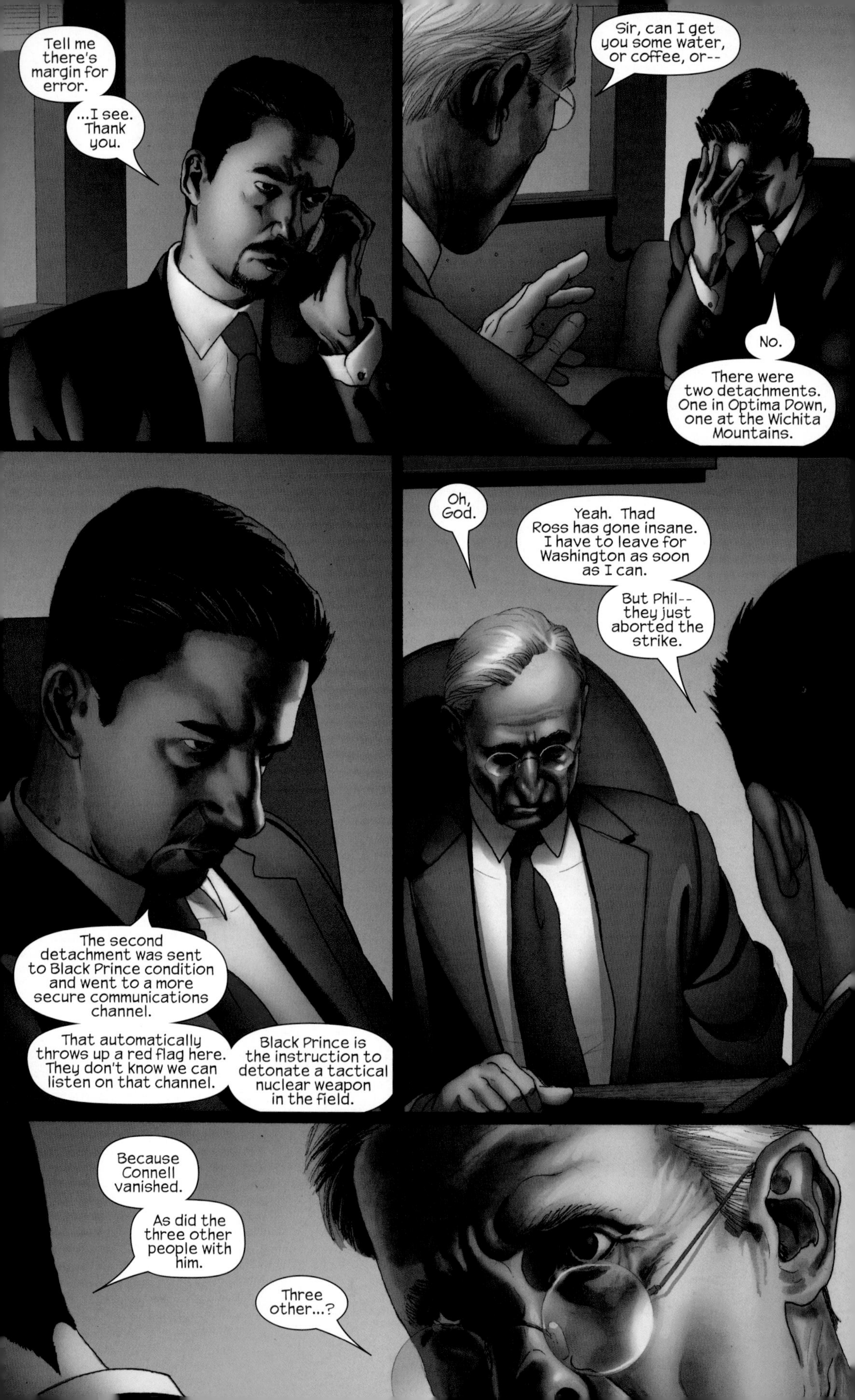

Tell me there's margin for error.
...I see. Thank you.
Sir, can I get you some water, or coffee, or--
No.
There were two detachments. One in Optima Down, one at the Wichita Mountains.
The second detachment was sent to Black Prince condition and went to a more secure communications channel.
That automatically throws up a red flag here. They don't know we can listen on that channel.
Black Prince is the instruction to detonate a tactical nuclear weapon in the field.
Oh, God.
Yeah. Thad Ross has gone insane. I have to leave for Washington as soon as I can.
But Phil-- they just aborted the strike.
Because Connell vanished.
As did the three other people with him.
Three other...?

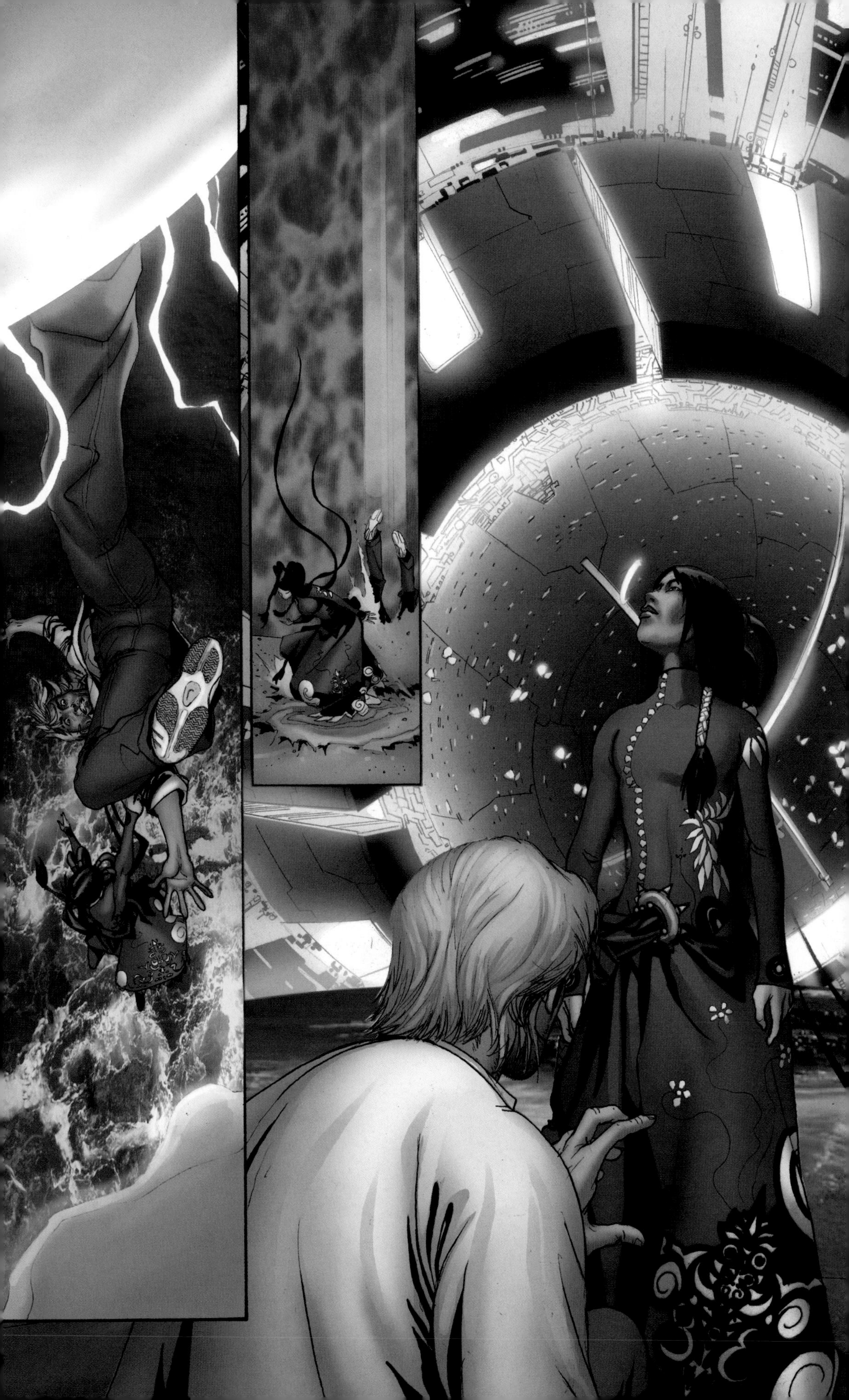

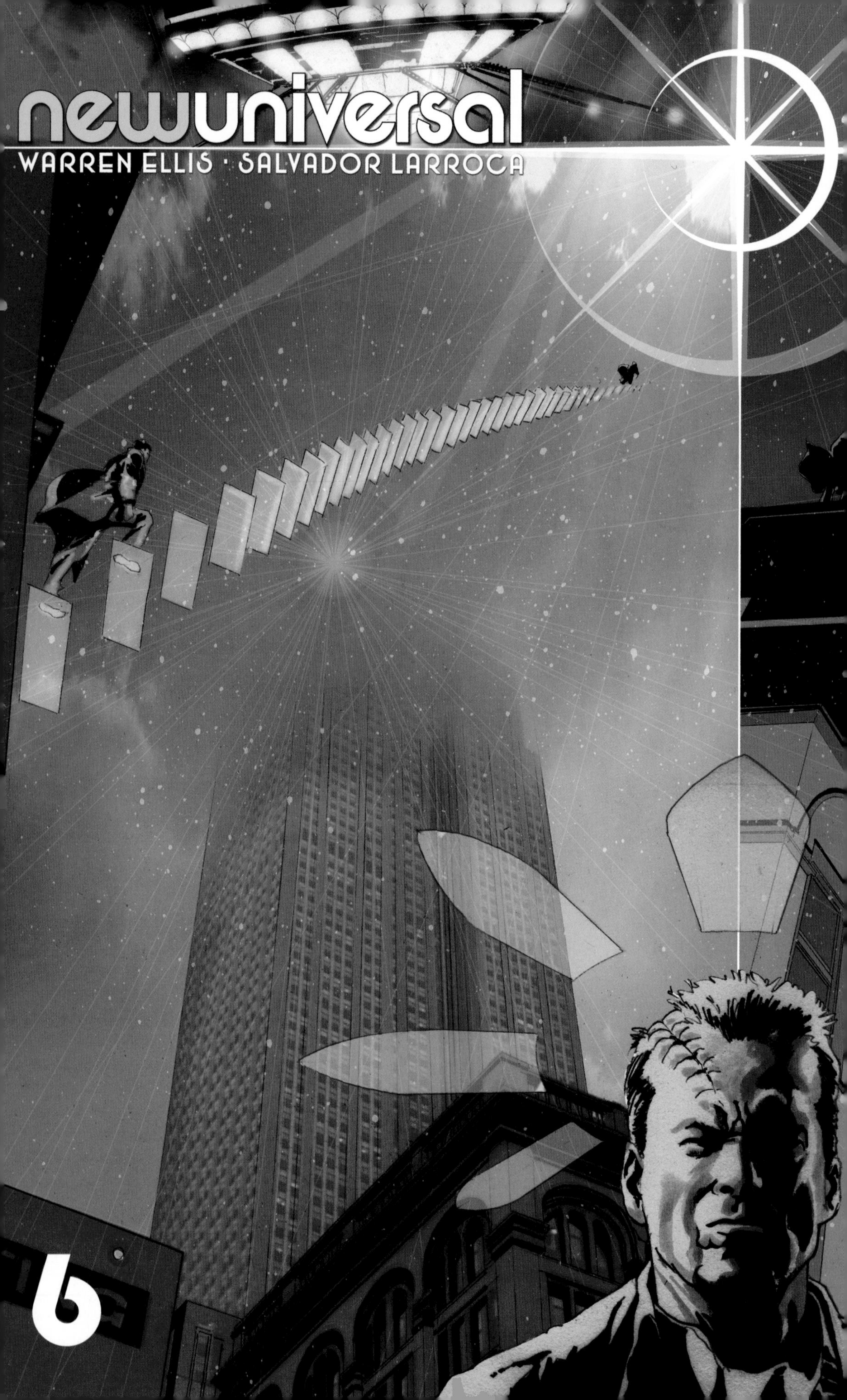
newuniversal
WARREN ELLIS · SALVADOR LARROCA
6

newuniversal
TUMBLE

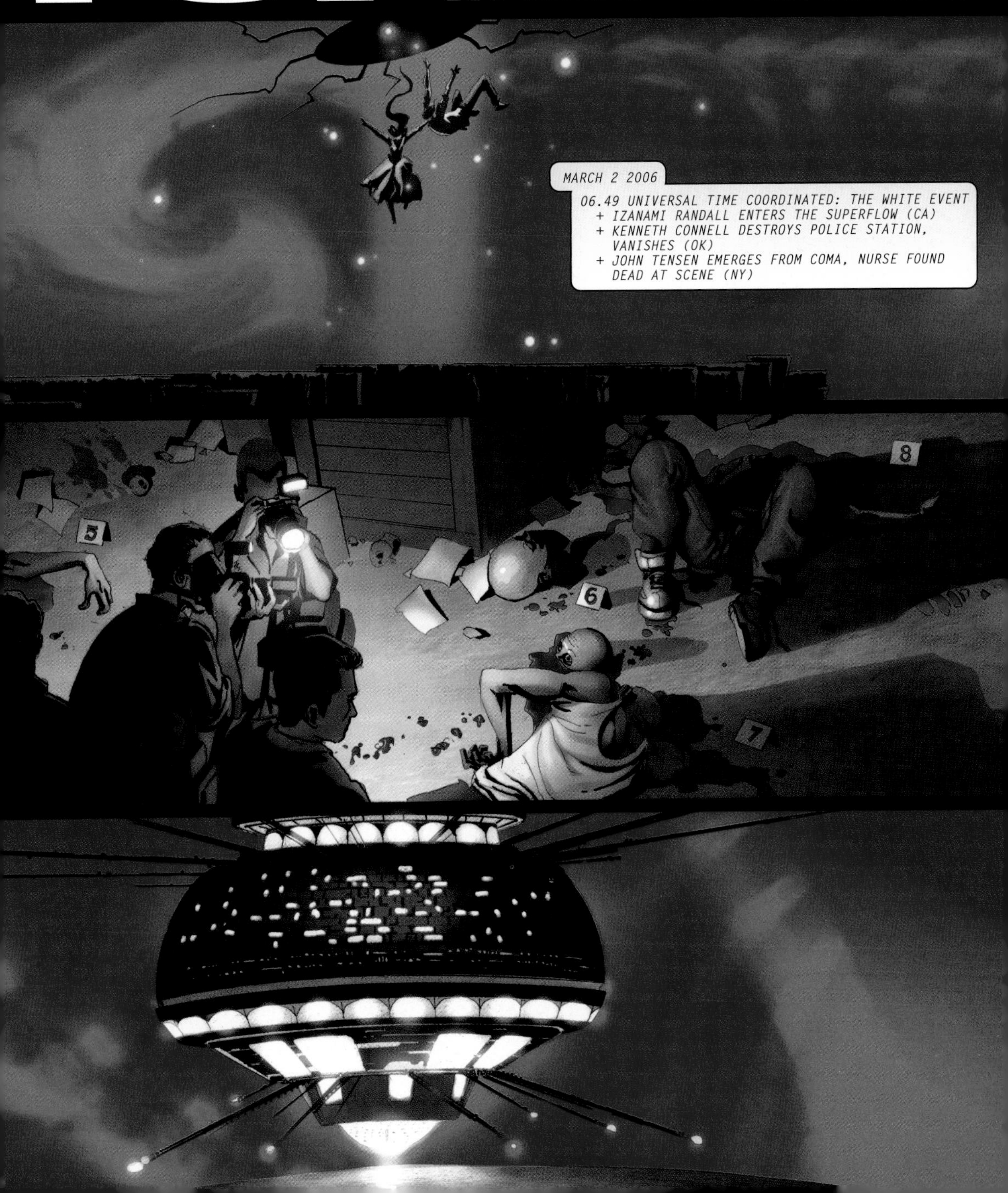
MARCH 2 2006
06.49 UNIVERSAL TIME COORDINATED: THE WHITE EVENT
+ IZANAMI RANDALL ENTERS THE SUPERFLOW (CA)
+ KENNETH CONNELL DESTROYS POLICE STATION, VANISHES (OK)
+ JOHN TENSEN EMERGES FROM COMA, NURSE FOUND DEAD AT SCENE (NY)
5
8
6
7

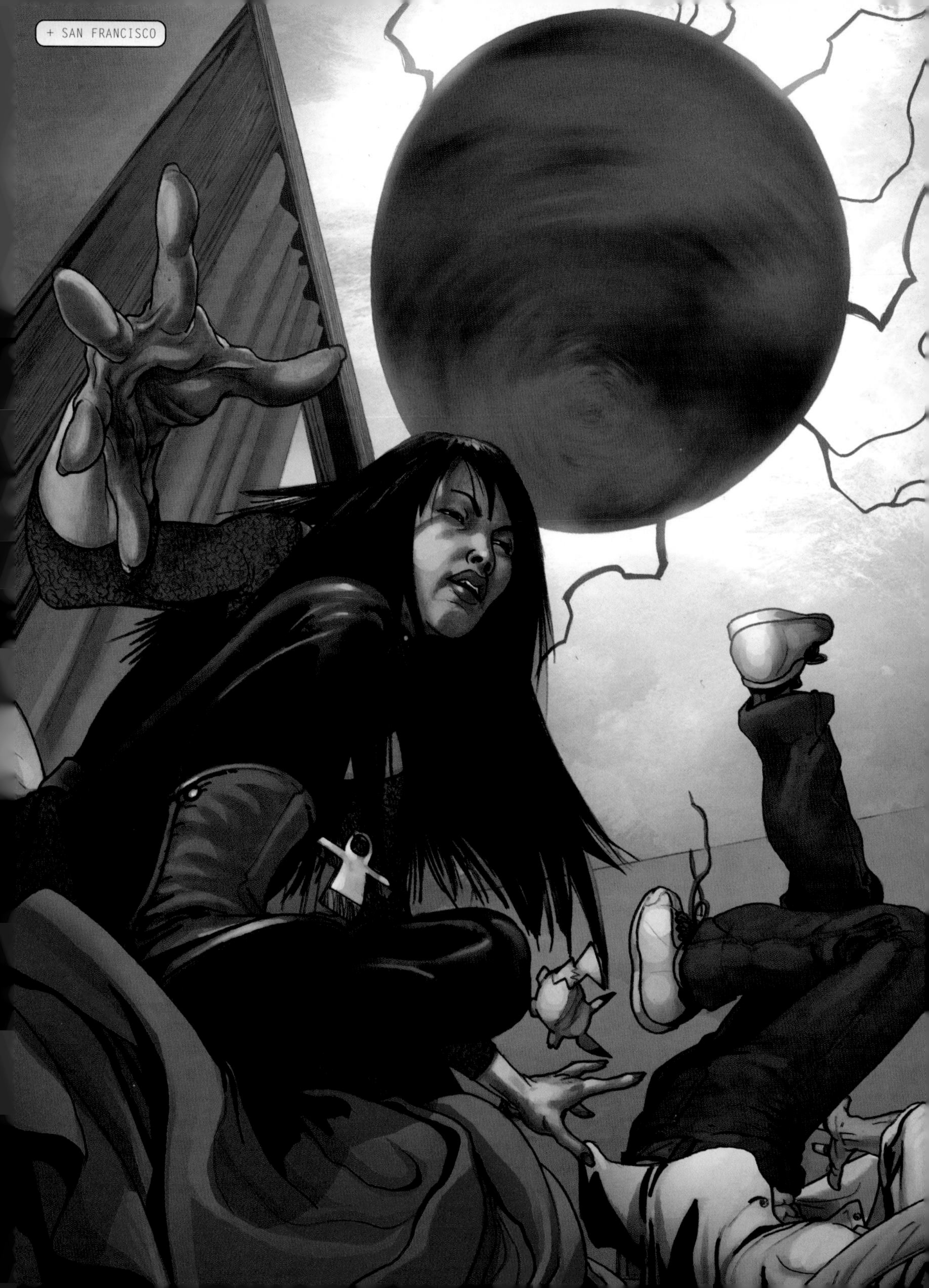
+ SAN FRANCISCO

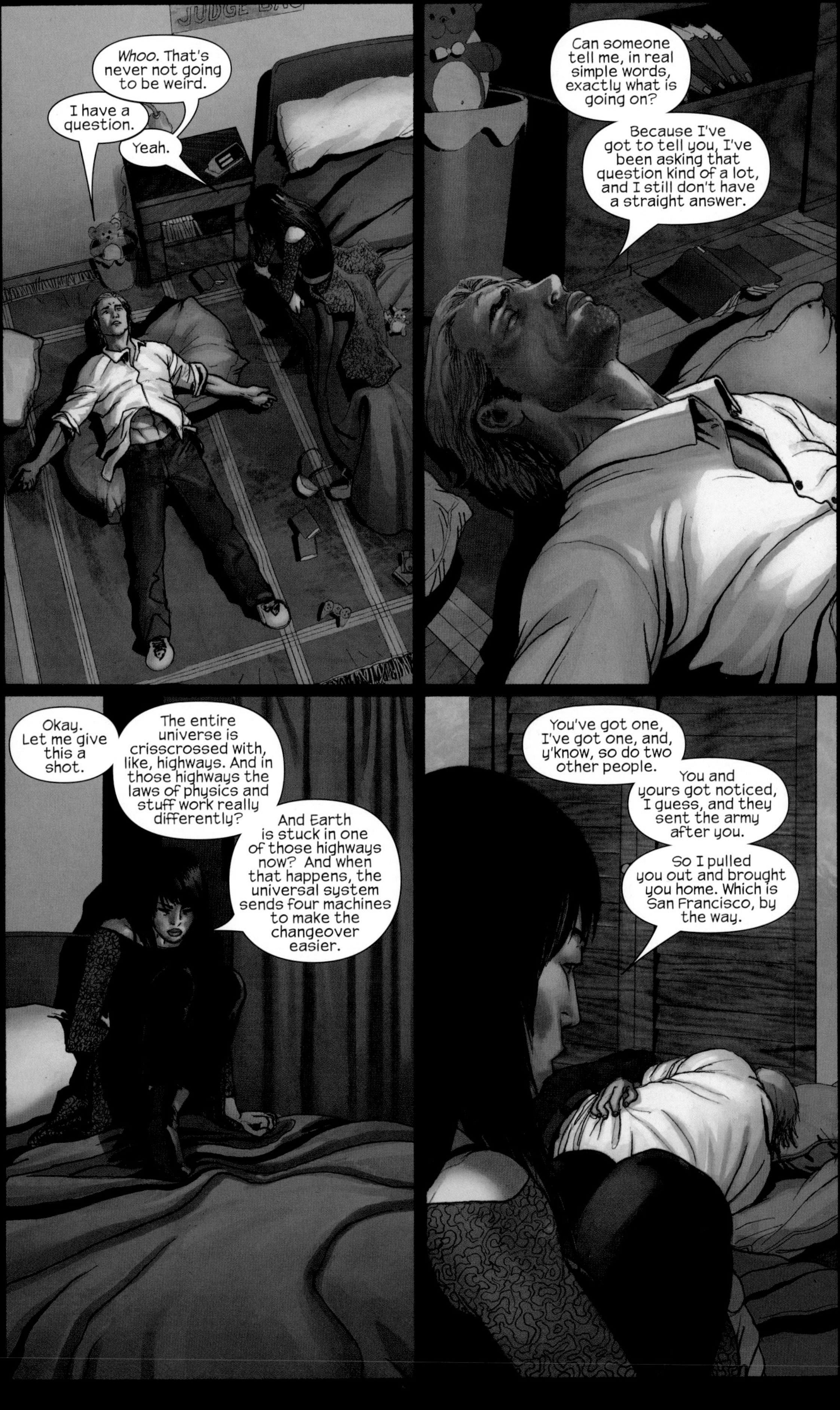
Whoo. That's never not going to be weird.
I have a question.
Yeah.
Can someone tell me, in real simple words, exactly what is going on?
Because I've got to tell you, I've been asking that question kind of a lot, and I still don't have a straight answer.
Okay. Let me give this a shot.
The entire universe is crisscrossed with, like, highways. And in those highways the laws of physics and stuff work really differently?
And Earth is stuck in one of those highways now? And when that happens, the universal system sends four machines to make the changeover easier.
You've got one, I've got one, and, y'know, so do two other people.
You and yours got noticed, I guess, and they sent the army after you.
So I pulled you out and brought you home. Which is San Francisco, by the way.

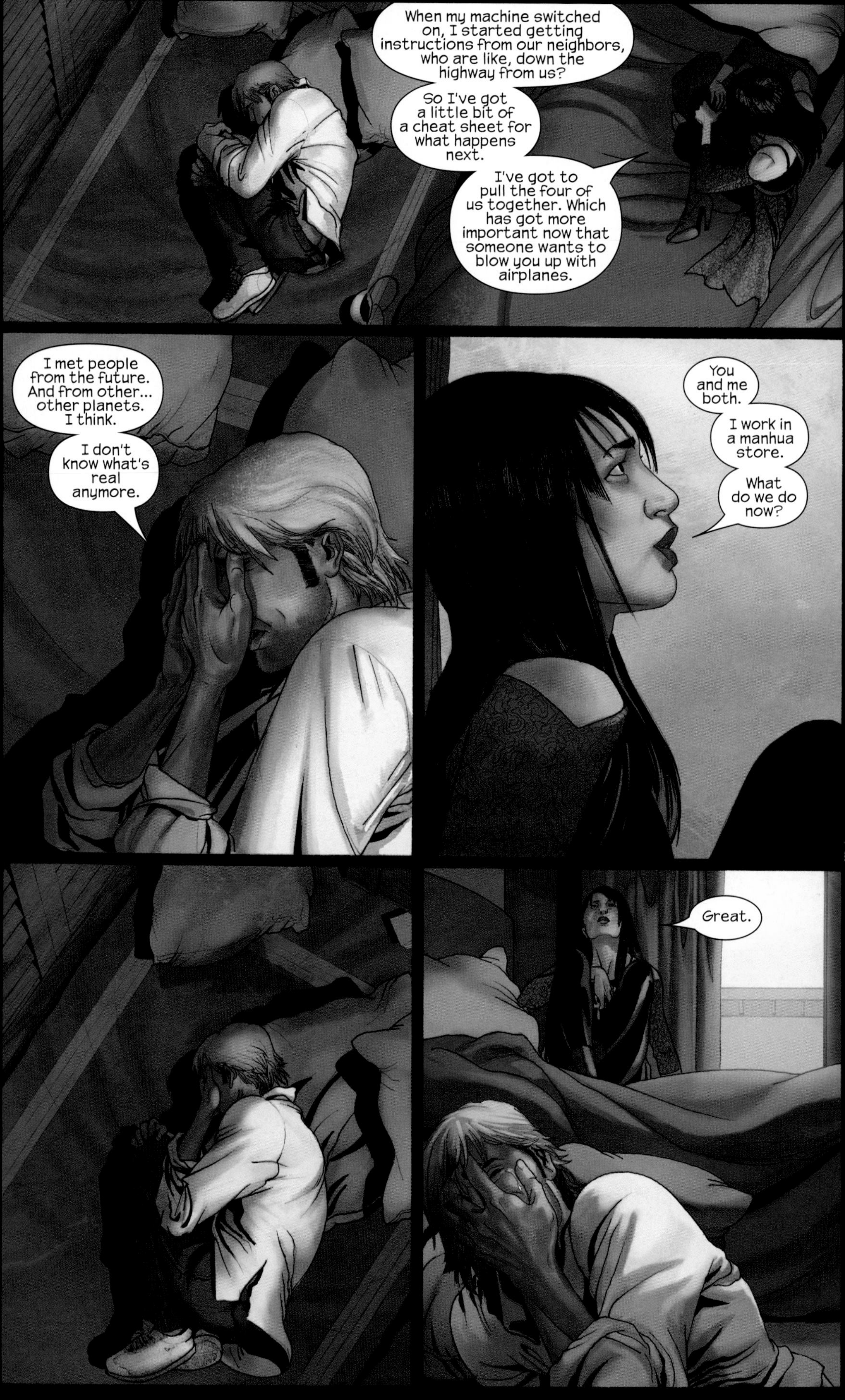
When my machine switched on, I started getting instructions from our neighbors, who are like, down the highway from us?
So I've got a little bit of a cheat sheet for what happens next.
I've got to pull the four of us together. Which has got more important now that someone wants to blow you up with airplanes.
I met people from the future. And from other... other planets. I think.
I don't know what's real anymore.
You and me both.
I work in a manhua store.
What do we do now?
Great.

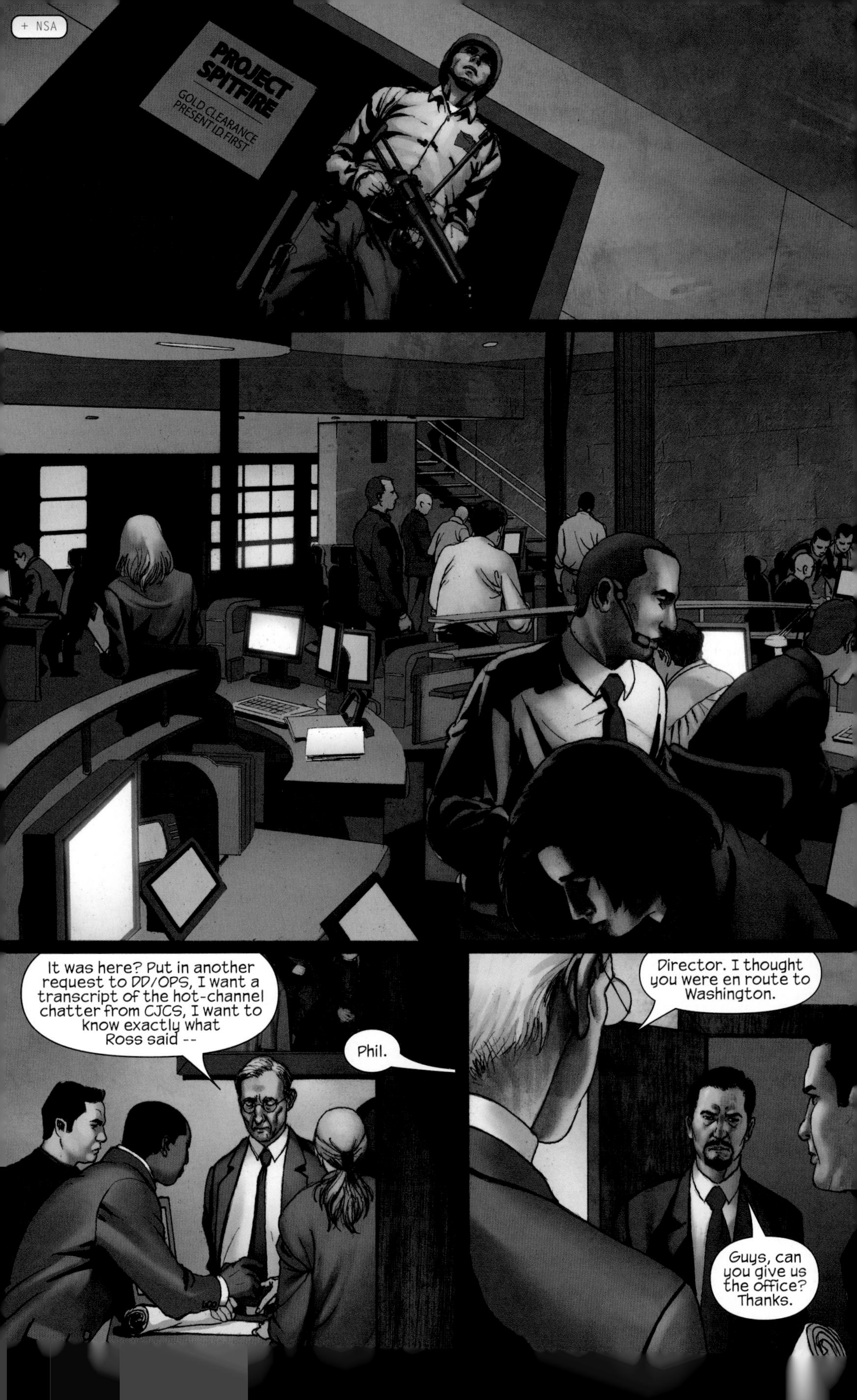
+ NSA
PROJECT SPITFIRE
GOLD CLEARANCE
PRESENT I.D. FIRST
It was here? Put in another request to DD/OPS, I want a transcript of the hot-channel chatter from CJCS, I want to know exactly what Ross said --
Phil.
Director. I thought you were en route to Washington.
Guys, can you give us the office? Thanks.

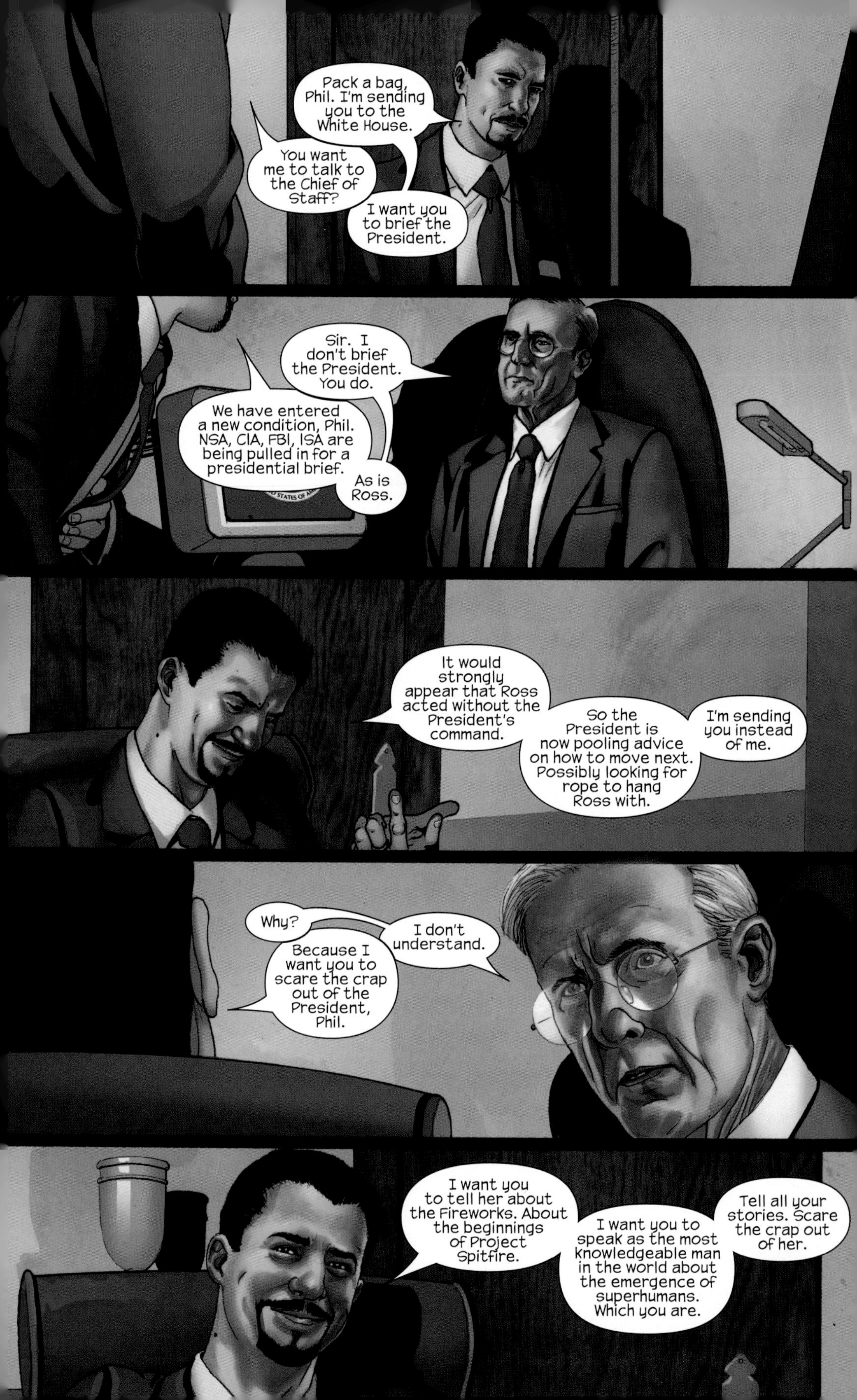
Pack a bag, Phil. I'm sending you to the White House.
You want me to talk to the Chief of Staff?
I want you to brief the President.
Sir. I don't brief the President. You do.
We have entered a new condition, Phil. NSA, CIA, FBI, ISA are being pulled in for a presidential brief.
As is Ross.
It would strongly appear that Ross acted without the President's command.
So the President is now pooling advice on how to move next. Possibly looking for rope to hang Ross with.
I'm sending you instead of me.
Why?
I don't understand.
Because I want you to scare the crap out of the President, Phil.
I want you to tell her about the Fireworks. About the beginnings of Project Spitfire.
I want you to speak as the most knowledgeable man in the world about the emergence of superhumans. Which you are.
Tell all your stories. Scare the crap out of her.

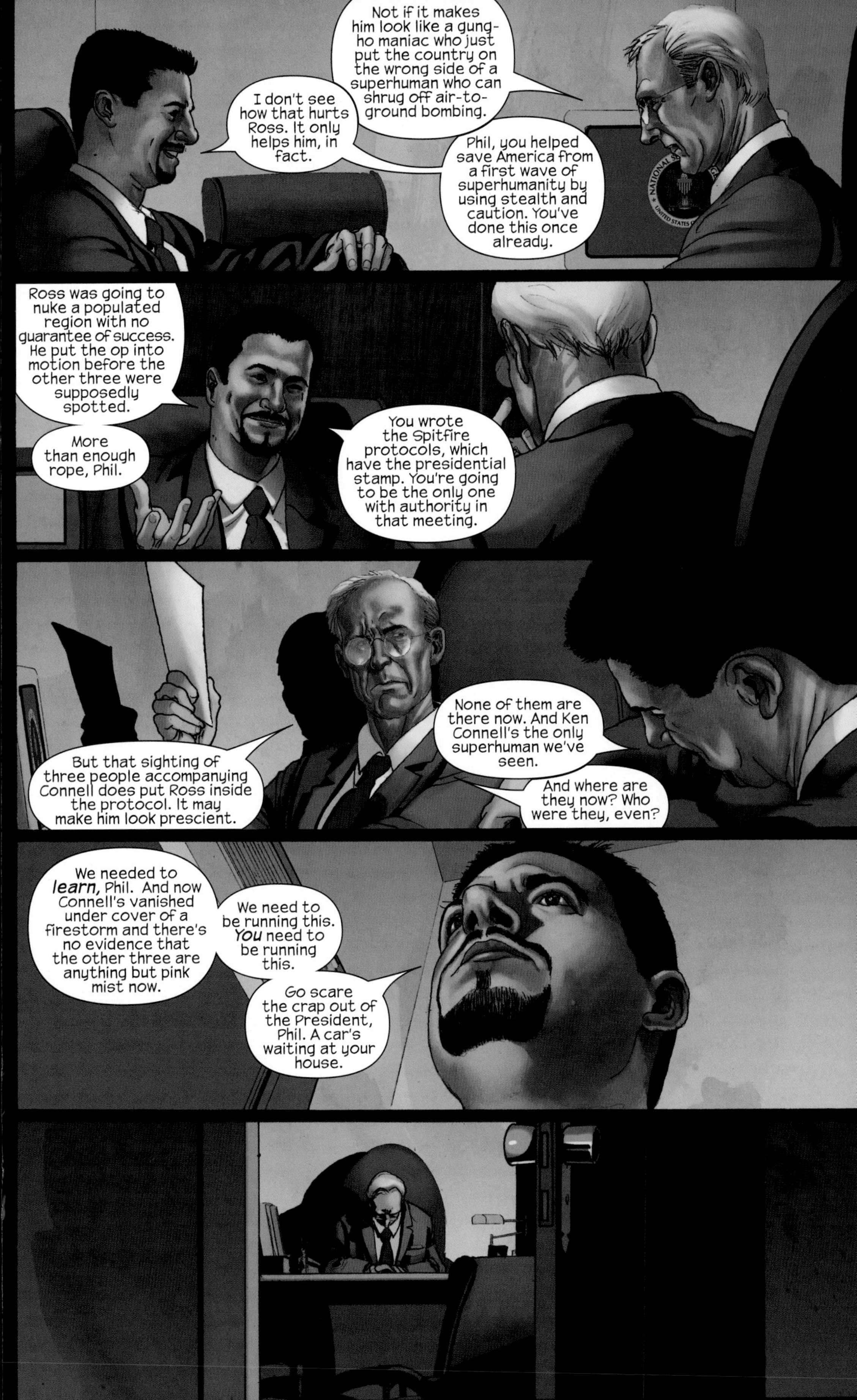
Not if it makes him look like a gung-ho maniac who just put the country on the wrong side of a superhuman who can shrug off air-to-ground bombing.
I don't see how that hurts Ross. It only helps him, in fact.
Phil, you helped save America from a first wave of superhumanity by using stealth and caution. You've done this once already.
NATIONAL SECURITY COUNCIL UNITED STATES
Ross was going to nuke a populated region with no guarantee of success. He put the op into motion before the other three were supposedly spotted.
More than enough rope, Phil.
You wrote the Spitfire protocols, which have the presidential stamp. You're going to be the only one with authority in that meeting.
But that sighting of three people accompanying Connell does put Ross inside the protocol. It may make him look prescient.
None of them are there now. And Ken Connell's the only superhuman we've seen.
And where are they now? Who were they, even?
We needed to *learn*, Phil. And now Connell's vanished under cover of a firestorm and there's no evidence that the other three are anything but pink mist now.
We need to be running this. *You* need to be running this.
Go scare the crap out of the President, Phil. A car's waiting at your house.

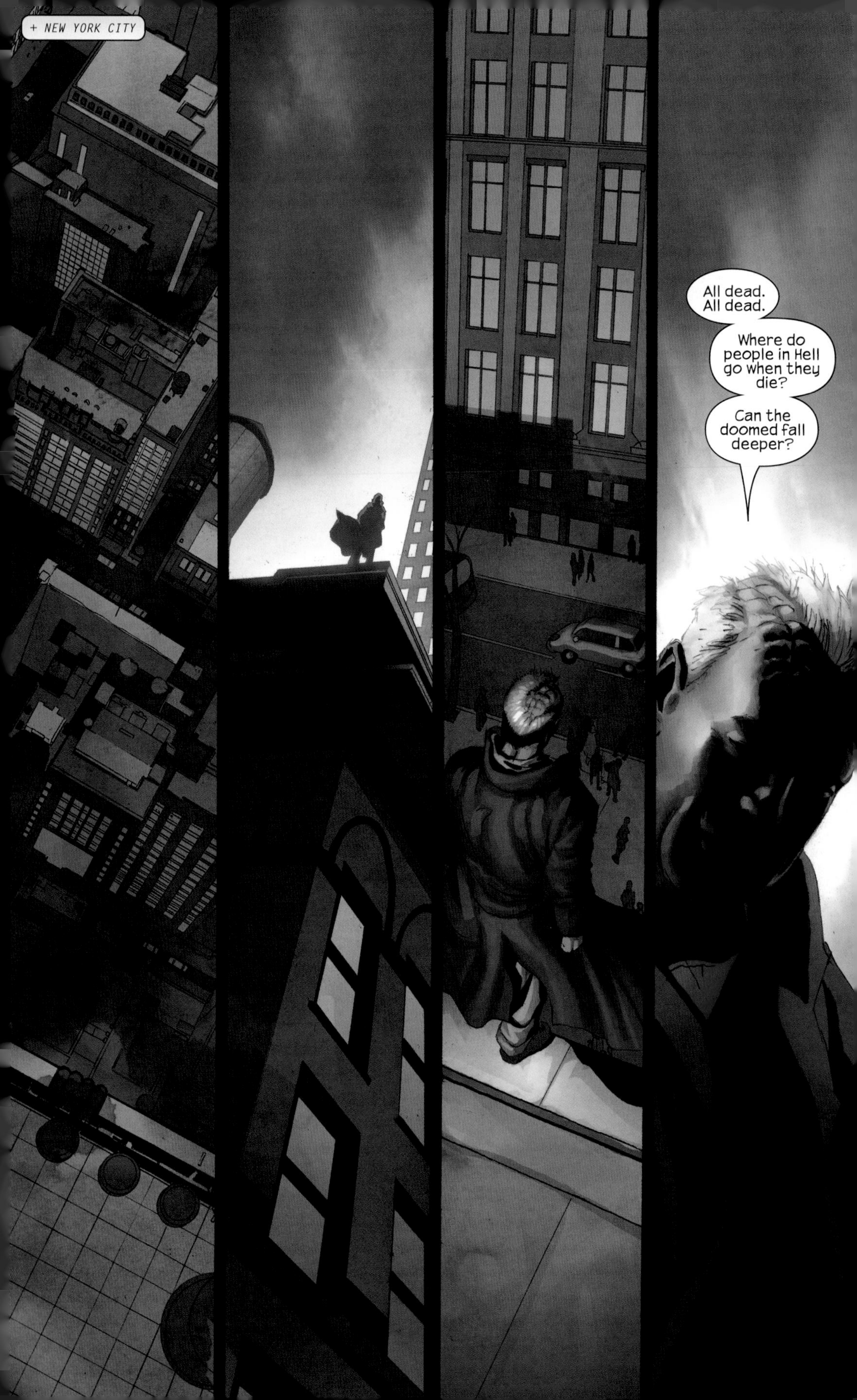
+ NEW YORK CITY
All dead. All dead.
Where do people in Hell go when they die?
Can the doomed fall deeper?

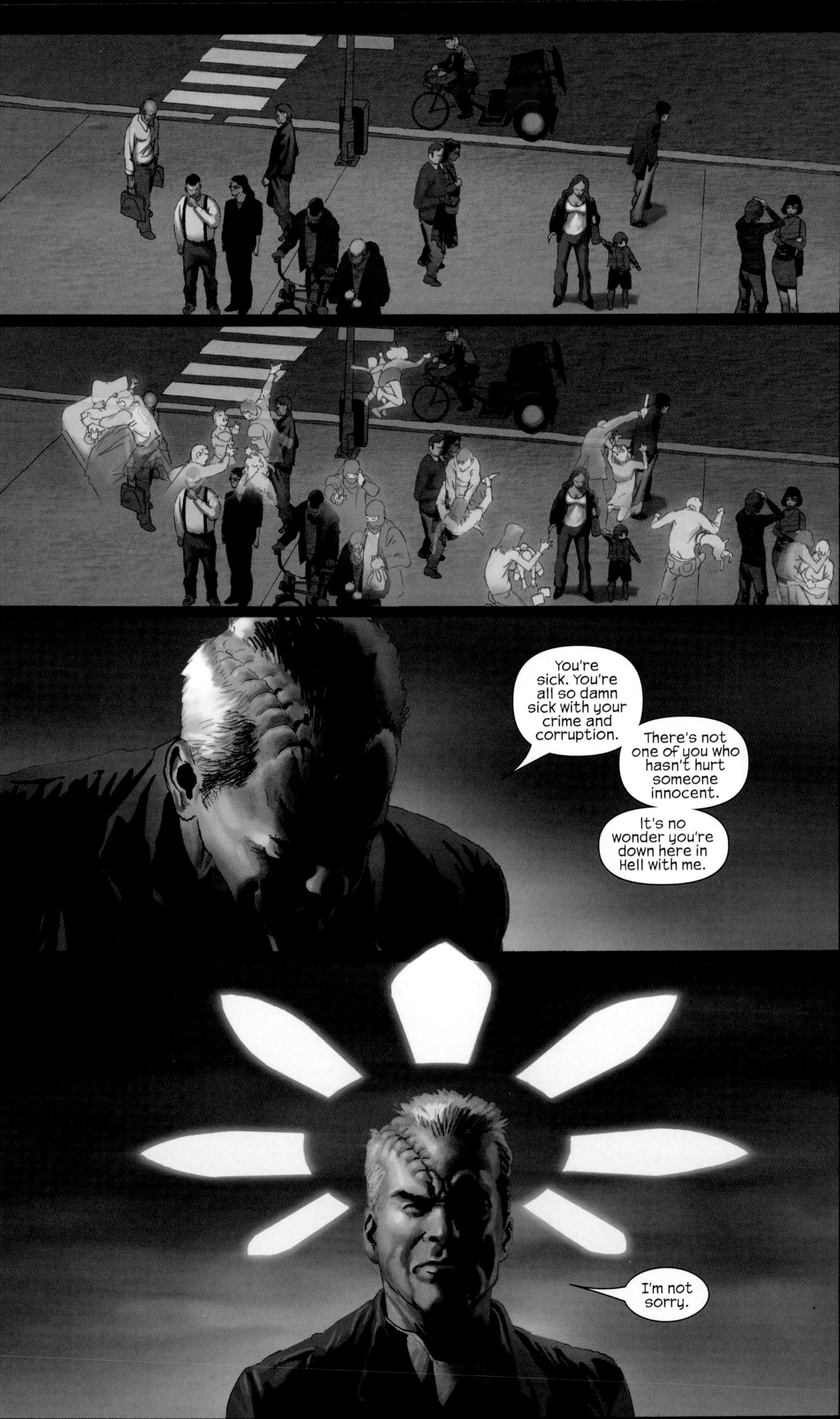
You're sick. You're all so damn sick with your crime and corruption.
There's not one of you who hasn't hurt someone innocent.
It's no wonder you're down here in Hell with me.
I'm not sorry.

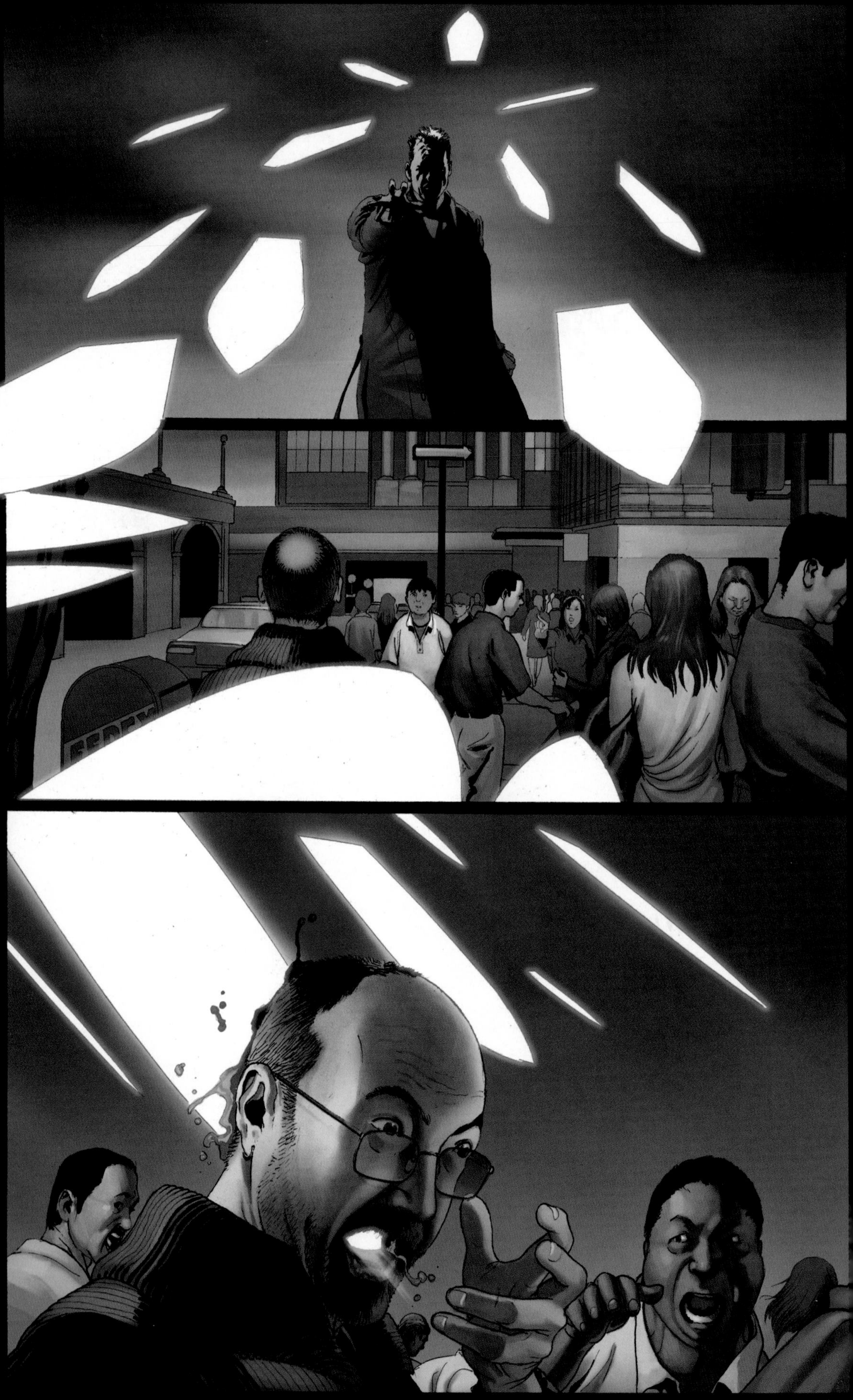

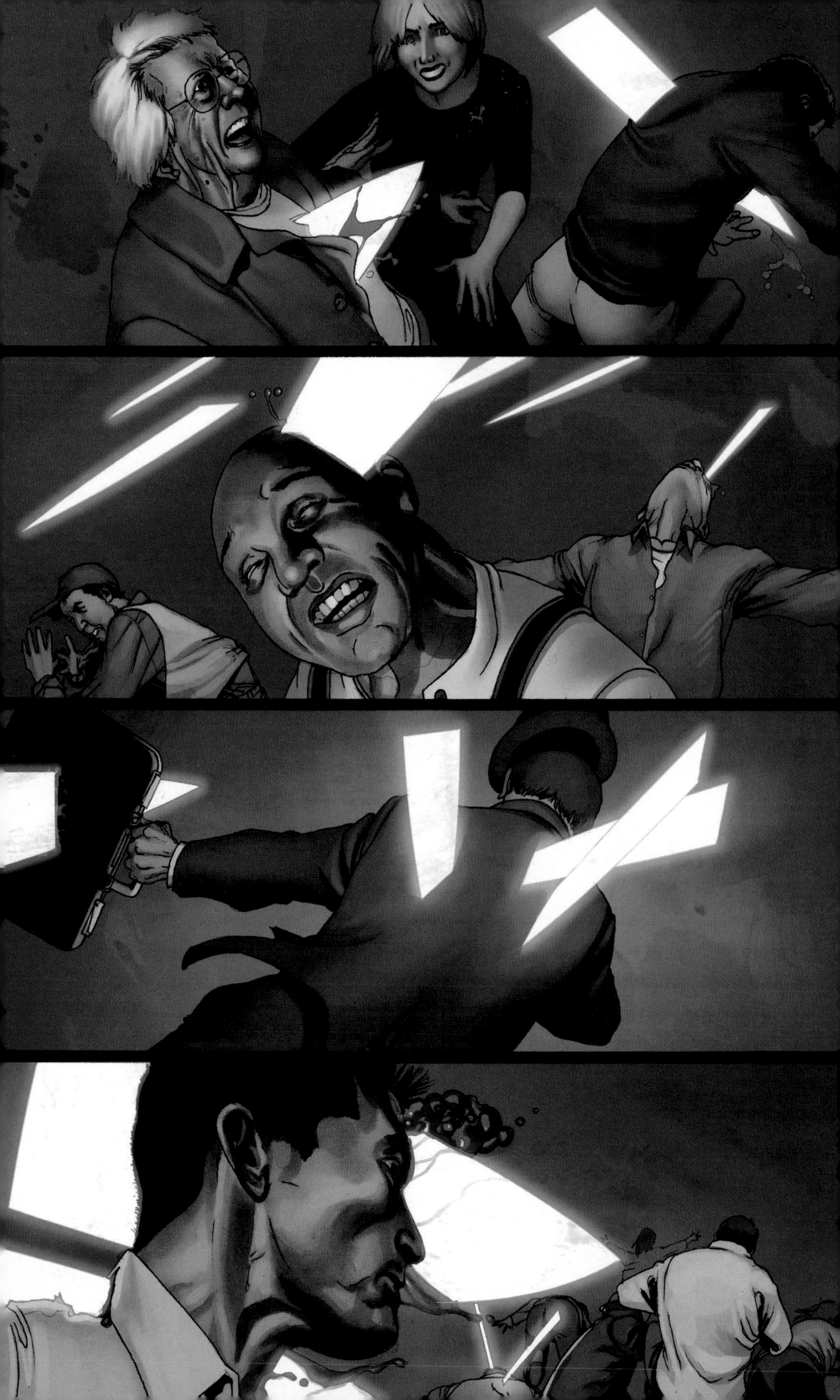

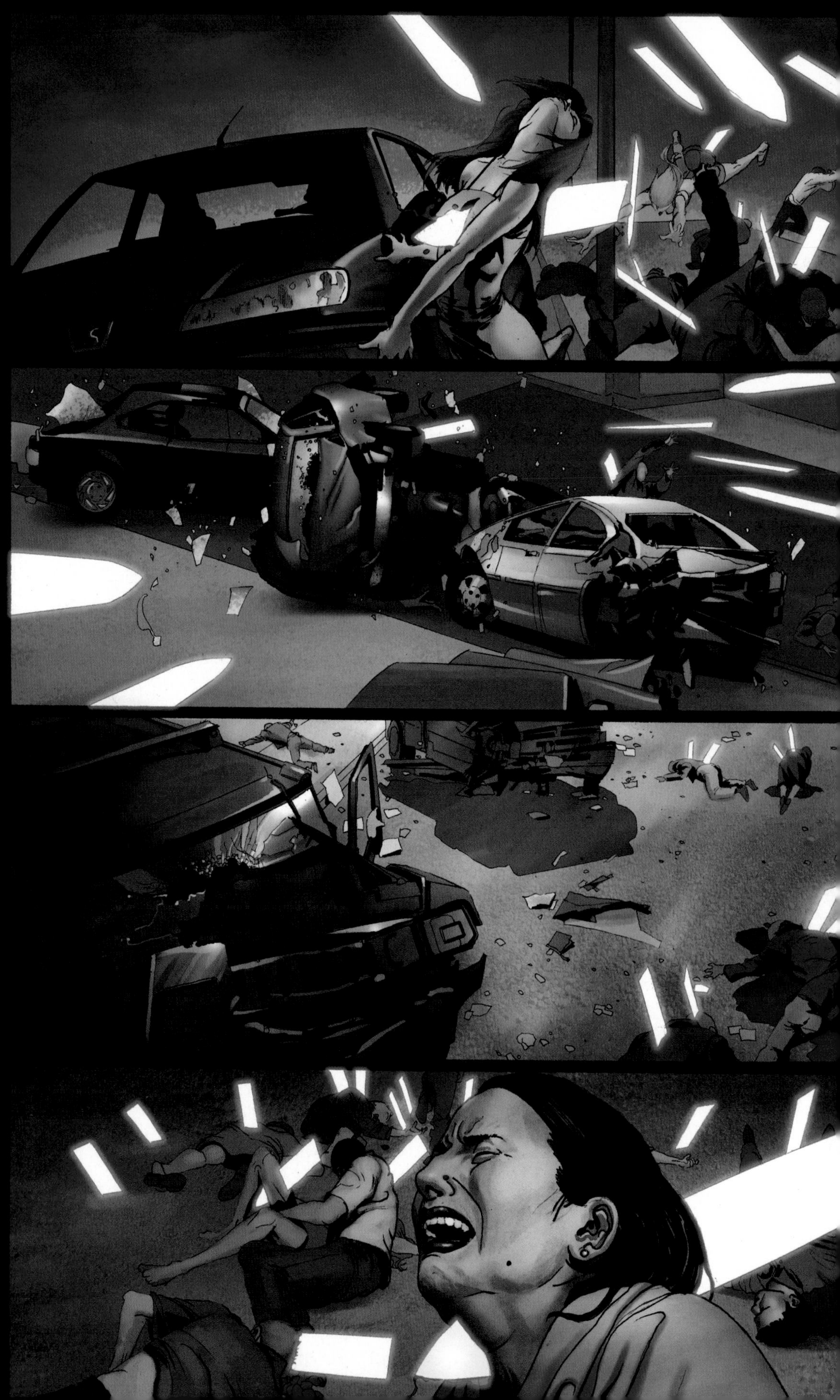

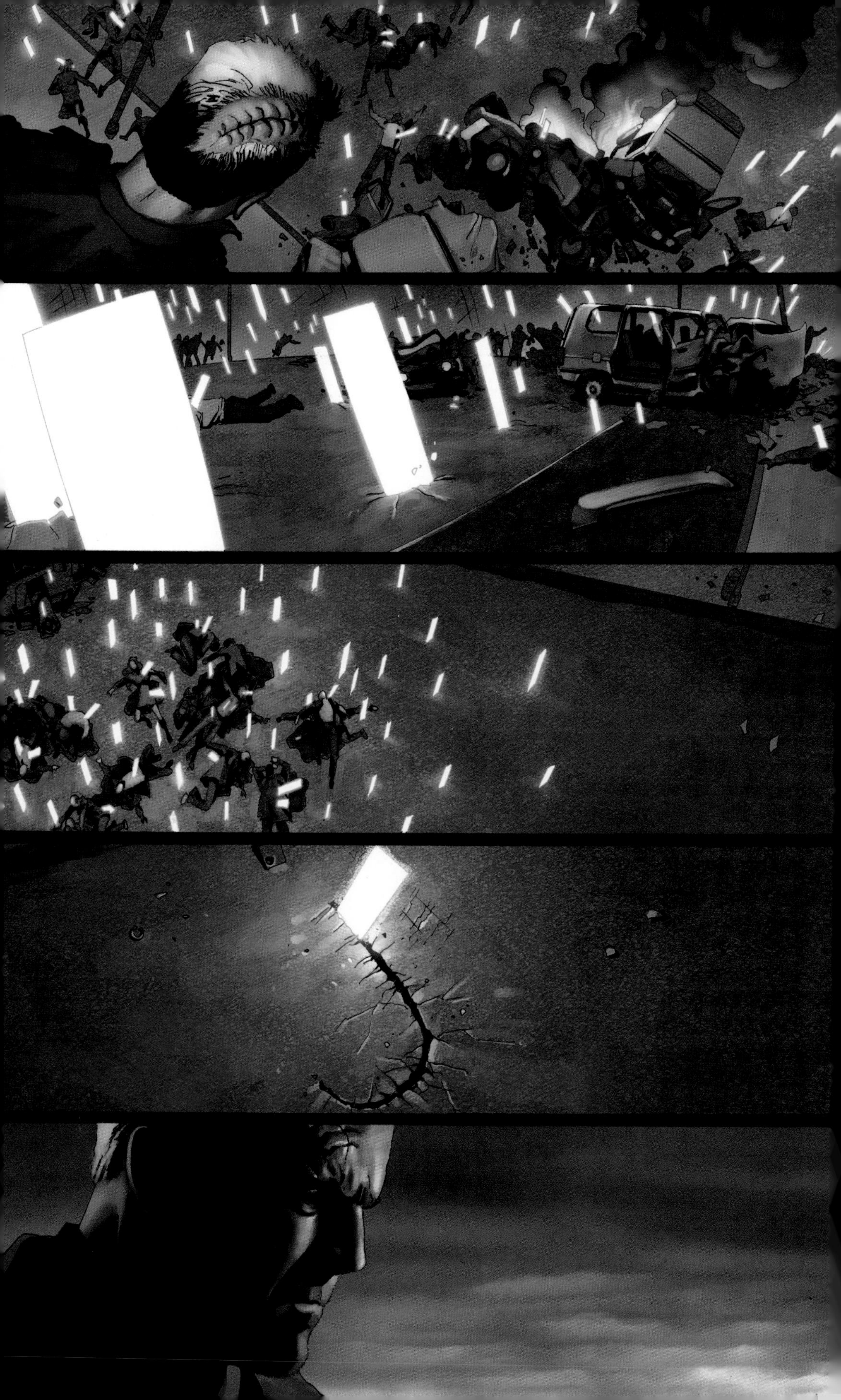

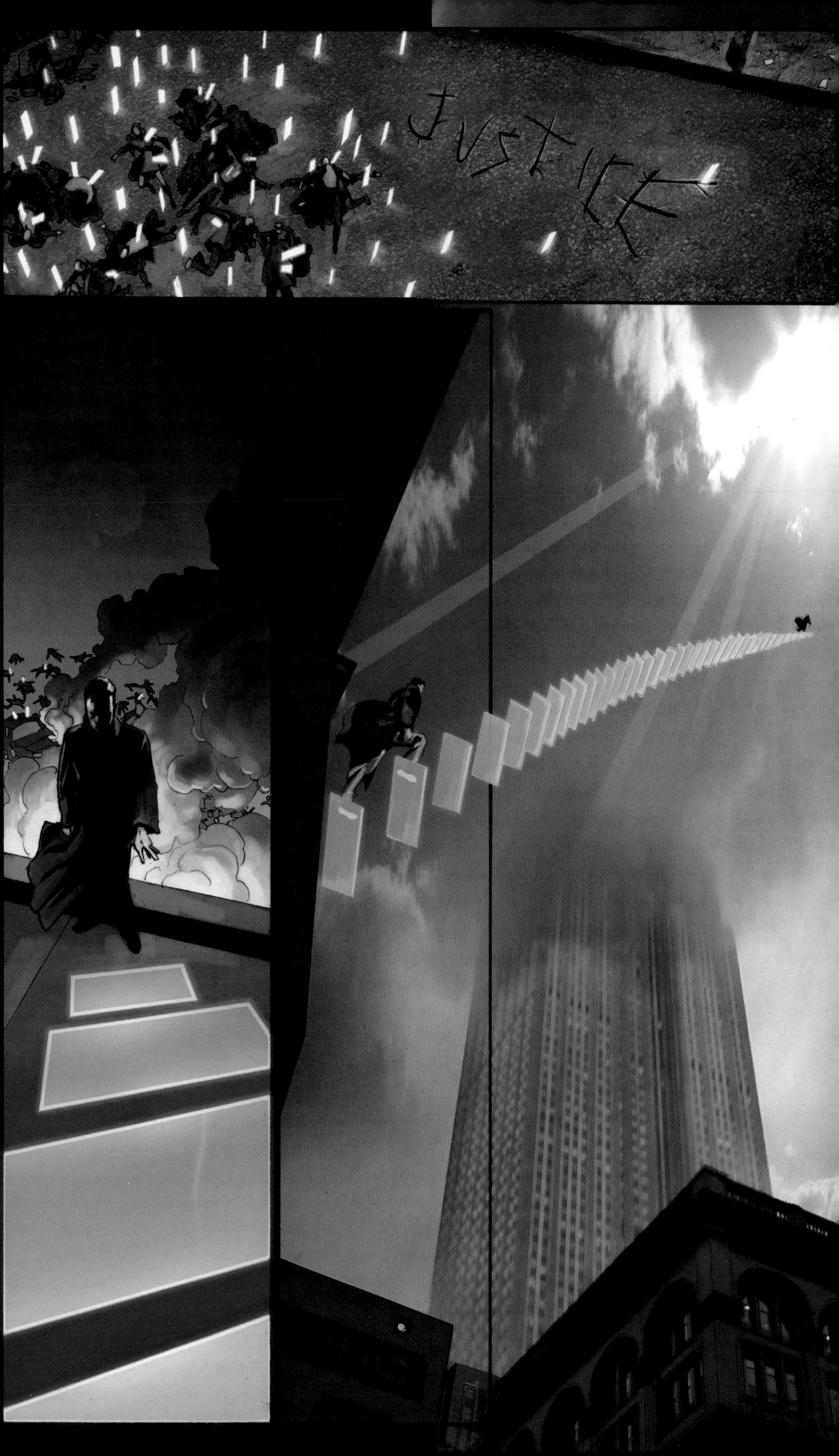
JUSTICE

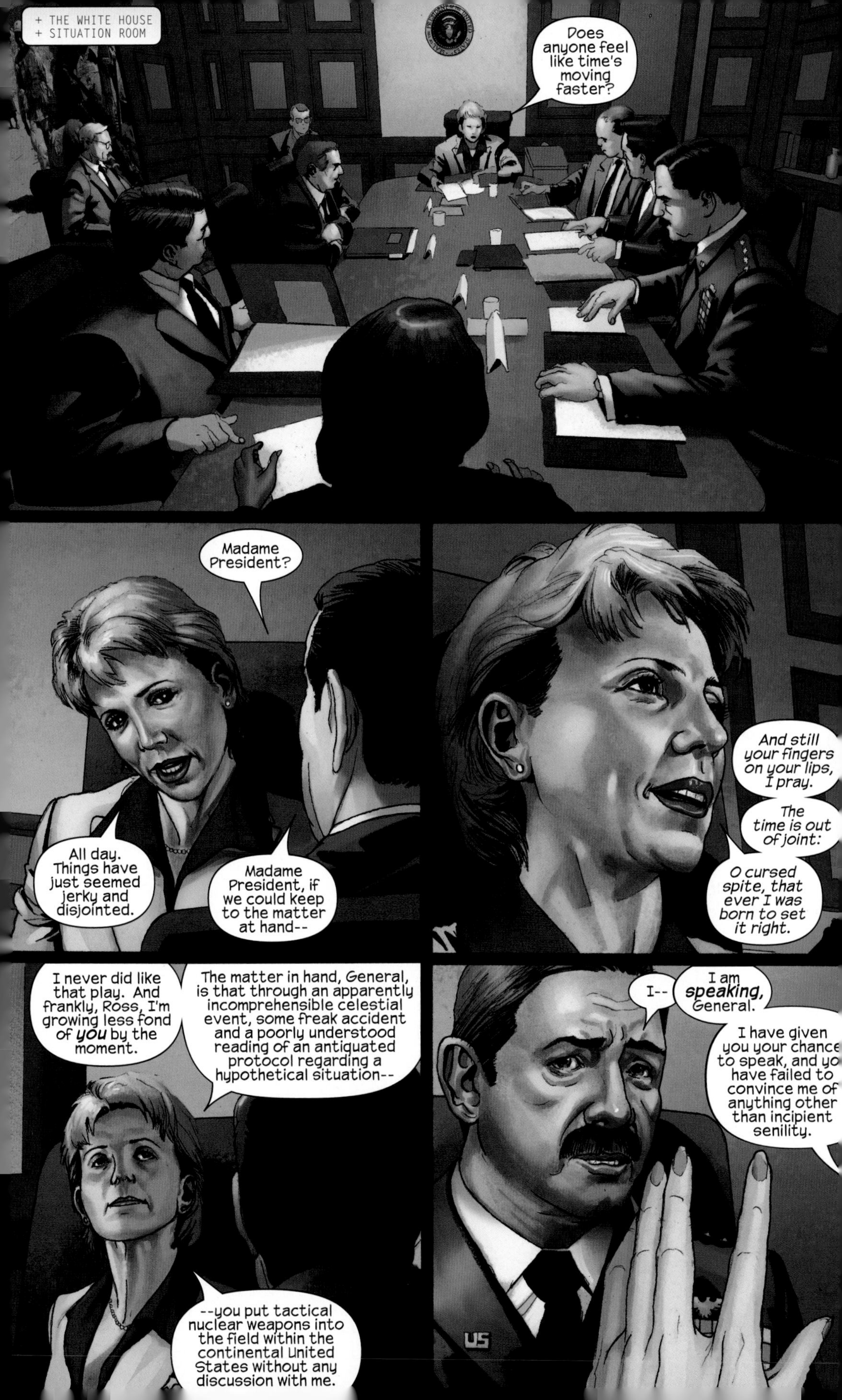

+ THE WHITE HOUSE
+ SITUATION ROOM
Does anyone feel like time's moving faster?
Madame President?
All day. Things have just seemed jerky and disjointed.
Madame President, if we could keep to the matter at hand--
And still your fingers on your lips, I pray.
The time is out of joint:
O cursed spite, that ever I was born to set it right.
I never did like that play. And frankly, Ross, I'm growing less fond of *you* by the moment.
The matter in hand, General, is that through an apparently incomprehensible celestial event, some freak accident and a poorly understood reading of an antiquated protocol regarding a hypothetical situation--
--you put tactical nuclear weapons into the field within the continental United States without any discussion with me.
I--
I am *speaking,* General.
I have given you your chance to speak, and yo have failed to convince me of anything other than incipient senility.

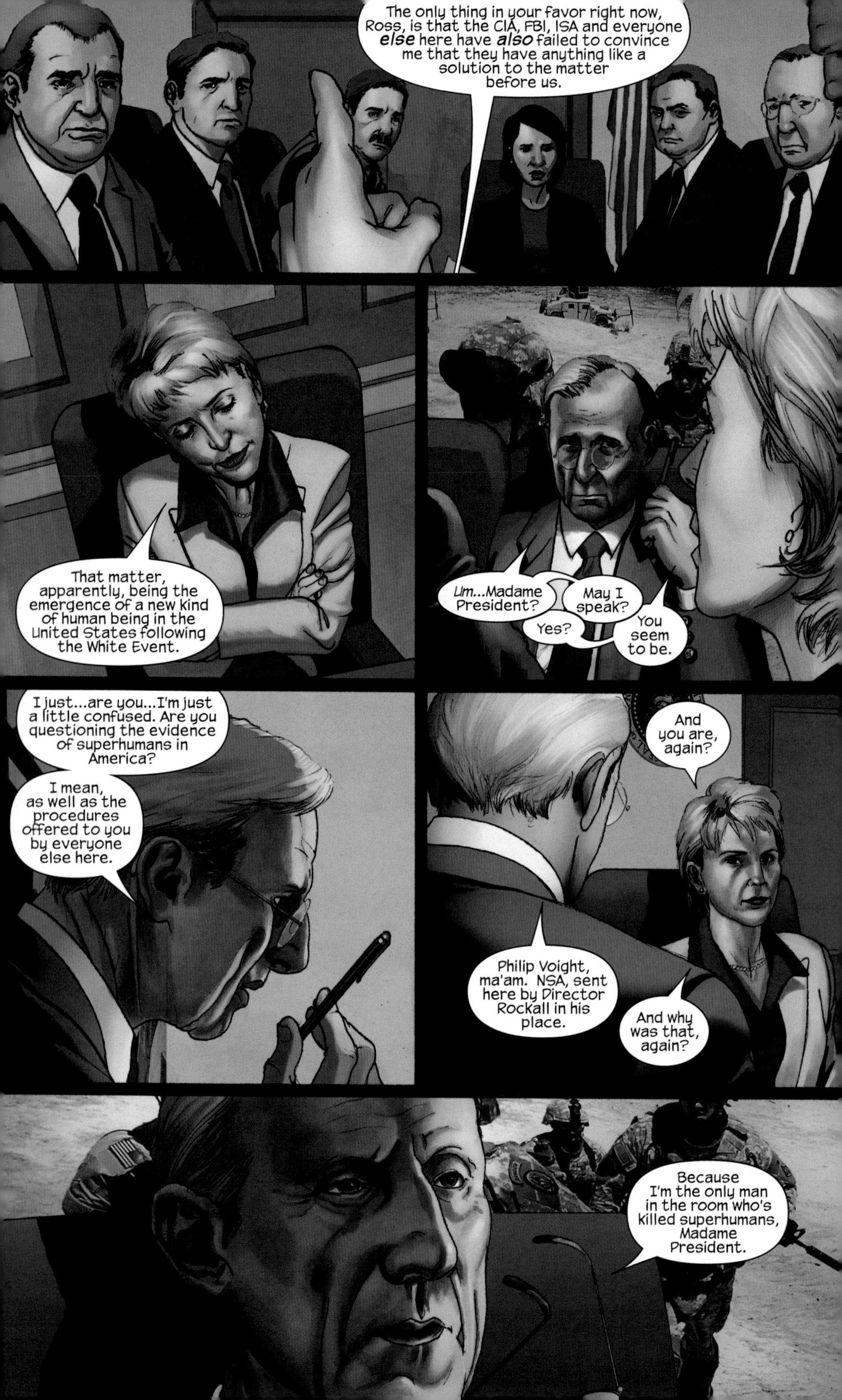

The only thing in your favor right now, Ross, is that the CIA, FBI, ISA and everyone *else* here have *also* failed to convince me that they have anything like a solution to the matter before us.
That matter, apparently, being the emergence of a new kind of human being in the United States following the White Event.
Um...Madame President?
May I speak?
Yes?
You seem to be.
I just...are you...I'm just a little confused. Are you questioning the evidence of superhumans in America?
I mean, as well as the procedures offered to you by everyone else here.
And you are, again?
Philip Voight, ma'am. NSA, sent here by Director Rockall in his place.
And why was that, again?
Because I'm the only man in the room who's killed superhumans, Madame President.

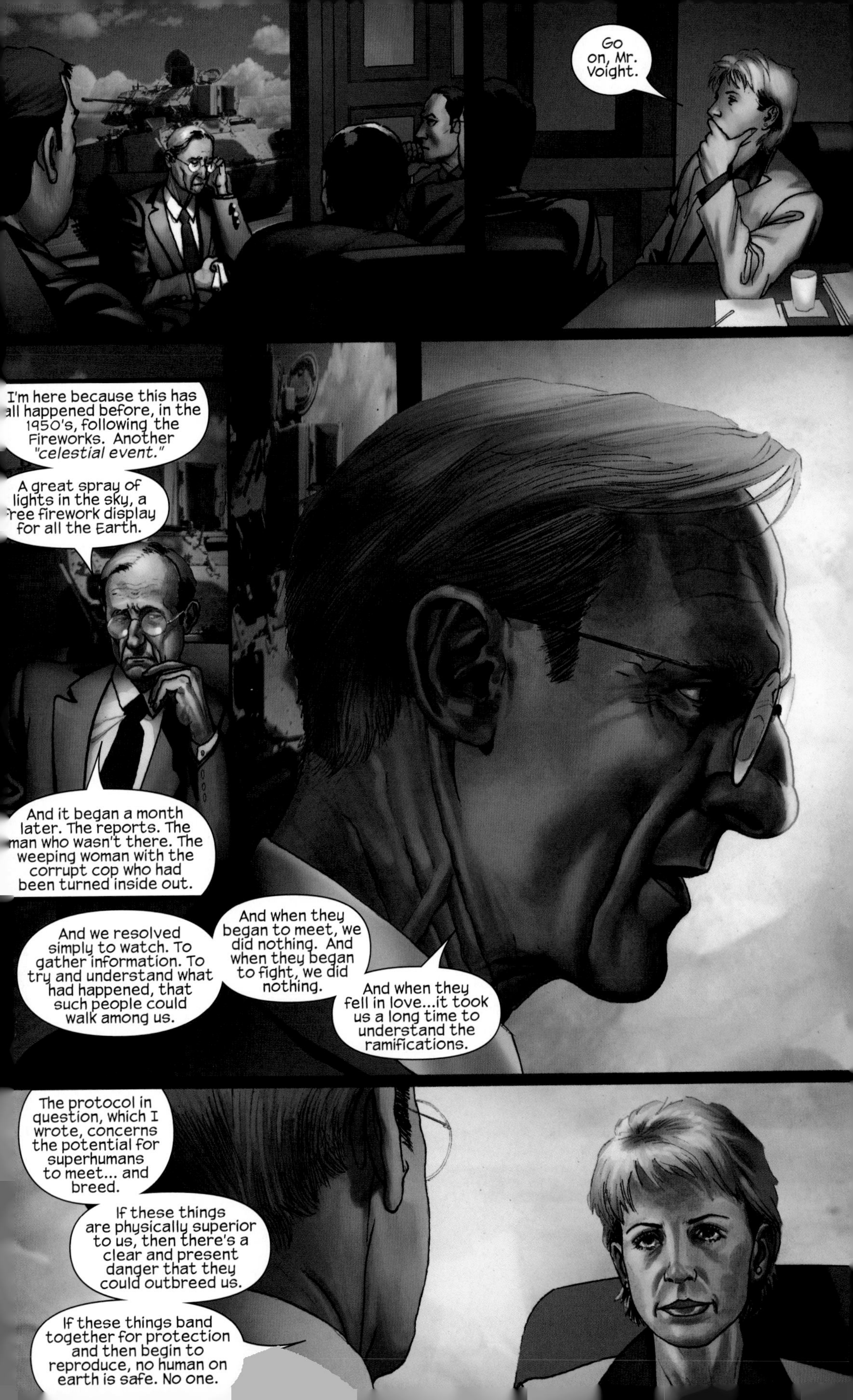
Go on, Mr. Voight.
I'm here because this has all happened before, in the 1950's, following the Fireworks. Another *"celestial event."*
A great spray of lights in the sky, a free firework display for all the Earth.
And it began a month later. The reports. The man who wasn't there. The weeping woman with the corrupt cop who had been turned inside out.
And we resolved simply to watch. To gather information. To try and understand what had happened, that such people could walk among us.
And when they began to meet, we did nothing. And when they began to fight, we did nothing.
And when they fell in love...it took us a long time to understand the ramifications.
The protocol in question, which I wrote, concerns the potential for superhumans to meet... and breed.
If these things are physically superior to us, then there's a clear and present danger that they could outbreed us.
If these things band together for protection and then begin to reproduce, no human on earth is safe. No one.

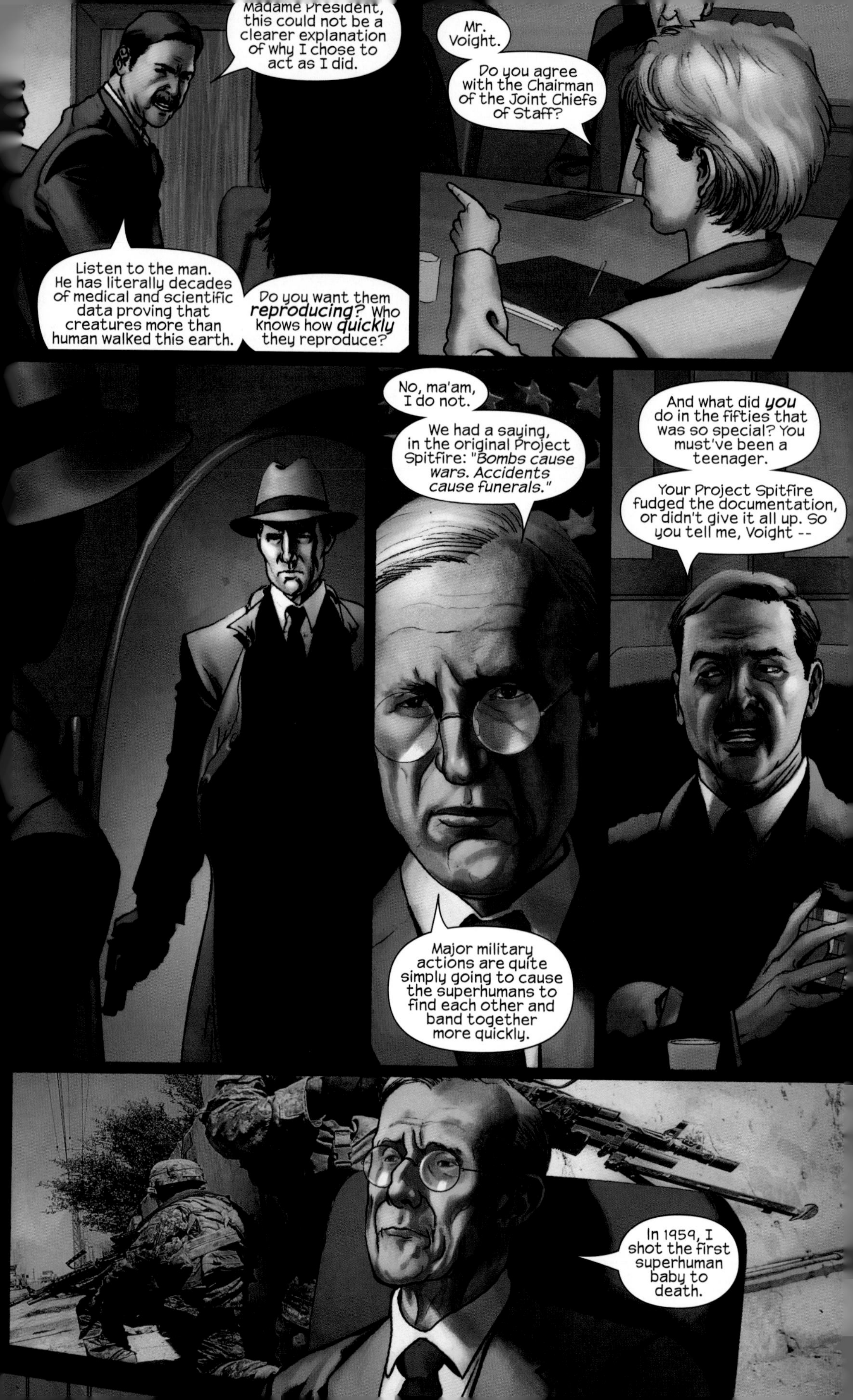
Madame President, this could not be a clearer explanation of why I chose to act as I did.
Listen to the man. He has literally decades of medical and scientific data proving that creatures more than human walked this earth.
Do you want them *reproducing?* Who knows how *quickly* they reproduce?
Mr. Voight.
Do you agree with the Chairman of the Joint Chiefs of Staff?
No, ma'am, I do not.
We had a saying, in the original Project Spitfire: "*Bombs cause wars. Accidents cause funerals.*"
Major military actions are quite simply going to cause the superhumans to find each other and band together more quickly.
And what did *you* do in the fifties that was so special? You must've been a teenager.
Your Project Spitfire fudged the documentation, or didn't give it all up. So you tell me, Voight --
In 1959, I shot the first superhuman baby to death.

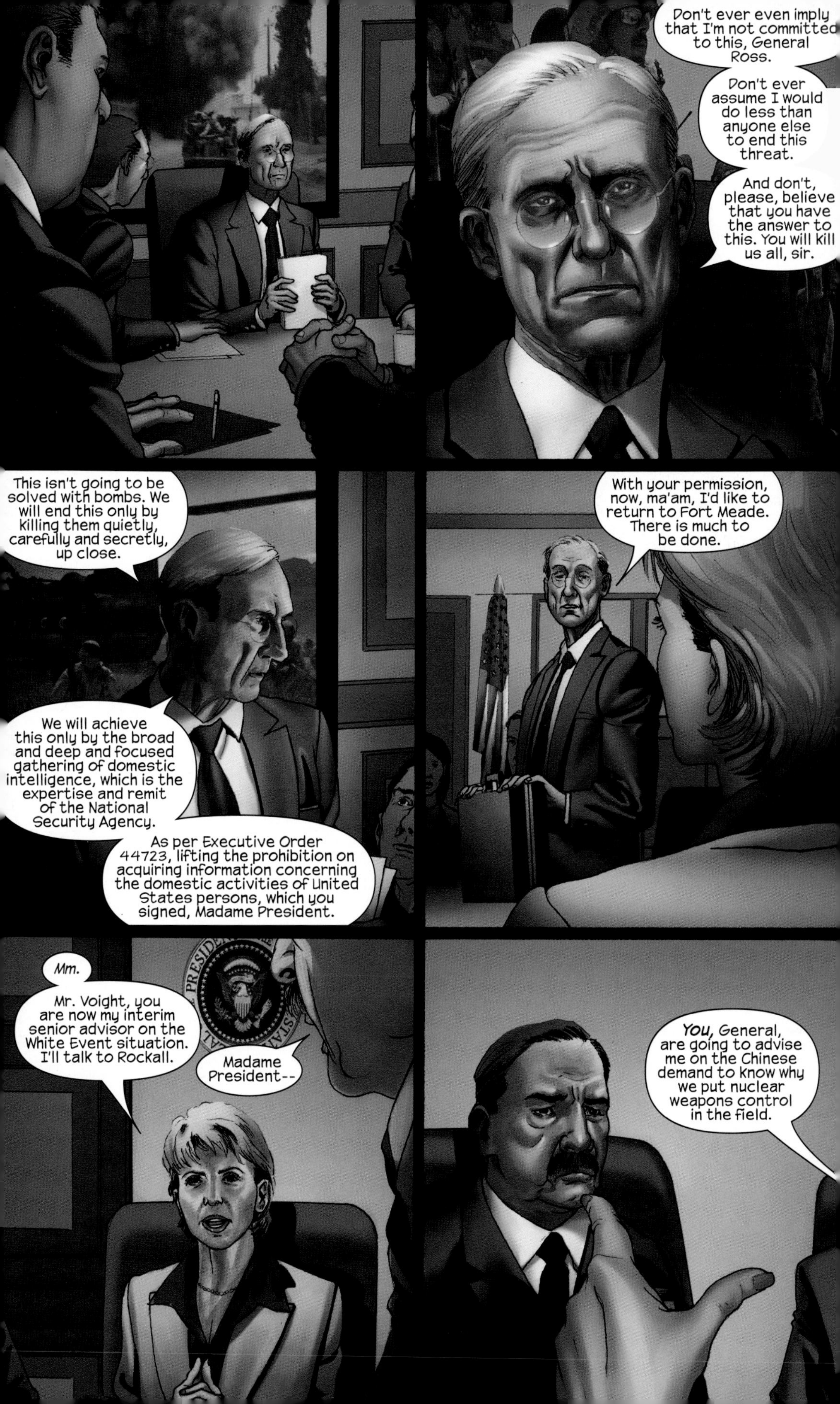

Don't ever even imply that I'm not committed to this, General Ross.
Don't ever assume I would do less than anyone else to end this threat.
And don't, please, believe that you have the answer to this. You will kill us all, sir.
This isn't going to be solved with bombs. We will end this only by killing them quietly, carefully and secretly, up close.
We will achieve this only by the broad and deep and focused gathering of domestic intelligence, which is the expertise and remit of the National Security Agency.
As per Executive Order 44723, lifting the prohibition on acquiring information concerning the domestic activities of United States persons, which you signed, Madame President.
With your permission, now, ma'am, I'd like to return to Fort Meade. There is much to be done.
Mm.
Mr. Voight, you are now my interim senior advisor on the White Event situation. I'll talk to Rockall.
Madame President--
You, General, are going to advise me on the Chinese demand to know why we put nuclear weapons control in the field.

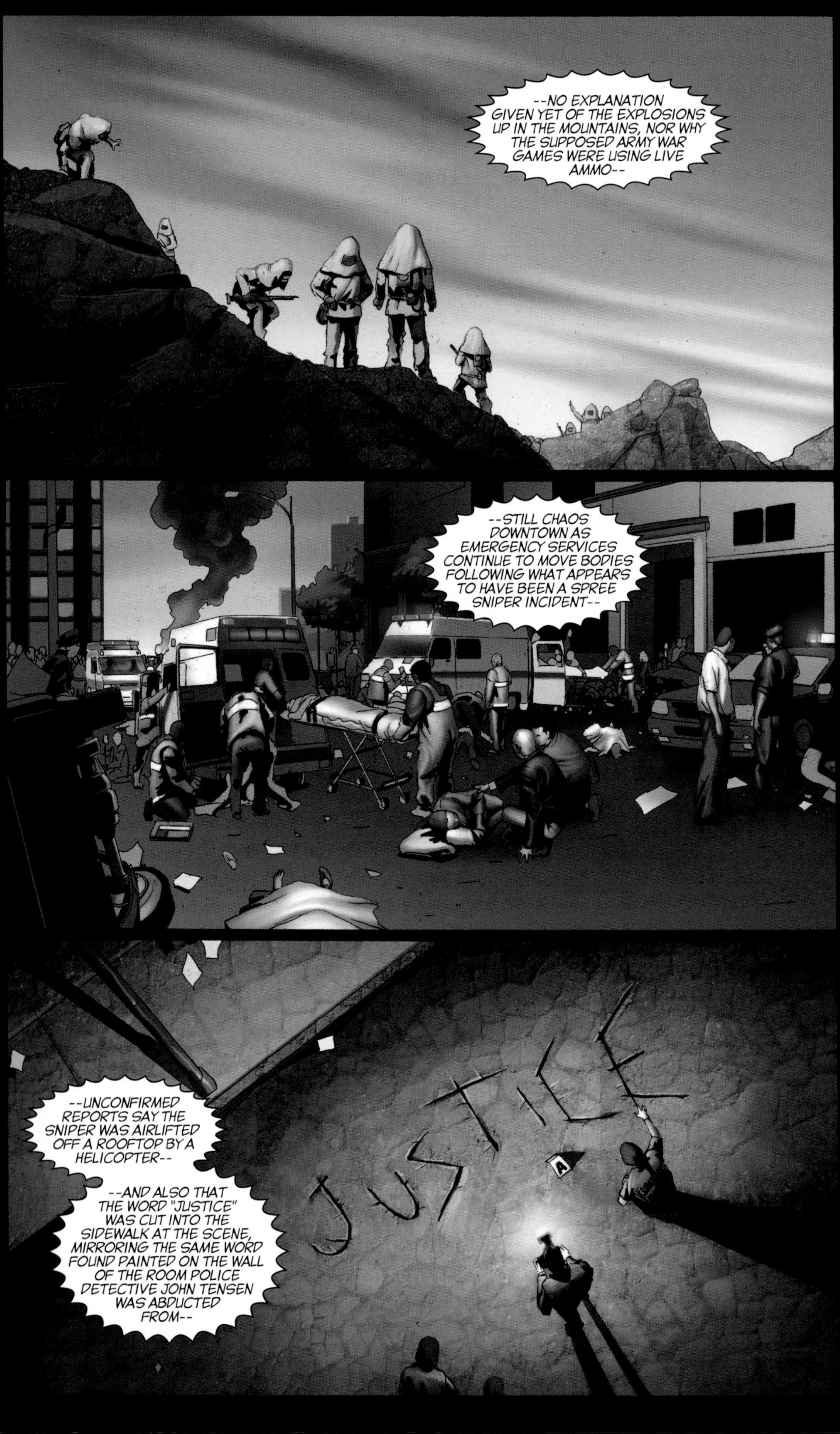
--NO EXPLANATION GIVEN YET OF THE EXPLOSIONS UP IN THE MOUNTAINS, NOR WHY THE SUPPOSED ARMY WAR GAMES WERE USING LIVE AMMO--
--STILL CHAOS DOWNTOWN AS EMERGENCY SERVICES CONTINUE TO MOVE BODIES FOLLOWING WHAT APPEARS TO HAVE BEEN A SPREE SNIPER INCIDENT--
--UNCONFIRMED REPORTS SAY THE SNIPER WAS AIRLIFTED OFF A ROOFTOP BY A HELICOPTER--
--AND ALSO THAT THE WORD "JUSTICE" WAS CUT INTO THE SIDEWALK AT THE SCENE, MIRRORING THE SAME WORD FOUND PAINTED ON THE WALL OF THE ROOM POLICE DETECTIVE JOHN TENSEN WAS ABDUCTED FROM--
JUSTICE

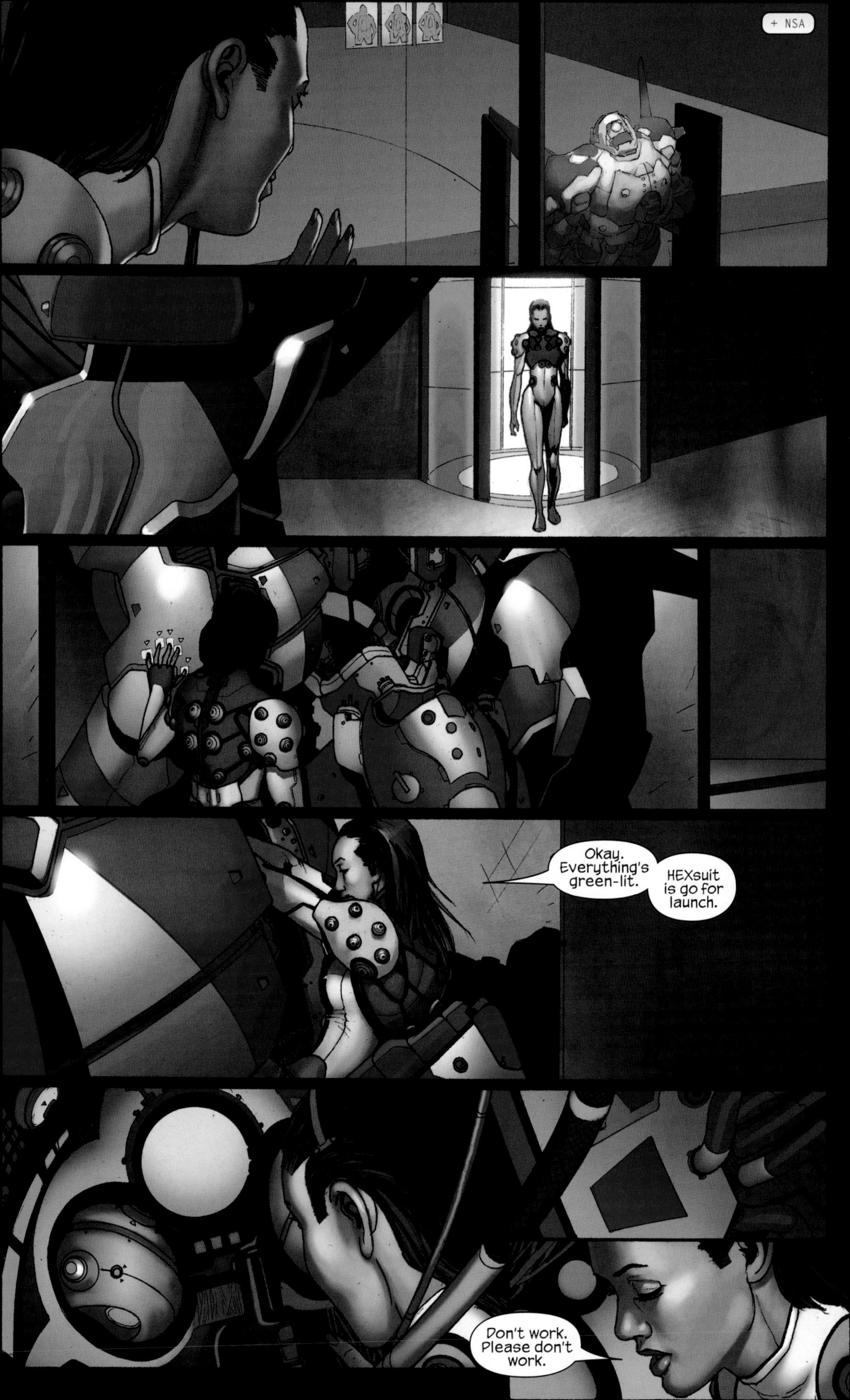
+ NSA
Okay. Everything's green-lit.
HEXsuit is go for launch.
Don't work. Please don't work.

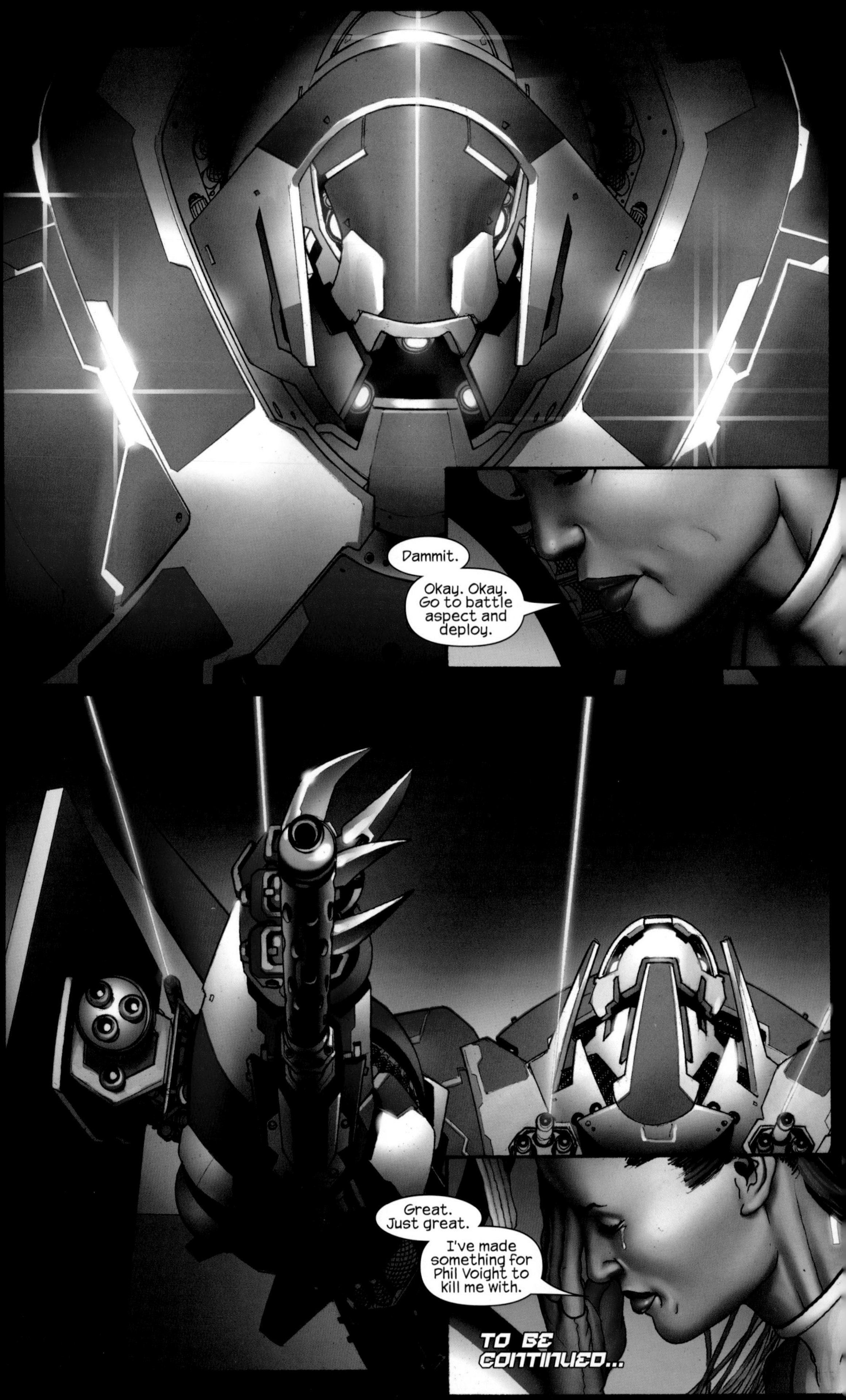
Dammit.
Okay. Okay. Go to battle aspect and deploy.
Great. Just great.
I've made something for Phil Voight to kill me with.
TO BE CONTINUED...

CHARACTER SKETCHES by SALVADOR LARROCA

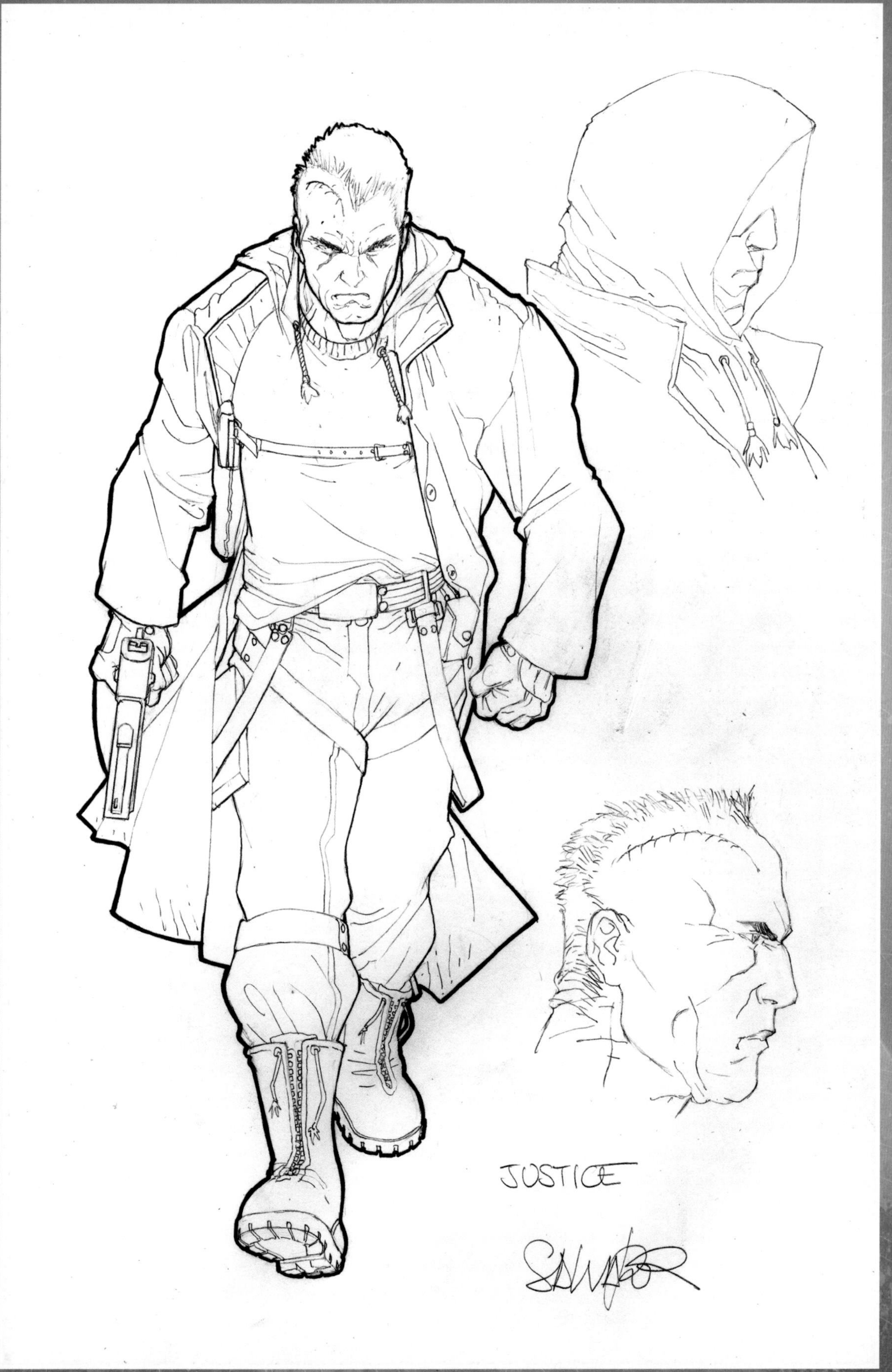
JUSTICE
SALVADOR

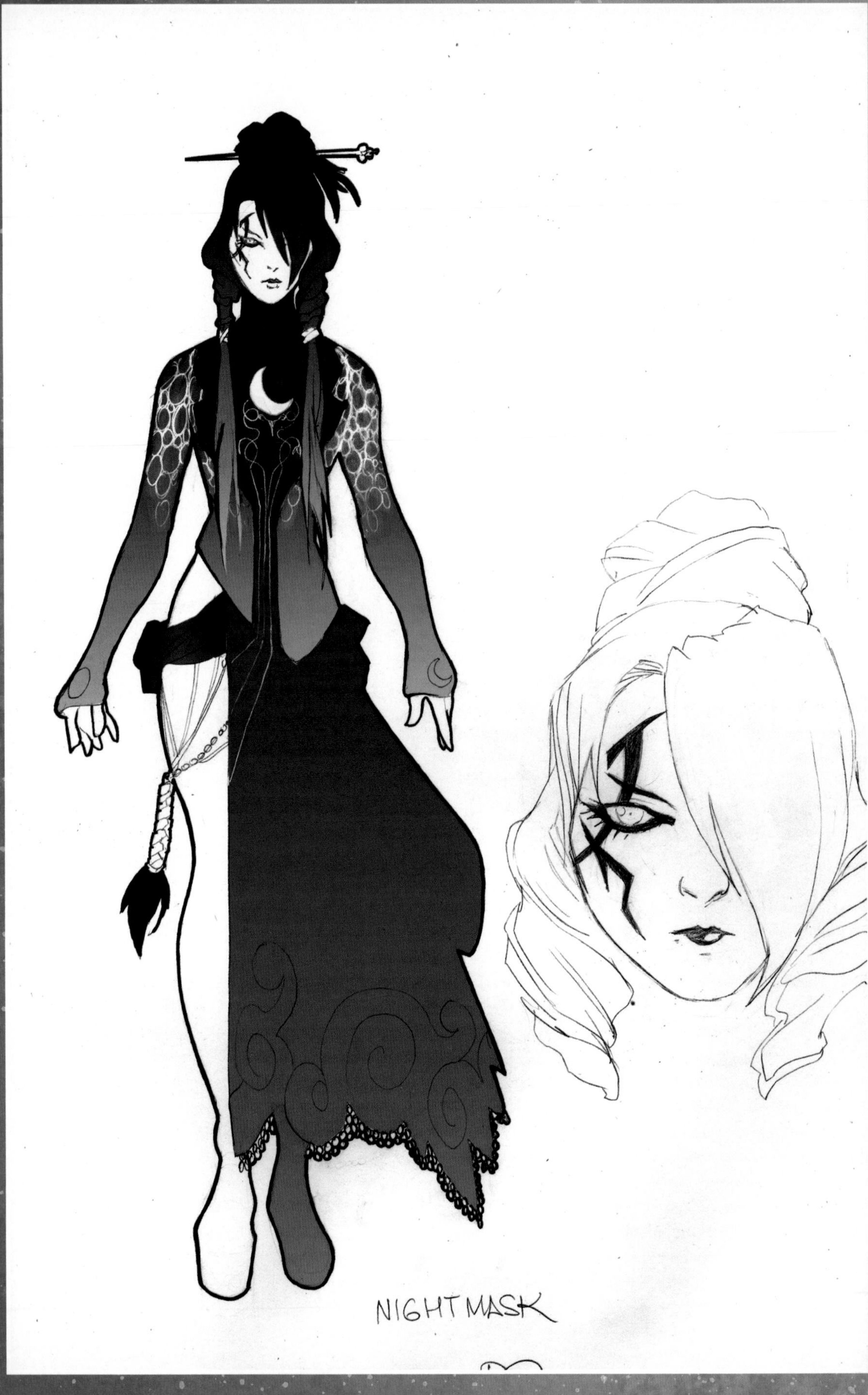
NIGHTMASK

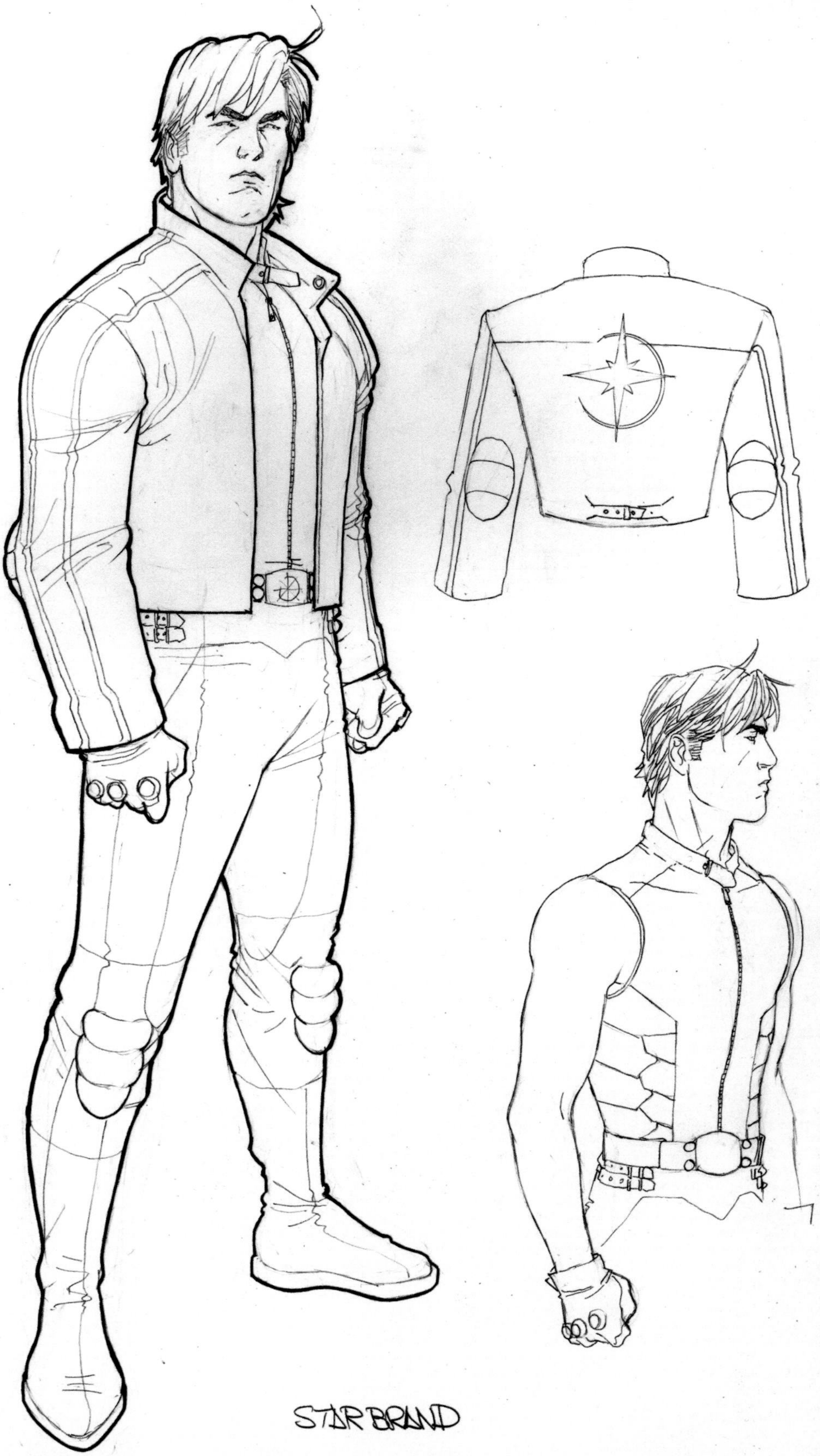
STAR BRAND

ISSUE #2 VARIANT COVER SKETCH by ESAD RIBIC

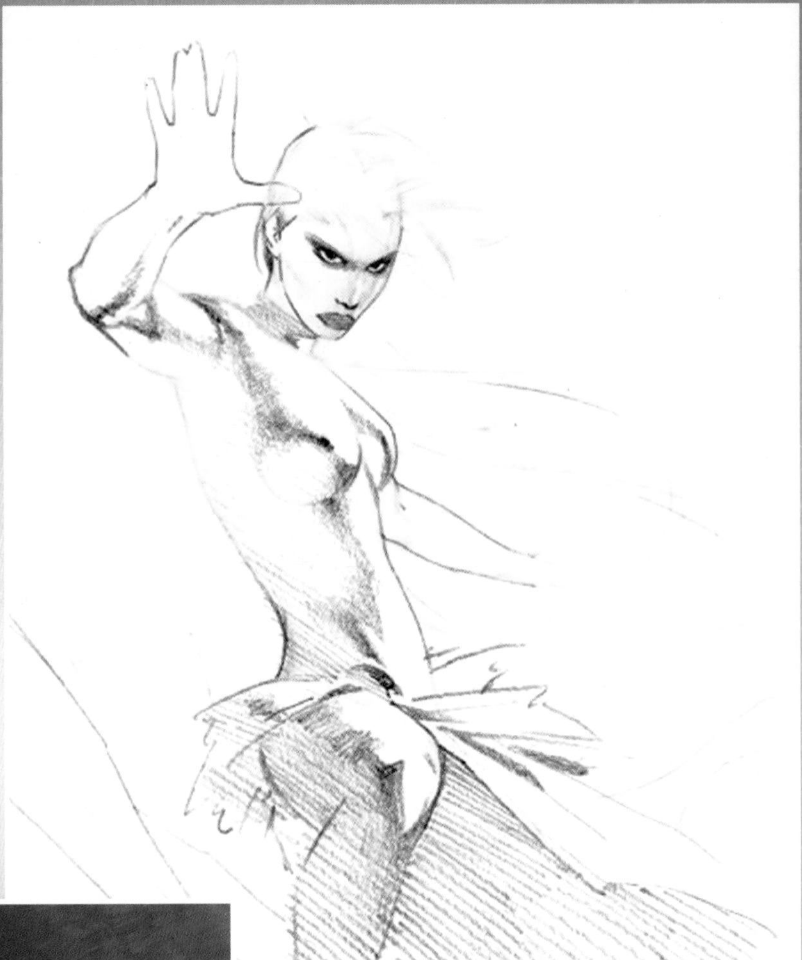

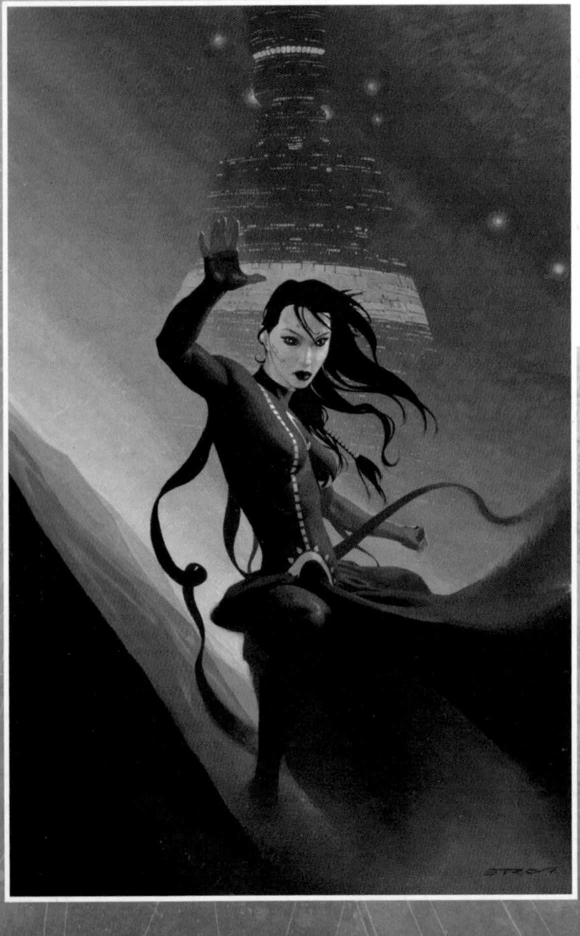

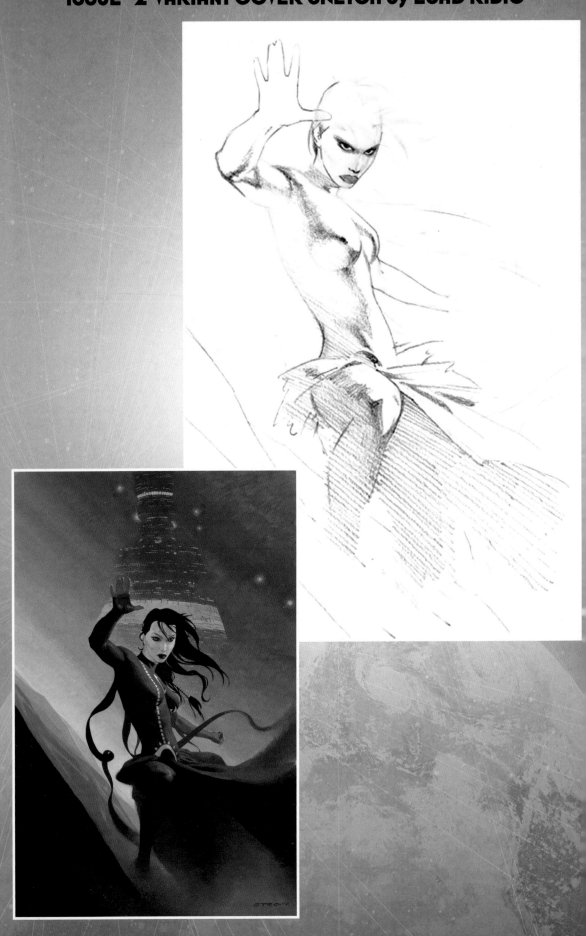